ECSTATIC SPONTANEITY

NANZAN STUDIES IN ASIAN RELIGIONS

Paul L. Swanson, General Editor

1. Jan NATTIER, *Once Upon a Future Time: Studies in a Buddhist Prophecy of Decline,* 1991.
2. David REID, *New Wine: The Cultural Shaping of Japanese Christianity*, 1991.
3. Minor and Ann ROGERS, *Rennyo: The Second Founder of Shin Buddhism,* 1991.
4. Herbert GUENTHER, *Ecstatic Spontaneity: Saraha's Three Cycles of Dohā*, 1993.

Ecstatic Spontaneity

Saraha's *Three Cycles of Dohā*

Herbert Guenther

ASIAN HUMANITIES PRESS
Berkeley, California

ASIAN HUMANITIES PRESS

Asian Humanities Press offers to the specialist and the general reader alike the best in new translations of major works and significant original contributions to enhance our understanding of Asian religions, cultures, and thought.

To the memory of

Pandit Jagannath Upadhyay

Printed in the United States of America

Library of Congress Cataloging-in-Publication Data

Guenther, Herbert V.
Ecstatic spontaneity: Saraha's three cycles of dohā / Herbert Guenther.
p. cm. — (Nanzan Studies in Asian Religions; 4)
Includes bibliographical references and index.
ISBN 0-89581-933-3 (cloth).
1. Sarahapāda, 8th cent. Dohākośa. 2. Religious life—Buddhism. 3. Buddhism—China—Tibet. I. Sarahapāda, 8th cent. Dohākośa. English. 1993. II. Guenther, Herbert V. III. Title. IV. Series.
BQ7775.G84 1993
294.3'44—dc20 92-43917
CIP

Contents

Foreword

Allan Combs

HERBERT GUENTHER IS A SCHOLAR and translator of the first order, one who is a master not only of the syntactic aspects of his subject, but also of the semantic ground from which it flows. This, combined with a deep understanding of process thinking in Western science and philosophy, places him in a unique position to interpret to the Western reader the profoundly process-oriented and holistic perspectives of Saraha's trilogy.

Process cannot exist without form. This seems apparent. Form, on the other hand, can present the illusion of standing free of process. Indeed, the modern mind has unwittingly invested deeply in form and the structural world views to which it gives birth. If certain historical analyses are to be believed, the advent of the ego as a central and widespread aspect of individual subjective life first came about during the Renaissance and the immediate following centuries.[1] The ego seeks security, but security is not to be had from process. Better to think of the cosmos as composed of static entities configured into reliable structures than to risk dissolution into the uncertainty of transformation. Better to cling to *being*, the noun, than to risk *becoming*, the verb.

Putting structure first in the reading of any system of thought fixes an emphasis on stability, puts virtue in conservation, and assures us of permanence. The Newtonian reading of the universe stresses stability in permanent systems, such as the solar system, and relegates process to events that occur within their structural constraints, or more narrowly,

---

[1] See J. Gebser, *The Ever-Present Origin*, N. Barstad and A. Mickunas, trans. Athens, Ohio: Ohio University Press, 1949/1968; R. F. Baumeister, "How the self became a problem: A psychological review of historical research," *Journal of Personality and Social Psychology* 52/1: 163–76, 1987.

to transformations of structure itself. Placing the emphasis on process, however, shifts our perspective to a view of structure as patterns of processes that can undergo multiple bifurcations into new structures without losing their identity. Consider, for instance, the evolution of a star, the metamorphosis of a caterpillar, or the growth of a child. Structure changes, but essence as process remains, taking on new forms. *Being*, the noun, becomes *becoming*, the verb. Transformation replaces stasis.

The possibility of a thoroughgoing process world view did not go unnoticed, even in ancient times, as evidenced by Heraclitus in the West and Lao Tzu in the East. What was needed, however, was a forum, a vehicle, to allow the translation of the process perspective into practical and diverse applications. Henri Bergson's turn-of-the-century evolutionary thought was a step in this direction, as was British philosopher Alfred North Whitehead's metaphysical theory, developed in the 1920s and based on the new scientific thinking of his day. The real breakthrough, however, came in the second half of this century with the marriage of the process perspective to systems theory.

General systems theory had been developing since the 1940s, for example in the writing of Ludwig von Bertalanffy, and had come under the influence of cybernetic theory, developed by mathematicians such as Norbert Wiener. The latter gave systems the new possibility of self-regulation through the action of cybernetic feedback loops. The marriage itself was brought about by theorists such as Erich Jantsch and Ervin Laszlo, who in the early seventies systematically and broadly explored a wide range of possibilities for understanding problems in philosophy and science in terms of dynamic evolving systems.

A major contribution to this conception was made by biologists Humberto Maturana and Francisco Varela, who proposed the idea of *autopoiesis*, according to which dynamic systems such as living organisms are constantly involved in the process of creating themselves. This notion leads to the concept of a system whose principal business is that of creating itself into the future—in other words, it is primarily involved not in being, but in becoming. Such ideas became quite real in the work of the chemist-mathematician Ilya Prigogine and his colleagues, who showed both theoretically and empirically that certain systems are able to utilize energy from their environments to self-organize toward increasing structural complexity. Examples of such systems include living organisms, ecologies, and the planet Earth. Prigogine calls these systems *dissipative structures*, because they utilize energy for transformation, dissipating heat (or disorder) as a by-product.

The process perspective that emerges from considerations such as the above gives us a new and radically different understanding of what it is to be human. Instead of a compact organism that preserves its integrity within the boundaries of its skin by homeostatic stabilizing mechanisms on the inside and manipulative engagements with the environment on the outside, we discover a flowing process that evolves into the future in a constant dynamic event of self-creation. In this process, all boundaries are arbitrary and ultimately artificial, for the process itself arises out of the whole fabric of reality, expressed through but not contained by the physical body itself. This process is not so much stabilized by the negative cybernetic feedback loops of homeostasis as it is actualized by the positive feedback loops of growth and transformation. It does not plan for the future based on what was learned in the past, but conserves its own history in such a fashion that in each moment it expresses the potential wisdom of its accumulated experience.

The fact that certain ancient Buddhist sages were able, through sheer penetration of direct personal experience, to come to a view fundamentally similar to that expressed above does honor both to them and to the modern architects of this perspective. Such a correspondence provides a remarkable cross-validation of a perspective that for most of us, in the East as well as the West, is dramatically different from our usual way of experiencing reality.

It is perhaps not surprising that the discovery of a process description of the human being would emerge from Buddhist thought. Perhaps no other tradition in the world has so relentlessly unmasked the façade of appearances, peeling back layer after layer of illusion in an uncompromising deconstruction of things-as-they-seem until nothing artificial remains. It is a tribute to Herbert Guenther that, despite the historical, cultural, and linguistic distance between ancient India and Tibet and the modern West, he was able not only to recognize the agreement between these perspectives, but also to translate the words as well as the concepts, from the one into the vernacular of the other.

Guenther also finds it useful to draw upon certain concepts from modern physics, most notably the notion of transformations that preserve or break symmetry. Considerations of symmetry, while in essence simple, have been very productive to physics and cosmology. A mirror is a useful device for discussing symmetry, performing a simple symmetry-conserving transformation on the object in front of it and preserving all of its structural relationships in the reversed image. On the other hand, if the mirror were less than perfect, exhibiting, for example, a slight curvature along one or another of its axes, it could be said to perform an approximate symmetry transformation. The image is not exactly that of the original object, but still related to it in a completely systematic way. On the other hand, were the mirror to shatter, the image would suddenly undergo a startling symmetry-breaking transformation.

Putting all this together, let us consider Guenther's description of the *buddha*, or *sangs-rgyas* in Tibetan.[2] The essential understanding here is not the notion of some historical person, but of the process of becoming spiritually awake. The nature of this process is suggested by the Tibetan concepts of darkness dissipating (*sangs*) and of light unfolding (*rgyas*)—two ideas indicative of a dissipative structure. This structure—or *process*, to speak correctly—can be understood as nothing less than an approximate symmetry transformation of Being itself.

---

[2] See Herbert Guenther, *From Reductionism to Creativity: rDzog-chen and the New Sciences of Mind*, Boston & Shatesbury: Shambhala, 1989.

Preface

MY FIRST EXPOSURE TO the elusive but fascinating figure of Saraha came during my study of Indian languages. Although my interest deepened in the course of my subsequent work in the fields of Indology and Tibetology, it was not until I left Vienna in 1950 to take up a teaching post in India that I was able to pursue the attraction more systematically. My research continued during my years at Lucknow University and the Vārāṇaseya Sanskrit Viśvavidyālaya (Benares Sanskrit University). In 1964 I was invited to Canada to head the newly established Department of Far Eastern Studies at the University of Saskatchewan, where I remained until my retirement as professor emeritus in 1984. Throughout those years, too, I continued to read and study the writings of Saraha.

During my long years in India, Acharya Narendra Dev, the late vice-chancellor of Lucknow University, and his disciple pundit Jagannath Upadhyay (to whose memory this book is dedicated), took a special interest in my work on Buddhist studies. Through their kind graces, I soon found myself in close contact with Indian scholars working in the field of Sanskrit studies. This contact made me realize the tremendous difference between Western reductionist tendencies to explain everything at one level (usually the lowest and most trivial level) and scholarship immersed in living tradition. Many of the scholars whom I came to know and to work with did not know a single word of English, but their depth of understanding was tremendous, and I am convinced my work would have been greatly impoverished had I not made efforts to converse with them in their native Sanskrit or Hindi.

Not long after my arrival in India, a young native of Lahul (culturally part of Tibet, politically part of India), whom I had helped gain admission to the Benares Hindu University, brought me and my family to his hometown of Kyelang. There I was introduced to his teacher, Lama Dam-chos rin-chen of the 'Brug-pa bka'-brgyud (dKar-brgyud) order, in whose monastery I would spend my university vacations in the years to come, far from the stifling heat of the plains. Year after year, in those remote surroundings at an altitude of 12,000 feet, I was introduced to original Tibetan texts, most of them unknown to the West. Among them was a rare commentary on Saraha's *Cycle of Dohā* by Karma 'Phrin-las-pa, which was to prove invaluable for understanding Saraha's mysticism. Needless to say, what I learned through discussion and instruction at the monastery proved every bit as valuable as the written texts put at my disposal.

I use the word "mysticism" guardedly in connection with Saraha because many of the connotations that have accrued to it in Western scholarship do not apply to his case. Broadly speaking, one may distinguish two kinds of mysticism: a *speculative* mysticism that remains within the compass of traditional theistic religion, and an *experiential* mysticism in which what is "lived through" erases the bordlerlines between subject and object. This latter form of mysticism has its roots not in discursive thinking but in the same principle of self-organization that characterizes everything that is alive. Here the opposition between religion and science falls away, and with it the whole static world view that the West inherited from Greek antiquity. Only with the collapse of this world view in modern times and the emergence of the "New Physics" has the gap between religion and science begun to close.

The fact is, modern physics has become ever more "mystical," not least of all because of the exposure of some of its most outstanding representatives to Eastern thought. David Bohm's association with J. Krishnamurti is well known; Erwin Schrödinger was deeply impressed by Indian philosophy; Niels Bohr chose as his emblem the Taoist yin-yang symbol; C. G. Jung's collaboration with Wolfgang Pauli led to the idea of synchronicity; and so on. Does it not seem fitting that these pioneers be called by the name that history has given to many of its great visionaries—mystics? Nor should the religious overtones of the name deter us. All of these thinkers in their own way were deeply religious in nature—*re-ligati* to wholeness and spontaneity rather than to an established canon of dogmas.

Things are quite different in the Indian context, particularly in Indian Buddhism. The oposition between religion and science is, of course, absent. It is not that India had no science—indeed the notion of zero goes back to Indian mathematicians—but that they did not oppose science to religion. For them, the key conflict lay rather between representational and hermeneutical thinking: on the one hand, philosophical systems constructed on carefully articulated logical reductions; on the other, the quest for the meaning of human life and human interiority through the exercise of creative imagination. Hermeneutical thinking poses a challenge to the hegemony of representational thinking, which in turn tends to dismiss it as the plaything of "eccentrics." Saraha was one such eccentric. The Buddhists had a different name for his kind. They called them *mahāsiddha*, "achievers." Ironically, they also restricted their number to eighty-four, thus reaffirming the inveterate bent towards reductionism that these thinkers had struggled to overcome.

Saraha stands out among the eccentric-achievers for the sheer volume of work he produced and the influence it had on later Tibetan works in the genre. For example, the first syllable of the first word in each stanza of his *Ka-khasya dohā* begins with one of the letters of the Indian alphabet, arranged in dictionary order. This literary device was taken up by the Tibetans, who took it a step further by having the initial letters run through the alphabet from beginning to end and then back again in reverse order. The practice continues in Tibet to this day, though I suspect that those who use it have no idea that it was introduced by Saraha.

The present book is divided into two parts, the first of which is intended to provide background material for the second. Part one opens with a brief account of Saraha's life, or what little we know of it, and a survey of the trilogy of songs that make up his *opus magnum*: the People, King, and Queen *Dohā*.[1] The chapters that follow deal with three basic and interlocking concepts that I consider central to appreciating the content of the songs: wholeness, body, and complexity. In composing these chapters, it has been necessary to supplement the often sketchy Indian source material with references to the far richer Tibetan tradition, in particular to the rDzogs-chen/sNying-thig teaching.

Wholeness is presented as the spontaneous dynamism of Being itself which is experienced by the individual as "ecstasy," that is, as an *Ek-stasis* that draws one out of one's fragmented particularity and into an undivided whole. For Saraha the experience of wholeness as an ecstatic spontaneity is situated in *the body* and resacralizes our image of the body. It is through our body that we reach up to the divine. Finally, in experiencing one's body as participating in a dynamic wholeness, one gains a fresh perspective on the *complexity* of ourselves and the world, important for living in the world without being enslaved to it.

Part two contains an annotated translation of Saraha's *Three Cycles*

---

[1] The information on Saraha in my previous book *The Royal Song of Saraha* (Seattle: University of Washington Press, 1969; reprint, Berkeley and London: Shambhala Publications, 1973), was abridged, revised, and updated for this chapter.

of Dohā. In translating the songs, I see myself as a mediator between two views of the world: the "old" world of Saraha (which is, after all, not so old) and the "new" world of contemporary "science" (which in turn is not all that new). Unless one is content with the mechanical transposition of words from one idiom to another, oblivious of the movements of history, such mediation is inevitable. In my own case, I have drawn heavily on what I see as clear affinities between modern "process thinking" and the ancient Buddhist notion of the Way in its dual role as process and guide.

In conclusion, I should like to thank the following persons for their abiding interest, encouragement, and support: my late friend and colleague pandit Jagannath Upadhyay at the Sanskrit University of Varanasi, India, for first recommending that I undertake a modern, phenomenological study of Saraha; Allan Combs, professor of psychology at the University of North Carolina at Asheville, for composing a foreword for this book; my former students and friends Kent Johnson, Jeannette Lavigne, Mariana Neves, and Candace Schuler for their invaluable suggestions on how to improve the presentation of the work; the Nanzan Institute for Religion and Culture, for inviting me to Japan to prepare the manuscript for publication, and Paul Swanson and James Heisig in particular for the care and enthusiasm with which they took up the challenge; and, above all, my wife Ilse, for her love and patience.

Herbert Guenther
March 1992
Nagoya, Japan

ECSTATIC SPONTANEITY

Chapter 1

Saraha

As is so often the case with major figures in the intellectual history of India, almost nothing factual is known about Saraha. And yet, to judge from the frequency with which his work is cited and the extent to which his style has been imitated, there is no denying his immense importance for the mystic philosophers and poets of Tibet as well as for certain thinkers in India. Since he is not reckoned as belonging to a line of succession in a particular spiritual tradition, it is hardly surprising that his name is mentioned but rarely in works dealing with Indian thought—works in any case that tend to emphasize the speculative rather than the experiential. The few indigenous Indian "biographies" of Saraha differ in details regarding his place of birth and the name of the ruler at that time, but they are agreed that there was a woman involved in the decisive turning-point of his life. By far the most interesting account of his life is given by Karma 'Phrin-las (1456–1539).[1] I cite it at length:

> The Great Brahmin Saraha was the youngest of five sons born to the Brahmin sPangs-pa phun-sum-tshogs and his wife, the Brahmini sPangs-ma phun-sum-tshogs,[2] in the South, in India, in

[1] Karma 'Phrin-las, *Do-hā skor gsum-gyi ṭī-kā sems-kyi rnam-thar ston-pa'i me-long*, a detailed commentary on Saraha's cycle of *Dohā* (hereafter cited as Karma 'Phrin-las). This is the only extant indigenous Tibetan commentary on Saraha's *Three Cycles of Dohā*.

[2] Tibetans tended to translate Indian names "interpretively." Literally these names mean "of excellent renunciation," the gender of the parents indicated by the suffix *pa* and *ma* respectively. The implication of these names is that Saraha—we do not know his "real" name—is, although a concrete human person, a "spiritual" being.

the country of Beta [Vidarbha]. The five brothers were well versed in many subjects, but excelled in the knowledge of the Vedas. Therefore King Mahāpāla was pleased to honor them as worthy persons. At this time Hayagrīva[3] had assumed the form of the Bodhisattva Sukhanātha in order to provide spiritual training for those capable of becoming instantly spiritually awakened. Thinking that the Great Brahmin might accomplish his purpose, he appeared in the guise of four Brahmin girls and one female arrowsmith, all of them beings of the spiritual world (*mkha'-'gro-ma*). Four of them took up their place in a park, while one remained behind in a marketplace. When the five brothers came to the park the four Brahmin girls approached them and asked them where they had come from, where they were going, and what they were doing. Being answered that they had not come from any particular place, were not going anywhere, and also were not doing anything special, the girls inquired about their caste. The brothers declared themselves to be Brahmins and recited the four Vedas on the spot. Four of them asked the girls whether they would like to have them as their consorts and when the girls consented they went away together.

The youngest brother thought of becoming a monk and asked the king for permission. Having obtained it, he entered the order under Mahāyāna Śrīkīrti, a disciple of Buddha's son Rāhulabhadra. Through intense studies he became a noted scholar in countless subjects. Not only did he become famous as the Brahmin Rāhula, he also became the spiritual master of the teacher Nāgārjuna and other illustrious persons.

Once when this Brahmin Rāhula was roaming in his district and had come to a garden, the four Brahmin girls approached him with cups of beer and begged him to drink them. Though protesting, he succumbed to their entreaties and drank the four cups in large gulps. He had four particularly pleasant sensations[4] and, as had been prophesied about him, he met the Bodhisattva Sukhanātha

---

[3] Hayagrīva (*rTa-mgrin*) is one of the protecting deities (*chos-skyong*) of Tibet. For a description see Alice Getty, *The Gods of Northern Buddhism* (Rutland, Vt.: Charles E. Tuttle Co., 1962), 162ff., and pl. xliv, fig. c; Antoinette K. Gordon, *The Iconography of Tibetan Lamaism* (rev. ed.; Rutland, Vt.: Charles E. Tuttle Co., 1959), 90 and plates; Raghu Vira and Lokesh Chandra, *A New Tibeto-Mongol Pantheon* (vol. 21 in the Śata-piṭaka Series of Indo-Asian Literatures, New Delhi: International Academy of Indian Culture, 1961), part 1, pl. 64; part 2, pls. 137–41; part 8, pl. 55.

[4] This is an allusion to the four kinds of delight sensed during the process of spiritual development and integration. See Herbert V. Guenther, *The Life and Teaching of Nāropa* (Oxford: Oxford University Press, 1963), 78, note 2, and below, note 126 in the translation of the "People *Dohā*."

face to face. Blessed by him he was exhorted: "In this city there lives a mysterious arrowsmith woman who is making a four-piece arrow. Go to her and many beings will profit by it." With these words the vision disappeared.

Through the sustaining power of this vision, the mystic awareness of the spontaneous coemergence of both transcendence and immanence was born in him. Thinking that he would have to act after this instantaneous realization of spiritual freedom, he went to the great marketplace and there saw a young woman cutting an arrow-shaft, looking neither to the right nor to the left, wholly concentrated on making an arrow. Coming closer he saw her carefully straightening a reed with three joints, cutting it both at the bottom and at the top, inserting a pointed arrowhead where she had cut the bottom into four sections and tying it with a tendon, putting four feathers where she had split the top into two pieces and then, closing one eye and opening the other, assuming the posture of aiming at a target. When he asked her whether she was a professional arrowsmith she said: "My dear young man, the Buddha's meaning can be known through symbols and actions, not through words and books." Then and there the spiritual significance of what she was doing dawned upon him.

The reed is the symbol of the uncreated; the three joints, that of the necessity to realize the three existential fore-structures;[5] the straightening of the shaft, that of straightening the path of spiritual growth; cutting the shaft at the bottom, that of the necessity to uproot samsara, and at the top, that of eradicating the belief in a self or an essence; the splitting of the bottom into four sections, that of "memory," "nonmemory," "unorigination," and "transcendence";[6] inserting the arrowhead, that of the necessity to use one's intelligence; tying it with a tendon, that of being fixed by the seal of unity; splitting the upper end into two, that of action and intelligence; inserting four feathers, that of looking, attending to the seen, acting on the basis of what has been seen and attended to, and their fruition in combination; opening one eye and closing the other, that of

---

[5] The three are the fore-structures of one's existentiality (*sku*) as intrinsically meaningful (*chos*) (*chos-sku, dharmakāya*); the gestalt through which one experiences oneself as a social being (*longs-spyod rdzogs-pa'i sku, sambhogakāya*); and our being, each in its own way, a guiding image (*sprul-p'ai sku, nirmāṇakāya*). The Tibetan term *sku* always implies the dynamic character of being and existing; the static aspect of "body" is termed *lus*.

[6] These are the key terms used in the elucidation of the progressive deepening of mystic insight and the felt knowledge of existence. As symbol terms they must not be confused with the connotations these words have in ordinary language.

shutting the eye of discursiveness and opening that of the a priori awareness; the posture of aiming at a target, that of the necessity to shoot the arrow of nonduality into the heart of the belief in duality.

Because of this understanding, Brahmin Rāhula's name was to become "Saraha"; in India, *sara* means "arrow" and *ha*(*n*) "to have shot." He became known as "He who has shot the arrow" (*mda'-bsnun*) because he had sent the arrow of nonduality into the heart of duality [which is the belief in subject and object as ultimate entities].

Then he said: "You are not an ordinary arrowsmith woman; you are a teacher of symbols."[7] He lived with her and engaged in yogic activities. "Till yesterday I was not a real Brahmin, from today I am"[8]—with these and similar words he departed with her to the cremation grounds.[9]

When on the occasion of some people celebrating a Tantric feast he sang some songs and when, singing many songs, he feasted in company with the arrowsmith woman in the cremation grounds, a great number of people who had gathered to watch in faith gained an understanding of the meaning of Reality by merely hearing the word "Reality" and went into ecstasy.[10]

At this time, many dirty-minded Indians vilified and slandered him: "The Brahmin Rāhula does not perform the time-honored rites and has given up celibacy. He indulges in shameful practices with a low-caste woman and runs around like a dog in all directions." When the king heard these slanders he issued orders to his subjects, headed by Saraha's four Brahmin brothers, that they should try to persuade the Great Brahmin to give up his scandalous behavior and, by acting decently, to help the people in the realm. It was then that on behalf of the people he sang the one hundred and sixty verses [constituting the "People *Dohā*"], thereby setting them

---

7 There is here a word-play between *mda'-mkhan-ma* (female arrowsmith) and *brda-mkhan-ma* (a woman well versed in symbols), the pronunciation of the two words being the same.

8 The same words are quoted in dPa'-bo gtsug-lag, *mKhas-pa'i dga'-ston*, ed. Lokesh Chandra (New Delhi: International Academy of Indian Culture, 1959), part 2, 349ff. In the account of Saraha's life in this work these words were spoken after his vision and before his meeting with the arrowsmith woman.

9 There is a double meaning involved here. Cremation grounds are frequented by people outside, or at the fringe of, the orthodox social milieu. Symbolically they intimate one's passing beyond the pale of consciousness that was conceived of as operating through eight perceptual patterns. For further details see my *From Reductionism to Creativity* (Boston and Shaftesbury: Shambhala, 1989).

10 Literally, "attained the faculty of walking in the sky."

on the right path. When the king's queens entreated him in like manner he sang the eighty verses [forming the "Queen *Dohā*"], making them understand the meaning of Reality. Finally, the king himself came to beg the Great Brahmin to revert to his earlier behavior, and it was for the sake of the king that Saraha sang the forty verses [known as the "King *Dohā*"].[11] As Saraha led the king and his entourage on the path of Reality the country of Beta [Vidarbha] became empty instantly [that is, the inhabitants lost interest in the common preoccupations of life].

Delightful as this biographical sketch is in poking fun at the puritanical tenor of Indian society, there is little of historical value in it. The reference to King Mahāpāla may be discounted for at least two reasons. First, other texts give the king's name as Ratnapāla or Candanapāla.[12] Since these names are as common in the Indian setting as Jones and Smith are in English, it is highly unlikely that any of them belonged to the Pāla dynasty, which ruled for about three centuries (from the ninth to the eleventh) in the eastern part of India. Second, "king" is an administrative title whose use is not restricted to persons who have earned themselves a place in history. This Mahāpāla may well have been no more than a local city magistrate. We may also note in passing that there is also no unanimity concerning the city where Saraha was born.[13]

---

[11] The arrangement of these three works reflects a progressive movement from the experiencer's preoccupation with the "effervescent," the sensuous-sensual; to the "internal," the exploration of the psychic dynamic and its imagery; to the "arcane," the organizing principle in the experiencer's wholeness.

[12] M. Shahidullah, *Les Chants Mystiques de Kāṇha et de Saraha* (Paris: Adrien-Maisonneuve, 1928), 31.

[13] According to the source used by M. Shahidullah, Saraha was born at Roli in Rajñi in the eastern part of India. But according to Padma dkar-po, *Phyag-rgya chen-po'i man-ngag-gi bshad-sbyar rgyal-ba'i gan-mdzod* (hereafter cited as *Phyag-chen gan-mdzod*), fol. 9b, he was born in Varanasi (Benares). Padma dkar-po lets him be a direct disciple of Buddha's son Rāhula and claims that he was born only thirty years after the Buddha's death, and that his early name was Rāhulabhadra according to the custom of the disciple taking part of the teacher's name. Padma dkar-po then attempts to explain away the period between Saraha's and Nāgārjuna's birth. The assumption that Mahāpāla is a misspelling for Mahīpāla, the name of the ninth king of the dynasty (circa 978–1030), also does not help because the popular memory has attached itself to this ruler more than to any other, so that he is more like a peg on which to hang any tradition about important persons.

TEXTS AND TEACHINGS

It has been argued that the language in which Saraha expressed his ideas is a late Apabhraṃśa form pointing to Bengal, and that for this reason he must belong to a late period of Buddhist thought. The argument would be convincing but for the fact that Saraha is quoted by Nāropa (1016–1100), and hence must have been recognized as an authority already by Nāropa's time. What is more—and this reflects rather unfavorably on the scholarliness of those involved—no one who has dealt with the "People *Dohā*" seems to have noticed that the Tibetan translation is not only longer than the alleged original but does not tally with the Apabhraṃśa version,[14] which studiously avoids all the technical terms characteristic of Saraha's thinking. Or again, the Indian thinker gNyis-med Avadhūtipa (of unknown date), whose work is available only in Tibetan translation but who himself used the Indian version, has also commented on a text from which the present Tibetan translation has been made and which cannot be identified with the available Apabhraṃśa version.[15]

Even if we grant that the Tibetan commentators read meanings into the text that were not there in the original, the fact remains that this "reading in" concerns words that are found in the Tibetan translation and must have been present also in the version from which the Tibetan translation was made (though not in the available Apabhraṃśa text).

---

[14] The original Apabhraṃśa version, preserved in a rather truncated state, has been edited and translated by M. Shahidullah in his *Les Chants Mystiques de Kāṇha et de Saraha*. Unfortunately, this otherwise pioneering work abounds in misspellings and mistranslations. These defects did not deter D. Snellgrove from transposing the French translation mechanically into English (*Saraha's Treasury of Songs*, in Conze's *Buddhist Texts through the Ages*) without any attention to the Apabhraṃśa text and its numerous Tibetan translations. Although Snellgrove would have us believe that he has consulted an original text, he leaves no doubt that he has grasped neither the subject-matter nor the structure of the Buddhist texts. The fact that he has taken no note of the numerous discrepancies between the Apabhraṃśa version and its Tibetan translations can only lead one to conclude that his familiarity with the Apabhraṃśa and Tibetan languages is less than adequate.

[15] *Do-hā mdzod-kyi snying-po don-gyi glu'i 'grel-pa* (*Dohākośa-hṛdaya-artha-gīti-ṭīkā*); bsTan-'gyur, Peking ed.: vol. *Tsi*, fols. 97a ff. (hereafter cited as *Do-hā mdzod-kyi snying-po*). If Advaya Avadhūti and Advayavajra are different names of a single person (Maitripa) at different periods of his life, as stated by Sog-po Khal-kha chos-rje Ngag-dbang dpal-ldan, *Grub-mtha' chen-mo'i mchan-'grel dka'-gnad mdud-grol blo-gsal gces-nor zhes-bya-ba-las dngos-smra-ba'i skabs*, fol. 2a, then Advaya Avadhūtipa's *Ṭīkā* would be the famous "Commentary by Maitripa."

It seems unlikely that the Tibetan translators, who proved adept at tranlating other Indian texts, should have misunderstood this particular text from the start. Moreover, since the Tibetan version contains more verses than the Apabhraṃśa text and since the grouping of individual lines into coherent verses differs from the available text, there is no alternative than to consider the Apabhraṃśa text a bowdlerized and fragmented version of an earlier work that has been lost.

This leaves us with the tradition, no doubt spurious, that Saraha became the teacher of Nāgārjuna when the latter was already an old man. Unfortunately the dates of Nāgārjuna are not known either. The hypothesis that he lived in the second century C.E. is highly plausible, but no exact proof can be adduced. Nāgārjuna, credited with initiating the much overvalued Madhyamaka system of philosophy, is certainly one of the greatest thinkers India has produced. So, too, is Saraha, who was well acquainted with the Madhyamaka line of thought and criticized it for its logical reductionism and its failure to account for the immediacy of experience.

Although the historicity of Saraha cannot be doubted, the elusiveness of the man is matched by that of his teaching. It is not that what he has to say is so abstruse as to be incomprehensible, but simply that the internal structure of his teaching is so baffling. This is partly a result of the genre of the song in which Saraha's thought is expressed, giving the effect of a collage of disconnected images. His thought progresses from one picture to the next, from one emotion to another, and therefore seems to lack the logical clarity of a didactic treatise. The failure to detect a progression of thought is certainly due to the fact that most philosophers have lost all vital contact with poetic modes of expression, and when they do aspire to poetry, end up with little more than representational thought in metrical form.

If it is difficult to detect a systematic progression of thought in one work, how much more difficult to find the common thread in three different works! Traditionally, the work of Saraha is known as *The Three Cycles of Dohā* (*do-hā skor-gsum*) consisting of what are otherwise known as "King *Dohā*," "Queen *Dohā*," and "People *Dohā*." These works are "songs" whose meter is technically known as *dohā*, most frequently used in compositions in the vernacular languages of India. Although each of these collections deals with a specific existential problem, there is some question as to whether the triple division was of Saraha's own making. According to Karma 'Phrin-las, some were of the opinion

> that *The Three Cycles of Dohā* were indeed sung by Saraha, but were not divided into larger and smaller poems as they all were merely

> expressive of his mystic experience. At a later time they were written down by Saraha's disciple Nāgārjuna and for the sake of instruction discussed in the form of three treatises varying in size. Others, however, claimed that Nāgārjuna cannot be held to have arranged the songs into treatises; they were put so by Saraha for the benefit of Maitripa, after Saraha had realized spiritual freedom and recited the songs to Maitripa as an instructive injunction.[16]

Karma 'Phrin-las himself rejects these views in favor of the position held by Rang-byung rdo-rje (1284–1339), for whom *The Three Cycles of Dohā* were the authentic works of Saraha.

In reading material that contains allusions to Saraha, one is struck at once by the fact that almost all quotations are taken from the "People *Dohā*."[17] This did not escape the attention of certain of the Tibetans who were driven to conclude that the "Queen *Dohā*" and "King *Dohā*" were not the works of Saraha at all. Karma 'Phrin-las rejects this claim and raises telling objections against the arbitrariness of all such "higher criticism."[18] Those who pretend to such criticism, he says, are "ignoble persons" in claiming that

> the "King *Dohā*" and "Queen *Dohā*" are not authentic works of Saraha, and that the term "Three Cycles of *Dohā*" does not refer to three distinct works but to a process of initiation necessary for spiritual maturation—a process which moves from instruction to guidance for appropriating the instruction into one's own life. [According to this veiw,] the first cycle is an initiation into the spiritual meaning of Vajravārāhī and proceeds by way of the four symbol-terms[19] used in the *Dohās*; the second stage is an explanation of the "People *Dohā*" along with Maitripa's commentary on it; and the third cycle makes use of the four symbol-terms to offer guidance or "instruction with pebbles." If this is the meaning of "Three Cycles of *Dohā*", then the two remaining works ["King *Dohā*" and "Queen

---

[16] Karma 'Phrin-las, 9.

[17] An exception is Klong-chen rab-'byams-pa, *Chos-dbyings rin-po-che'i mdzod-kyi 'grel-pa lung-gi gter-mdzod* (hereafter cited as *Chos-dbyings rin-po-che'i mdzod*, fol. 54b), where the first line of stanza 8 of the "King *Dohā*" is quoted. Stanza 17 is quoted in full by Thub-bstan 'bar-ba in his *Nges-don phyag-rgya-chen-po'i sgom-rim gsal-bar byed-pa'i legs-bshad zla-ba'i 'od-zer*, fol. 5ab.

[18] On the unsound methods of "higher criticism" in general, see Walter Kaufmann, *Critique of Religion and Philosophy* (London: Faber and Faber, 1958), 265ff.

[19] These are literally rendered in the traditional objectivist's reduction as "memory," "nonmemory," "unorigination," and "transcendence," but as symbol-terms their connotations are much wider.

> *Dohā*"] are forgeries. To substantiate their case, these critics note that the index to the bsTan-'gyur by Bu-ston [1219–1364] includes only the "People *Dohā*" and that there is no Indian commentary on the other two works. They further observe that while in India Ras-chung-pa [1083–1161] found only the "People *Dohā*"—because gLing-ras-pa [1128–1188], an authority on mysticism, had written a commentary on this *Dohā*" but not on the other two—whereas on return to Tibet he found all three works with Bal-po A-su. They conclude that the two additional works may well have been composed by Lama Bal-po himself.
>
> All this sort of subversive talk reflects on the ignorance [of those who hold such views], for even though the verses do not occur in gLing's commentary, they do appear after the main body of the text in other works. Moreover, many entries have been omitted in the index to the bsTan'gyur. Were this proof that they had never been written, or were the mere absence of an Indian commentary sufficient to argue against the authenticity of a text, the number of spurious works would increase greatly. Hence the works *are* of Indian origin. They must be considered authentic since such wise persons as Rang-byung rdo-rje and others have written commentaries on them based on older commentaries by scholars such as Par-phu-ba[20] and Tsang nag-po which are known to be authentic, and since many later scholars such as Mati paṇ-chen [ca. 1334] and Yid-bzang rtse-pa have continued to produce commentaries on them.[21]

The tradition of the *Dohās* in Tibet goes back to Mar-pa (1012–1097), who studied them in India under Maitripa and later transmitted his knowledge to his favorite disciple Mi-la ras-pa (1040–1123). In so doing, it would appear that he did not provide Mi-la ras-pa with anything like a detailed explanation. In this regard Karma 'Phrin-las notes:

> Of the four illustrious and famous disciples of Maitripa, Lord Mar-pa distinguished himself in the study of the *Dohās*. Having experienced for himself what the teaching was about, he handed it down to Mi-la ras-pa and others, though he did not translate the three works or offer instruction on their content.[22]

---

[20] His summary of Saraha's instructions, the *dPal Saraha'i gdams-pa doha'i bsdus-don*, has been photostatically reproduced in *A Treasury of Instructions and Techniques for Spiritual Realization*, compiled by 'Jam-mgon Kong-sprul, in vol. 5, 22–28, of the *gDams-ngag-mdzod*, ed. N. Lungtok and N. Gyaltsan, Delhi, 1971.

[21] Karma 'Phrin-las, 9–11.

[22] Karma 'Phrin-las, 11.

Atīśa (982–1054) also studied the *Dohās* and was about to teach them when he was requested by 'Brom-ston not to do so, on the grounds that the Tibetans might take them too literally and endanger their morals in the process. Thus Maitripa's commentary was translated into Tibetan, but the *Dohās* themselves were not taught as such. Similarly the Zhi-byed system,[23] which goes back to Dam-pa Sangs-rgyas (eleventh century) and accepts the *Dohās*, was more concerned with appropriation of the content of the *Dohās* than with their actual promulgation.

Continuity in the teaching of their content is accredited to the Indian Vajrapāṇi (b. 1017), who was the teacher of several Tibetans. His exploits are merely hinted at by Karma 'Phrin-las, but a more detailed and intelligible account is found in 'Gos lotsava's *sDeb-ther sngon-po*.[24] Without the latter, much of what Karma 'Phrin-las writes remains unintelligible. Vajrapāṇi's influence centered on three persons who were to acquire great fame and contribute much to the development of Buddhist thought in Tibet. They were the Nepalese A-su (commonly known as Lama Bal-po), Ras-chung-pa, and mNga'-ris-pa, through whom the continuation of the teaching as well as the practice of realization was established. Karma 'Phrin-las again informs us:

> The tradition that originated with Bal-po A-su came to be known as the Bal method of the *Dohās*; that which derived from Ras-chung-pa, who had studied the subject under Ti-phu-ba, was known as the Ras-chung method; and that which spread through Gru-shul-ba, who had studied under mNga'-ris-pa, became known as the Par method, since it was Par-phu-ba [a direct disciple of Gru-shul-ba] who had arranged the *Three Cycles of Dohā* into treatises with accompanying manuals. As these three methods were developing, mNga'-ris-pa and Ras-chung-pa also studied under Lama Bal-po. Thus although the methods of teaching appear to be different in each case, the latter two traditions [of mNga'-ris-pa and Ras-chung-pa] stem from Bal-po, who had studied under Vajrapāṇi, and accept Bal-po's interpretation. This is how our own tradition came to be considered as consisting of three methods. My teacher, 'Khrul-zhig

---

[23] A short account of this system, which aims at the total annihilation of suffering, is given in Thu'u-kvan bLo-bzang chos-kyi nyi-ma dpal bzang-po, *Grub-mtha' thams-cad-kyi khungs dang 'dod-tshul ston-pa legs-bshad shel-gyi me-long*, part 5.

[24] George N. Roerich, *The Blue Annals* (Calcutta: Royal Asiatic Society of Bengal, 1949), 858.

chen-po, explained solely the Par method and followed the text as embodied in the latter's commentary.[25]

mNga'-ris-pa[26] had studied in India, but on the advice of Vajrapāṇi went to Lama Bal-po for further studies. At first he thought he detected a difference between Vajrapāṇi's and Bal-po A-su's teaching, but the deeper he searched the more he realized that there was no essential difference between them, and therefore accepted Bal-po A-su's interpretation. The implication is that Bal-po, a native Nepalese probably of Tibetan stock, had interpreted the teaching of Vajrapāṇi in the light of his Tibetan background. mNga'-ris-pa recognized the difference but justified it on the assumtion that the Indian and the Tibetan scholars shared Buddhism as a common ground and ultimate aim, which then cleared the way for him to accept the Nepalese-Tibetan way as more suited to his Tibetan character.[27]

It is significant that mNga'-ris-pa noted the difference between Indian and Nepalese-Tibetan modes of thought. It does much to discredit the long-cherished myth that the Tibetans were mechanical translators of Indian texts who considered the ideas and images behind the words as discrete entities that could be simply lifted out of one context and placed into another with no loss in meaning—a myth, one might add, that is not without its adherents among modern dictionary fundamentalists. The Tibetans were well aware of the fact that the words through which concepts are communicated belong to a specific realm of discourse, and that although "one word may have two or more functions, one of its functions cannot change places with another."[28]

mNga'-ris-pa's direct disciple was Gru-shul-ba, about whom little is known. Gru-shul-ba's disciple was Par-phu-ba, who was born in gYor-po and belonged to the ancient family of rNga. His proper name

---

[25] Karma 'Phrin-las, 12.

[26] His full name was mNga'-ris Jo-stan Chos-kyi tshul-khrims: mNga'-ris after the name of his birthplace; Jo-stan, short for Jo-bo stan-gcig-pa, in recognition of the quality of his studies; Chos-kyi tshul-khrims is his monastic name.

[27] Karma 'Phrin-las, 4.

[28] Gilbert Ryle, *Dilemmas* (Cambridge: Cambridge University Press, 1954), 32. It seems that many of the pseudoscholarly translations of Buddhist philosophical texts, by linguists who deliberately close their eyes to the fact that an etymological dissection of an isolated word is not a meaningful proposition, mask an attempt to ridicule and demean civilizations different from our own, because their so-called "objective" approach is but a euphemism for their ego-centered feeling of superiority.

was bLo-gros seng-ge, but he became known as Par-phu-ba because he had founded a monastery at Par-phu. Under Gru-shul-ba, Par-phu-ba was introduced to the teaching of mysticism, as a number of commentaries and explanatory works on the *Dohās* testify. Under Bu lotsava he studied logic and epistemology, and then met Phag-mo gru-pa ('Gro-mgon Phag-mo gru-pa rDo-rje rgyal-po, 1110–1170), who was a follower of one of the idealistic-mentalistic schools of Buddhism (*sems-tsam*). This idealistic-mentalistic interpretation was taken over by Par-phu-ba in his writings about the *Dohās*. Karma 'Phrin-las's teacher also taught the Par method, which accounts for a similar strain in the latter's writings. Here again it should be noted that the Tibetans developed this line of thinking in their own way, so that several distinct variations from the Indian prototype can be observed.

After Par-phu-ba the tradition of the *Dohās* continued through his direct disciple dGyer-sgom of sNye-phu shugs-gseb, a monastery dGyer-sgom had founded and resided at for some twenty-six years. dGyer-sgom's disciple was Sangs-rgyas dbon, alias Rin-chen snying-po, who served as abbot of sNye-phu shugs-gseb for many years. He was succeeded by his disciple Brag-'bur-ba, the latter by Ri-la gzhon-rin, better known as Shugs-gseb ri-rab because of his time as abbot at the Shugs-gseb monastery. Thereafter the tradition passed through Bla-ma dKon-mchog rdo-rje, Chos-sgo-ba dPal shes-rab, rDza-khol-ba Jo-stan, Bla-ma sMon-lam-pa, sTag-lung Chos-rje Ngag-gi dbang-po, rJe Sha-ra rab-'byams-pa bSod-nams seng-ge, and 'Khrul-zhig Sangs-rgyas bsam-grub, who was the teacher of Karma 'Phrin-las.[29]

While following in the line of his teacher Sangs-rgyas bsam-grub, 'Phrin-las also incorporated the teaching of Chos-grags rgya-mtsho (1454–1505), the seventh Karma-pa hierarch and an adherent of the Kar method that had begun with Ras-chung-pa and continued through Dus-gsum mkhyen-pa, 'Gro-mgon Ras-chen (the first Karma-pa hierarch), and his successors.[30] Since Karma 'Phrin-las expresses his indebtedness to the seventh Karma-pa, whose instruction he says he frequently obtained, we may safely date his commentary on the "King *Dohā*" to the second half of the fifteenth century. From Karma 'Phrin-las's works it also becomes evident that Bal-po Asu and sKye-med bd-chen are one and the same person. In two places Karma 'Phrin-las

[29] Karma 'Phrin-las, 4.

[30] Karma 'Phrin-las, 4. Another tradition also derived from Ras-chung-pa. It was developed by rGyal-ba Lo (1187–1250), Sum-pa, and, in particular, gLing-ras-pa (born 1128). In this tradition special attention was given to the "People *Dohā*."

refers to the "previous commentary" and there he quotes the exact words of sKye-med bde-chen.[31]

> > >

Even so brief a survey as the above should serve to underline the importance of Saraha in the intellectual history of Tibet. His insistence on the immediacy of experience—its spontaneity, its wholeness, its ecstasy—marked a quest for the authentic Self that resolutely refuses to lose itself in abstract speculations about the self. In so doing, Saraha set himself squarely within the ancient Indian tradition of "inwardly directed" thought, a tradition whose offshoots include Buddhism and whose stress on the transformation of the self continues in our times in ideas like the "process of individuation."

By all accounts Saraha was a Brahmin, a member of the social class whose duty it was to study (to learn more about oneself) and to teach (to transmit to others the fruits of one's own experience). These "others" of course belonged to the upper strata of society, the "sons and daughters of good social standing" (*kulaputra*, *kuladuhitṛ*, Tib. *rigs-kyi bu*, *rigs-kyi bu-mo*) as the early Buddhists called them. As a Buddhist, Saraha believed and taught that the spiritual essence of the human being lay beyond the reach of caste distinctions, much to the chagrin of his fellow Brahmins.

Judged by the standards of modern historiography, our account of Saraha's life is obscure if not outright suspect. Judged in terms of the Tibetan idea of biography (*rnam-thar*), which focuses on the spiritual development of the individual, we are on much surer ground. Even the little biographical material we have, read in the light of his "Queen *Dohā*," show us a person who had risen above the bonds of social nexus to the full stature of his humanity. To his fellow Brahmins, Saraha was a maverick. To his fellow seekers for the true Self, he was and still is a light shining in the darkness.

---

[31] For a translation of this commentary see Guenther, *The Royal Song of Saraha* (Seattle: University of Washington Press, 1969), pp. 89–91, 169–71.

Chapter 2

Wholeness

WE HUMANS ARE FRAGMENTED and divided beings, at odds with ourselves and our surrounding world. We suffer from our ongoing fragmentation and yearn for a wholeness whose presence we somehow sense as the driving force in our quest for its recovery. This wholeness, not reducible to any of its parts and yet neither simply their sum, has been given different names at different times in human history.

Hermetic philosophy, one of the oldest of Western worldviews, spoke of wholeness residing in itself as the All. In Gnosticism, particularly in the teaching of Valentinus (d. 160 C.E.), it was called *pleroma*, "the fullness that is the same as nothingness." In our own times this ancient term has been revived by thinkers such as Carl Gustav Jung[1] and Gregory Bateson.[2] The idea of wholeness also resurfaced in the mathematician and process philosopher Alfred North Whitehead,[3] as the idea of "extensive continuum," and has also figured prominently in the writings of twentieth-century physicists like David Bohm.[4]

In India, specifically in Buddhist India, and later in Tibet, this idea of wholeness was given the name Mahāmudrā (*phyag-rgya chen-po,* "a Seal than which none could be greater"). Other names, varying with the various traditions and approaches to this problem, were "Being—a ground that is without a ground" (*gzhi rtsa-med-pa*), "abidingnesss"

---

[1] See his *Septem Sermones ad Mortuos*, included as Appendix V in his *Memories, Dreams, Reflections* (New York: Vintage Books, 1961); and Stephan A. Hoeller, *The Gnostic Jung* (Wheaton: The Theosophical Publishing House, 1985), part 2.

[2] See *Mind and Nature: A Necessary Unity* (New York: E.P Dutton, 1979), 7, 94.

[3] See his *Process and Reality* (New York: Harper Torchbooks, 1960).

[4] See his *Wholeness and the Implicate Order* (London: Routledge & Kegan Paul, 1980).

(*gnas-lugs*), and "supercompleteness" (*rdzogs-pa chen-po*, now referred to by Western works in its abbreviated form, rDzogs-chen).

WHOLENESS AS A "SEAL"

In Tibetan Buddhism, talk of wholeness as a "seal" turns an otherwise static notion into a dynamic one. The emphasis is shifted away from the physical thing designated as seal to the act of seal*ing*. Mechanical though the act of marking with a seal may appear at first glance, this change in emphasis has important implications. For one thing, the seal is thought to remain in touch with the source that makes it perform its function: it stays in the hand of the one who marks something. But who is this "one"? Tibetan Buddhism looks beyond the mere agent for an experiential whole, a "one" that appears to itself through archetypal images. The principal such images in this context are the king (representing the political dimension), the authentic Self (representing the psychological dimension), and the inner mentor (representing the personal dimension). This latter, to which we will return shortly, introduces a "felt" relationship between one's deep sense of finiteness and a dim sense of openness that beckons one from afar to move into the infiniteness of Being.

All these images are, strictly speaking, guiding images that help the experiencer along the journey to wholeness. In particular it is the image of the authentic Self that has left its indelible mark—stamped on the one who is in search of it. It is in this sense of an indelible mark that Rong-zom Chos-kyi bzang-po (eleventh century) defines the term "seal":

> Seal means that the mark reveals the [threefold presence of the] authentic Self's gestalt, [inner] voice, and [engaged] spirituality.[5]

A further implication of this shift from the static notion of a *thing*-seal to the dynamic notion of a seal*ing* (*mudraṇa*) is the inclusion of joyfulness as an integral element in the act of seal*ing*. In interpersonal relationships, this joy shows up primarily as a mutual pleasing (*modana*).[6] In a male-dominated psychology, the mutuality is one-sided and pleasing is distorted into a mere duty for women—in spite of the fact that "seal" (*mudrā*) is a feminine noun. Indeed, to stress the feminine

---

[5] *gSang-'grel*, fol. 26a.
[6] *gSang-'grel*, fol. 26a.

character of this seal/sealing, Tibetans have spoken of a *phyag-rgya-ma*. As Klong-chen rab-'byams-pa (1308–1363/4) explains,

> *Phyag* means to hold (back)—to hold [one] back from lapsing into samsara and to keep one on the level of spiritual wakefulness; *rgya* means to seal—to seal samsara with the seal of spirituality; *ma* means nourishing food, for just as one who goes without food will die, so too without attending to the *phyag-rgya-ma*, there is no deep understanding [into Being], without which one will remain fettered to the three realms of worldly attachment.[7]

In addition to these two senses of *mudrā*, the physical seal and the act of sealing, there is a third level of meaning that encompasses and penetrates the other two. There the seal is understood as a tension between bondage and freedom. From Buddhism's characteristically dynamic perspective, this tension of opposites energizes a thrust forward, propelling one into what we might call, with Heidegger, the "beingness of Being," or *ek-stasis*. This is the sense in which Rong-zom Chos-kyi bzang-po explains the term *mudrā*:

> *Mu* means freedom and *drā* means bondage. The function [of the seal] is both to fetter oneself and to free oneself and others, to break the individual [forms of] bondage. Hence one speaks of the "seal" as a bondage-freedom.[8]

For the Buddhist, wholeness is an openness out of which other wholes are able to emerge, each full and complete in itself. This idea is a direct continuation of an idea stated, perhaps for the first time, in the opening section of the *Īśā-Upaniṣad*:

> That is full;
> This is full.
> From the full emerges the full;
> Fullness coming from fullness, fullness still remains.

Wholeness, fullness, completeness, or whatever name we give it, cannot but point to itself. In the idiom of logic so dear to the Indians, the specifier is the specified and vice-versa. This self-reflexivity of wholeness implies that the experiencer is an integral aspect of wholeness and experiences wholeness through an inner affinity and sensitivity to it.

---

[7] *Theg-mchog*, vol. 1, 216–17.
[8] *gSang-'grel*, fol. 26b.

THE FOUR SEALS

Traditionally four "seals" – always to be understood functionally, leaving an *impression* and creating an *expression* – have been distinguished. Their Indian names are *karmamudrā, dharmamudrā, mahāmudrā,* and *samayamudrā*; their Tibetan equivalents are *las-kyi phyag-rgya, chos-kyi phyag-rgya, phyag-rgya chen-po,* and *dam-tshig-gi phyag-rgya,* respectively.

The first, *karmamudrā*, was defined as a woman whose physical appearance and presence was never, except among inveterate reductionists, conceived of as only physical, and hence not as something that could be manipulated like a tool or a toy. Within the triarchic framework of Buddhist thought, she was seen, from "without," as a member of a particular social setting or caste. Seen from "within," she became a divine maiden or, as we might say in the idiom of depth psychology, an anima-figure conveying "meaning" (*dharma,* Tib. *chos*), one who acts (*karma, las*) as a mediator between the realms of naive reality and the imaginal-symbolic. Finally, in the realm of the "arcane," she represented instinct, dispositional traits, vital functions of biological human nature.[9]

The correlation of the realm of the imaginal-symbolic with that of the naive-real, the former imparting meaningfulness to the latter, was summed up in the code term *dharmamudrā.* In actual life we deal with meanings rather than with things (unless, of course, one happens to think of oneself as a mindless "thing"). But to become aware of meaning requires something beyond a rational calculus that "grasps" things and cannot see beyond the lifeless and impersonal "it." Meanings are rather to be "understood" by *aisthesis,* the capacity for perceiving wholes and wholeness. This capacity or sensitivity to meaning is something *sui generis* and rooted in our spiritual nature. It is not, as Freud would have us believe, a mere derivative of biological instinct. Awareness of meaning signals the working of what in Sanskrit is termed *jñāna*, the Tibetan term for which, *ye-shes*, implies a cognitive capacity (*shes*) that has been operative from time before time (*ye*). It is from this perspective that the *dharmamudrā* is also referred to, though rarely, by the term *jñānamudrā* (*ye-shes-kyi phyag-rgya*).[10]

The third seal, *mahāmudrā*, points to a wholeness that can be experienced in the immediacy of ecstasy as a connectedness with the beingness-of-being. It does not connote anything like "pure immediacy" or "totality" in the sense in which traditional metaphysics has

[9] On this triarchic pattern, see *Theg-mchog*, vol. 1, 298–300.

[10] *gSang-'grel*, fol. 27a.

used these terms to turn wholeness into a thing or object of reason. Rather, in the words of Rong-zom Chos-kyi bzang-po:

> *Phyag-rgya chen-po* (*mahāmudrā*) is the as yet undifferentiated field-like expanse of Being where meanings are born.[11]

The realization of wholeness might seem to mark the end of the road, the crowning achievement of experience. In fact, it is a kind of turning point to a fourth and final seal where the experiencer begins a new and enriched life whose energy is contagious. This stage of revitalization is called *samayamudrā* (*dam-tshig-gi phyag-rgya*). Rong-zom Chos-kyi bzang-po speaks of it this way:

> *Dam-tshig* is the pristine awareness that is the mystery of the authentic Self's spirituality and *phyag-rgya* is the mark [it leaves on everything with which it comes into contact].[12]

The relationship among these four "seals" is succinctly stated by Saraha[13] in what we may call his *Vajragīti* trilogy, a virtual panegyric of the Mahāmudrā experience:

> The *karmamudrā* is an analogy; the *dharmamudrā* is the way;
> The *mahāmudrā* is the culmination; the *samayamudrā* is other-enrichment.
> By attending to what is on a lower level than the *dharmamudrā* one will not come to the end of one's journey.
> Falling into the extremes of hopes and fears there is [for such a person] too much of aimless activity.[14]

And later, in the same work, he is still more forthright:

> The [sensuously felt] experience that comes in the wake of attending to the *karmamudrā*
> Has arisen through the power of circumstances, because it is an artificially planned one;

---

[11] *gSang-'grel*, fol. 27a.

[12] *gSang-'grel*, fol. 27a.

[13] Concerning the unresolved problem of Saraha's dates, see chapter 1.

[14] *Kāyakośa-amṛta-vajragīti* (in bsTan-'gyur, vol. *Tsi*, fol. 80b). The two other works in this trilogy are the *Vākkośa-rucirasvara-vajragīti* and the *Cittakośa-aja-vajragīti*, to which a summary, the *Kāya-vāk-citta-amanasikāra*, is added in order to emphasize that none of the topics discussed in the trilogy are matters of representational thought. The original Indian versions of all of these works have been lost. It is an unresolved problem why this trilogy or cycle of songs (*gīti*), which specifically deals with the Mahāmudrā, has found no Indian or Tibetan commentaries.

It is not the beingness [of ecstasy], because it depends on something other [than itself].
Although the *dharmamudrā* (experience) is not some artificially planned one,
Its [sensuously felt] experience does not "see" what is not given [as an object for its gaze].
But when the [sensuously felt] experience of the *mahāmudrā* comes about
One knows the multiplicity of [the creations of one's] organismic thinking to be such as never having come into existence [as independent entities].[15]

The culminating Māhamudrā experience of which Saraha speaks is, as he had stated earlier, the "authentic Self." It is a whole whose realization comes about through something approaching what C. G. Jung called "active imagination," namely a spontaneous flow of images in which the subject participates rather than merely observes objectively. Insofar as this imaginative activity becomes ever more self-reflexive, and thereby ever more "whole," the *dharmamudrā* is—again to borrow a term from Jungian psychology—a kind of individuation, a "process by which a person becomes a psychological in-dividual," that is, a separate, indivisible unity or "whole."[16]

COMPLEMENTARITY-IN-SPONTANEITY

Surveying the various attempts to "define" *mahāmudrā* as a wholeness that does not admit of reduction to anything else, we are left with an impression of what we might call "pure potential," an as-yet-unfolded on the verge of unfolding and leaving its indelible mark on the unfolded. It is this unfolding that Saraha calls *sahaja* (*lhan-cig-skyes-pa*), which is explained in the first part of the trilogy, the translation of which follows in part 2.[17]

---

[15] *Kāyakośa-amṛta-vajragīti* (in bsTan-'gyur, vol. *Mi*, fol. 82a).

[16] C. G. Jung, *Collected Works* (Princeton: Princeton University Press, 1957–1970), vol. 9, 275. The authentic or individuated Self is not an absolute or One as postulated by metaphysical philosophies. Hence in the passage cited in the text Rong-zom Chos-kyi bzang-po speaks of the "authentic Self" (*bdag-nyid chen-po*) in the plural.

[17] It is interesting to note that the term *mahāmudrā* that figures so prominently in Saraha's *Kāyakośa-amṛta-vajragīti* (it appears no less than 39 times) does not appear at all in this part of the present trilogy, consisting of the "People *Dohā*," the "Queen *Dohā*," and the "King *Dohā*."

Literally, *sahaja* means "co-emergent" (it can be read as noun or adjective) where emergence (*ja*) is a spontaneous and uncaused manifestation of what we might call the principle of "complementarity" (*saha*). As an immediate experience, co-emergence entails a feeling of "togetherness" (*saha*) whose numinosity erases all sense of separation. A precise rendering of the term *sahaja* would therefore have to be something like "complementarity-in-spontaneity," a translation which I have adopted throughout.

For Saraha, complementarity-in-spontaneity has three aspects, based on the distinction between ordinary body, speech, and mind. As phenomenal (*snang-ba*), it is at once physical and psychic, and exhibits different degrees of density: mind is relatively transparent, speech is semi-transparent, and body is opaque.[18] The phenomenal, whatever its degree of intensity, is always and forever inseparable from the noumenal. In their "togetherness" the two give the experiencing individual a sense of meaning and connectedness with a universal process that vanquishes the fear of death. Saraha is credited with the words:[19]

> Hey-ho friends! This complementarity-in-spontaneity
> Is not gained from [any] other source[20] than from the trustworthy innermost mentor's mouth.
> If you deeply feel and understand this supreme value, the energy [that flows from his] mouth,
> There is no death to your mind (*yid*)[21] and there is no nihility to your body (*lus*).[22]

---

[18] The idea of treating mind as a physical phenomenon presents considerable difficulties to Western thinking because of a deeply ingrained dualism that pits the psychic/mental against the physical/material. In Buddhist thought body, speech, and mind represent our "physical" side, while "pleasure" (*bde-ba*), "luminosity" (*gsal-ba*), and "undividedness by concepts" (*mi-rtog-pa*) represent our "psychic" side. The idea of degrees of intensity and density reflects a dynamic or "process" mode of thought. Even among the Buddhists, of course, there were those who persisted in thinking of the universe as a static entity. For example, in his *Grub-mtha'* (382), Klong-chen rab-'byams-pa informs us that adherents of the teaching contained in the earlier ("lower") Tantras interpreted the threefold dynamic of *lhan-cig-skyes-pa* as a state of equilibrium not unlike the three "strands" (*guṇa*) of the Sāṃkhya system.

[19] *Grub-thob brgyad-cu-rtsa-bzhi'i rtogs-pa'i snying-po rdo-rje'i glu*, 126; see also the commentary in Abhayaśri's *Grub-thob brgyad-cu-rtsa-bzhi'i dohā 'grel-bcas*, 151–52.

[20] The commentator has in mind words and propositions about it.

[21] I have used the English word *mind* to render the Tibetan term *yid* (*manas*) in an attempt to highlight the contrast with *body* (*lus*, *deha*). Both *yid* and *lus* describe processes, the former referring to mind as essentially a *Denkvorgang*

In this passage, and indeed throughout the first two parts of his *Dohākośa* trilogy, Saraha stresses the importance of the "innermost mentor." Let us look more closely at this image.

THE INNERMOST MENTOR

For Sahara, the "innermost mentor" (*bla-ma*) is an archetypal figure and guiding image dominant in one's process of coming to self-realization. It rises to the surface when one begins to interact with the forces acting in and through oneself. These forces need to be exteriorized in order to be faced and addressed in dialogue. In this process of exteriorization they acquire a human face, but this transformation of the innermost mentor into an outer force remains, when all is said and done, part of one's own spirituality (*sems-nyid*). That is, there is a dynamic at work here ordering cosmos and psyche into a single, undivided whole whose symbolic expression reverts back finally to the archetypal figure of an innermost mentor.

Although lexically the Tibetan term *bla-ma* corresponds to the Indian term *guru* (a term I have come to abhor because of the cheap associations that have often eclipsed its true meaning), it has been interpreted by the Tibetans as meaning both "heavy" and "wide-open": "heavy" because of its many and brightly shining qualities, and "wide-open" because of its lack of all limiting and obscuring negativities.[23]

(thinking process) that comes to birth with the ego. As far as we can talk about *yid* at all, it refers to an "ego-inclined awareness" with at least some degree of ego-centeredness. *Lus* refers to the body as the final phase of a process of embodiment. The commentator thus understands *yid* to mean that one's ego-inclined awareness, ruptured by rational dichotomies and tossed around by emotional vicissitudes, has through insight become an occasion for the unceasing presence of Being in its ungenerated, original state.

[22] The commentator understands *lus* to mean that the (overt) dichotomies and their (latent) tendencies create the impression that it is they who constitute bodily existence and they who destroy it in order to make room for a new constitution. The discontinuity implied in thus seeing the body as a "complex of instincts and discursive ventures" (*rnam-rtog bag-chags-kyi lus*), eclipses the view of body as the expression of a pristine awareness of a greater whole of which we are but a part (*ye-shes-kyi lus*). The body-mind problem, only touched on here in passing allusion to the words *yid* and *lus*, merits closer comparison with the fresh approach taken by Merleau-Ponty in his *Phenomenology of Perception* (London: Routledge & Kegan Paul, 1962, 216; see also 12, 267, 327, 352) and by David Michael Levin in *The Opening of Vision* (London: Routledge & Kegan Paul, 1988, 203).

[23] See, for example, g.Yung-mgon rdo-rje's *rDo-rje-tshig-gi zab-don*, 429.

What distinguishes the *bla-ma* from the *guru*, however, is its dynamic structure that seems to be partly psychic and, at least potentially, partly physical. There are three elements to this structure. The first is the energizing force that flows from the whole of Being itself. This is called the *brgyud-pa'i bla-ma*. When this whole "speaks" to us, what we hear is not so much a transmission of information as an inner voice that speaks with conviction and bids us pay heed. This voice, the second element, is called *bka'i bla-ma*. The third and final element in the *bla-ma* dynamic is the impact it has on the mind, wiping it clean of fictions about reality and laying our spirituality naked before us. This is called the *dngos-kyi bla-ma*.[24]

From even so brief a discussion of *bla-ma*, it is clear that when the earlier Buddhists, and Saraha in particular, speak of an innermost mentor, they are not referring to an idea but to an experience. The same may be said of Saraha's use of the term "guardian lord" (*nātha*, Apabhraṃśa *nāha* or *ṇāha*, *mgon-po*), which adds an element of numinosity to the experience of the innermost mentor. And as the sense of the numinous is often accompanied by a perception of intense luminosity, the guardian lord is also referred to as the "guardian lord Light-invariant" (*mgon-po 'od mi-'gyur-ba*).[25] Here again, the guardian

---

[24] *Grub-thob brgyad-cu-rtsa-bzhi'i dohā 'grel-bcas*, 151.

[25] The phrase *mgon-po 'od mi-'gyur-ba*, "the guardian lord Light-invariant," is often expanded to *gdod-ma'i mgon-po 'od mi-'gyur-ba*, "the primordial lord Light-invariant." In this latter phrase *gdod-ma* refers to the birth of time from out of the inner dynamics of Being itself. The idea is that a rupture occurred within the unity and symmetry of Being, and that this rupture gave rise to the space-time continuum. This eruption of Being into time and space was accompanied by a massive wave of intense, supracognitive energy that found its way into the heart of every embodied being (*lus-can*), where it serves as the organizing principle for the bodily evolution of that being. See *mKha'-yang*, vol. 2, 195–96, 201.

In his *Zab-mo yang-tig*, vol. 1, 280, Klong-chen rab-'byams-pa speaks of this "primordial guardian lord Light-invariant" as the spiritual awakening (*sangs-rgyas*) of the whole, be it at the level of the individual or the universe—a process that has been going on since "time before time":

> *gdod-ma'i mgon-po 'od mi-'gyur-ba ni*
> *'khor-'das gang-du'ang ma-chad-cing*
> *sngar sangs snga-nas rgyas-pa'o*

> The primordial lord Light-invariant,
> Not fragmented into either samsara or nirvana,
> Has since time before time [been a process of darkness] dissipating
> and [of light] expanding.

lord is not seen as something absolute and beyond the reach of human experience. Such absoluteness may be fitting in high theological and metaphysical speculation, but here it is an obstacle. The turning of experiential images into abstract concepts protects the fundamental biases and delusions of the ego by deliberately reifying what is encountered in experience.[26] Saraha leaves no doubt that there is nothing abstract and absolute about his idea of the innermost mentor or guardian lord, and even goes so far as to claim that the guardian-lord is none other than one's own "authentic (in Jungian terminology, individuated) Self" (*bdag-nyid*).

THE AUTHENTICITY OF BEING

As *mahāmudrā*, wholeness marks everything it touches with the indelible seal of Being. As *sahaja*, complementarity-in-spontaneity, wholeness manifests itself as the inseparable togetherness of the experiencer and the experienced. Let us now go a step further and consider what we might call "the authenticity of Being as an uncontrived wholeness." In this connection, Sahara favors the term *ṇia* (*nija*, *gnyug-ma*), a word that appears only rarely in the Indian context.[27] Although *ṇia* may be

---

Although the term *sangs-rgyas* never lost its verbal character in the Tibetan context, as the corresponding Sanskrit word *buddha* did in the Western tradition by being turned into a noun denoting a Buddha-thing, it was used to replace *mgon-po*. Thus in the *Rig-pa rang-shar*, 535, 639–40, and in the *Seng-ge rtsal-rdzogs*, 377 we find the phrase *sangs-rgyas 'od mi-'gyur-ba*. In place of *mgon-po* or *sangs-rgyas* we may even find even *ston-pa*, "teacher" (*Rig-pa rang-shar*, 575). That it is the ecstatic, supracognitive intensity of Being (*rig-pa*) that "constitutes" itself as primordial guardian lord or *sangs-rgyas* is well attested by a passage in the *Spros-bral don-gsal chen-po'i rgyud*, 389 (in: *rNying-rgyud*, vol. 6, 374–608). Its ideas are said to have been transmitted from dGa'-rab rdo-rje (of unknown date but believed to have lived in the first century of the common era) through a number of persons to Padmasambhava, who gave them their final form in this monumental work. In the abbreviated version, the *Thig-le kun-gsal* (in: *rNying-rgyud*, vol. 5, 124–289), the passage in question can be found on page 133.

26 This critique is already found in g.Yung-mgon rdo-rje, *rDo-rje tshig-gi zab-don*, 431.

27 I have found it only twice, both in the same author, Kotali (Tog-tse-pa), one of the eighty-four eccentrics (*mahāsiddha*), among whom Saraha is also numbered, and author of the very short *Sahajānanta-svabhāva* (in bsTan-'gyur, vol. *Tshi*, fol. 58ab.) Kotali expressed his understanding of reality in these words, recorded in *Grub-thob brgyad-cu-rtsa-bzhi'i rtogs-pa'i snying-po rdo-rje'i glu*, 131 and *Grub-thob brgyad-cu-rtsa-bzhi'i dohā 'grel-bcas*, 191–92:

taken as either noun or adjective, Saraha's Indian and Tibetan commentaries are agreed in interpreting it primarily as a noun, meaning something like "Being-in-its-beingness" (*de-[kho-na]-nyid*) or "Being's abidingness" (*gnas-lugs*). The adjectival connotation gives it the added quality of something that is "uncontrived" (*ma-bcos-pa*).[28] Like the

---

All pleasures and pains arise from the mind—
With this admonition by the innermost mentor I have hoed the mountain of the mind, [for]
Should an intelligent person [merely] hoe the physical mountain
He would not win the deeply felt understanding of the ecstasy of Being's genuineness (*gnyug-ma'i bde-ba chen-po*) in himself.
This as-yet undifferentiated psychic potential awakens in one's heart;
When the six perceptual patterns have been cleared ecstasy flows uninterruptedly.
All one's postulates have turned out to be meaningless and the cause of one's frustrations.
Dispose of your active and passive imaginations in the dimension [of yours] that is Being's genuineness (*gnyug-ma'i ngang*).

[28] It appears in this qualitative sense in a number of other terms as well. An outstanding example is Klong-chen rab-'byams-pa's *Nam-mkha' rab-'byams*, 398 (in: *mKha'-yang*, vol.1, 397–411):

so-ma gnyug-ma ma-bcos rang-ka-ma
rang-bzhin lhug-pa ye-grol chos-nyid-la
bcings dang grol med nam-mkha'i mdud-pa bzhin
spang dang 'khrul-pa'i byung-khungs zad-pa yin

In Being's possibilizing dynamics, fresh, genuine, uncontrived, plain,
Continuing being-itself, relaxed, and since time before time having exercised its freedom,
There has never existed [something that might be called] bondage or freedom—like a knot in the sky.
The source for something to be given up and for going astray has dried up.

The same "painting with words" occurs in his *Khyung-chen gshog-rdzogs*, 271 (in: *Zab-yang*, vol. 1, 265–74):

so-ma gnyug-ma ma-bcos rang-ga-ma
tha-mal shes-pa rang-grol rgyal-ba'i lam
rang-rig rang-grol gnyen-pos bcos mi-dgos
skye-med lhun-rdzogs ye-grol rig-pa'i klong
gang snang grogs-su 'char-ba'i rang-bzhin-la
spang-blang 'khrul-pa'i byung-khungs zad-pa yin

Fresh, genuine, uncontrived, plain,
This as-yet undifferentiated psychic potential, exercising its

other terms for wholeness already discussed, *ṇia* carries a sense of dynamism, best understood as referring to an intense intrapsychic presence. In this regard, it is not a barren, passive quality but a creative, active feeling-tone.

Ṇia performs two functions. On the one hand, it *deconstructs* the normal tendency of ego-consciousness (*yid*) to busy itself with reified presences, thus opening one up to a new and wider horizon of vision. In this sense Saraha speaks of *ṇia-mana* (*gnyug-ma'i yid*), an "ego-consciousness whose reifying tendencies have been deconstructed by the authenticity of Being as an uncontrived wholeness and presence." On the other hand, *ṇia* heightens our capacity to awaken to our own wholeness. In this sense Saraha speaks of *gnyug-ma'i ye-shes*, a "pristine awareness heightened in its sensibility by the authenticity of Being as an uncontrived wholeness and presence."

The former term, *ṇia-mana*, appears only in his "People *Dohā*," a work concerned with the initial expansion of one's horizon. The latter term, *gnyug-ma'i ye-shes*, is reserved for the "Queen *Dohā*," a work devoted more to the intensification of vision through active imagination. It should be noted here that the use of the genitive to juxtapose *ṇia* and *mana* (*gnyug-ma'i yid*) and *gnyug-ma* and *ye-shes* (the Apabhraṃśa version in which this term occurs has been lost) does not imply the possession of one thing by another. There are no "things" here at all, but only relationships whose inner tension keeps the process of individuation alive.

---

freedom by itself, is the royal road;
To be experienced by one's self in an ecstatic supracognitive intensity,
exercising its freedom by itself, it need not be "improved" by
[extraneous] helpful devices.
In this vortex of an ecstatic supracognitive intensity that is without
birth, complete in its thereness, and having since time before
time exercised its freedom
Whatever comes-to-presence continues doing so as being a friend
The source for straying into [the mistaken notions of] acceptance
and rejection has dried up.

Strictly speaking, the two terms *ye-grol* and *rang-grol* can only be paraphrased, not translated. They are "adverbs" designating what in Whiteheadian terminology we might call "vector feeling-tones" which cannot be abstracted from the process of experiencing. The first term indicates that the process has been going on since "time before time" (*ye*); the second, that the process does so by itself (*rang*).

THE "OWNMOSTNESS" OF WHOLENESS

Saraha's concern with the experience of wholeness expresses itself in his frequent use of the term *sahāba* (*svabhāva, rang-bzhin*). The term suggests a kind of energy state, corresponding quite literally to what quantum physics calls eigenstate or eigenvalue (stationary value), or, from a more dynamic perspective, *eigenfunction*. That is, *sahāba* denotes something primarily taken up with its *own* (*rang*) ability to continue functioning (*bzhin*). This "ownmostness" or "ownmost dynamics," as I propose to render the Indian/Tibetan term, is also a kind of wholeness. More precisely, it is an articulation of the original wholeness of Being that itself is beyond all articulation. For did not the early *Īśā-Upaniṣad* already state, "From the full [wholeness] emerges the full [wholeness]"?

Saraha's insight into the functional dimension of wholeness has far-reaching implications that seem to counter the traditional Buddhist claim that what we call reality has no *eigenstate* or *eigenfunction* or *eigenvalue* (*niḥsvabhāva, rang-bzhin med-pa*).[29] In the course of time this metaphysical claim became absolutized into a dogma whose truth was beyond question. Ironically, this seems in effect to perpetuate the very reifying and dichotomizing tendencies of ordinary representational thought that Buddhism set out to overcome, and thus to draw perilously close to a nihilism in which Being itself is negated.

By conceiving of *svabhāva* as an energy state with a specific value (grammatically expressed as a compound with *sahāba* as the second term) Saraha can speak of the ownmostness or *eigenfunction* of "complementarity-in-spontaneity" (*sahaja-sahāba, lhan-cig-skyes-pa'i rang-bzhin*) and of the "ownmostness of the authenticity of Being as its *eigenfunction*" (*ṇia-sahāba, gnyug-ma'i rang-bzhin*) in the same vein that he speaks of the "ownmostness or *eigenfunction* of samsara " (*saṃsāraha bhaṅge, 'khor-ba'i rang-bzhin*) or of "the ownmost dynamic or *eigenfunction* of enchantment" (*māyāmaya parama, sgyu-ma'i rang-bzhin*).[30]

---

[29] The term *niḥsvabhāva* occurs in this traditional sense only twice in Saraha's *Dohākośa-nāma mahāmudrā-upadeśa* (*Do-hā-mdzod ces-bya-ba phyag-rgya chen-po'i man-ngag*). Lost in its original Apabhraṃśa, the Tibetan translation has been preserved in the bsTan-'gyur, vol. *Tsi*, fols. 95a–97a. The term *rang-bzhin med-pa* is found on fol. 96a. It is interesting to note that this small work is attributed to the "Hermit (*ri-khrod-pa*) Saraha." This altogether magnificent work gives the distinct impression of being a compilation of the basic ideas of Saraha. Could it have been a later work written by Saraha? We know too little about his life to answer that question, but, to judge from the colophons, he seems to have set out as an "instructor" (*slob-dpon*), became an outstanding visionary (*rnal-'byor-gyi dbang-phyug*), and finally a hermit (*ri-khrod-pa*).

[30] Literally translated the Apabhraṃśa phrase means "the highest reality,

The English phrasing here gives an ostentatious tone to the original Tibetan, but Saraha's aim was just the opposite: to draw attention to what can be apprehended directly in the immediacy of experience. We who are more concerned with what is *not* directly apprehended but hypothetically inferred on the basis of the directly apprehended, would prefer a formulation that begins, "What is meant by complementarity-in-spontaneity (or authenticity) is . . . " But this renders Saraha's accent on immediate experience as at best incidental. Although *rang-bzhin* serves as the first term in what looks to the Sanskrit eye to be a compound, it actually retains its independence in such a way that what follows is more in the nature of an explanation or emphasis.[31]

Clearly Saraha's principal ideas did not originate in a vacuum. Traces of earlier Upanishadic thought, for example, are discernible throughout. More intriguing is the fact that Saraha's ideas have their counterpart in Gauḍapāda's *Āgamaśāstra*. The critical passage runs as follows:

> *sāṃsiddhikī svābhāvikī sahajāpy akṛtā ca yā*
> *prakṛtiḥ seti vijñeyā svabhāvaṃ na jahāti yā*[32]

---

consisting of enchantment." The apparent discrepancy between the Apabhraṃśa version and the Tibetan translation is another strike against the myth, perpetuated in academic circles, that the Tibetans translated the Indian texts mechanically into their own language. Quite the contrary, they thought a great deal about the content of what they were translating. The often acrimonious controversy between "translation" and "interpretation" is, to follow in the footsteps of Saraha's bluntness, just so much "hogwash."

[31] The few cases in which this occurs are *rang-bzhin gnyug-ma* in stanza 18, where the Apabhraṃśa has the more common *ṇia-sahāba*; *rang-bzhin lhan-cig-skyes-pa* in stanza 93, where the Apabhraṃśa also has the more common *sahaja-sahāba*. The phrase *rang-bzhin gnyug-ma* is, however, well attested by its occurrence in Saraha's *Kāyakośa-amṛta-vajragīti* (see note 17 above, fol. 81b). But without the Apabhraṃśa version, there is no way to determine what the original wording was. The emphatic character is most evident in stanza 19:

> *rang-bzhin dag-pa'i sems-la bsam-gtan-dag-gis mi bslad-de*
>
> Your mind that by virtue of its presenting Being's ownmostness is pure should not be ruined by concentrative meditations.

The Apabhraṃśa version merely has: *asamala citta* "(a) mind without blemishes," which is a far cry from the Tibetan *rang-bzhin dag-pa*, which, in the light of similar compounds, we might "reconstruct into Sanskrit"—a pastime many Indians take great delight in—as *prakṛti-viśuddha*.

[32] *Āgamaśāstra*, IV, 9.

That is to be known as matter/energy (*prakṛti*) that is
efficacious,[33] expressive of its own dynamics, spontaneous,
uncontrived and
That does not forsake its ownmostness.

We do not know what, if any, contact there was between Saraha and Gauḍapāda,[34] but both authors emphasize the dynamic, rather than static, character of Being. This alone makes them both unique in the rich world of early Indian thinking, which eventually fell into stagnation and repetitiveness. It is an irony of history that Śankara, though recognizing the importance of Gauḍapāda's work, was bent on eliminating all traces of Buddhism in his particular brand of Vedanta, while Saraha's work remained practically unnoticed by Buddhist philosophers, who foundered in the interminable subtleties of logical disputations.

THE FOURFOLD FUNCTION OF MIND

The idea of relating individuals to their surrounding world according to a triarchic model, so characteristic of Buddhist thought, is also reflected in the way the individual as such is understood. For example, the pursuit of truth is likened to a journey with a starting point (a tension or restlessness that prompts one to depart the world of the familiar for the unknown), a path or way (the process of spiritual growth stimulated by the interplay of perception and insight, of operacy[35] and appreciation), and a culmination or goal (the realization of authenticity in self-fulfillment and other-enrichment).

Another such triarchic model (already alluded to in connection

---

[33] The adjective *sāmsiddhikī* is derived from the noun *saṃsiddhi*, meaning "success," and implies that matter-energy (in Gauḍapāda's diction) is bound to produce the desired effect. This idea of effecting a desired result (*sgrub*) is also found in stanza 115 of Saraha's *Dohākośa-upadeśa-gīti*.

[34] If language is a criterion, Saraha would be earlier than Gauḍapāda. He makes extensive use of the term *manas* (*yid*) that figures prominently in the older *Chāndogya-Upaniṣad*, while Gauḍapāda favors *citta* (*sems*), which is a more recent term characteristic of the *Bṛhadāraṇyaka-Upaniṣad*. Both the *Chāndogya-Upaniṣad* and the *Bṛhadāraṇyaka-Upaniṣad* are "early" Upanishads. In time, the term *citta* was to carry the day.

[35] This term was coined by Edward de Bono, *I Am Right—You Are Wrong* (New York: Viking Penguin Inc., 1990), 26. As a dynamic term that applies to a living system as a whole its use is most suited to convey what the Buddhists understood by *thabs*.

with the first of the seals, the *karmamudrā*) sees the individual as functioning in three interdependent dimensions: the external, the internal, and the arcane. No one dimension can exist apart from the others, nor can any one be reduced to any other. The "external" dimension (*phyi*) refers literally to the phenomenal world as that which "lights up" (*snang-ba*), but insofar as it always lights up in mistaken identifications (*'khrul-snang*) it sets up a wealth of "meanings in material concreteness," that is, a world of things and reified ideas (*chos, chos-can*).[36] The "internal" dimension (*nang*) refers to the mental and imaginal capacity (*shes-pa*) for entertaining meanings, ceaselessly giving birth to "new" meanings in material concreteness while dissolving "old" ones (*chos-nyid*).[37] The "arcane" or "secret" (*gsang*)[38] is the dimension of ecstatic and supracognitive intensity (*rig-pa*), a dimension where knowledge is fully experiential.

Over and above this triarchy of dimensions rests a "fourth dimension," which in sNying-thig texts and texts deriving from them is called *yang-gsang*, "arcaner-than-arcane,"[39] or *kho-na-nyid*, "the holistic."[40] Saraha is familiar with this progression, even if he does not refer to it explicitly. In general, references to the fourfold dynamic are phrased in such a way that to the uninitiated they would sound like conventional language, even though they are expressly stated to be "symbolic expressions" (*brda*) in the mythical idiom of the Ḍākas and

---

[36] See, for instance, *Bla-ma yang-ting* vol. 1, 419–29.; *Chos-dbyings*, 272–73. According to *mKha'-yang*, vol. 2, 199, the "external" are the projections of psychic contents in fierce and calm shapes.

[37] According to *mKha'-yang*, vol. 2, 199, the "internal" are the Ḍāka-Ḍākinī syzygies. The ancient term *syzygy*, which, as June Singer has shown (*Androgyny: The Opposites Within*, Boston: Sigo Press, 1989), means "a pair, the existence of which is maintained by its essential complementarity," was reintroduced into modern psychoanalytic thought by C. G. Jung. The Buddhist conception is thus radically different from the Hindu notion of Śiva as half male and half female (*ardhanarīśvara*).

[38] As was the case in medieval Western mysticism, the word *secret* here did not refer to something obscurely mysterious or to be kept hidden. It merely indicates something that must be experienced to be known. Alas, all too often mysticism has been confused with dark mystification and the term *secret* has not infrequently served to masquerade the most abominable ignorance. According to *mKha'-yang*, vol. 2, 199, the "arcane" is the phoneme (*yi-ge*), a vibrational complex, that is first uttered to call the world of meanings into being.

[39] See *mKha'-yang*, vol. 2, 199, where it is defined as *thig-le nyag-gcig*, "information singularity." On this latter term, see my *Matrix of Mystery* (Boulder & London: Shambhala, 1984), 47, 49, 53.

[40] *Chos-dbyings*, 273, where it is defined as *gnas-lugs*, "abidingness."

Ḍākinīs.[41] The aim of this symbolic code is to bypass the intellect's tendency to break the world up into quantifiable fragments and thereby to stimulate awareness of a world of qualities and the accompanying insight into oneself as an organismic-instinctive-apperceptive-spiritual manifold.[42]

That these symbolic expressions have mentalistic overtones is hardly surprising. From its first beginnings, in varying degrees of explicitness, Buddhism has insisted on the fact that mind or spirit is a dynamic principle lying at the very heart of a universe in which the human individual is an integral part. Indeed, for the Buddhist the pure intensity of mind is the very stuff of which the universe, and we in it, are made.[43]

These four dimensions of symbolic expression, as interrelated to each other and as referring to a world that is itself interrelated, function like vectorial connectives for mind. Their Tibetan names, *dran-pa, dran-med, skye(-ba) med(-pa),* and *blo(-las) 'das(-pa),* are rendered in English as memory, non-memory, non-origin (or without an origin),[44] and transcendence (literally, beyond the intellect). While these dictionary equivalents are not incorrect, they fail to do justice to the richer connotations of each term. Each belongs to a greater whole. Each makes wholeness present in a way that the re-presentations of our ego-centered, time-and-space oriented thinking cannot. Sahara makes the

---

[41] Linguistically speaking, (masculine) *ḍāka* and (feminine) *ḍākinī* are so-called *deśī* words or local non-Sanskritic expressions. They designate mythological figures who are felt to be symbolic manifestations of modes of pristine awareness (*jñāna, ye-shes*). The Tibetan terms *mkha'-spyod* and *mkha'-spyod-ma* are literal translations of the Sanskrit *khecara* and *khecarī*, "roaming over the sky." Here the word "sky" (*kha*), like other Sanskrit synonyms such as *ākāśa* and *gagana,* is a metaphorical expression to indicate the fullness of the openness or nothingness of Being. The "roaming" of these mythological figures over the openness of Being suggests more subtly their "enjoyment" of the fullness of Being.

[42] For further details see figures 1, 2, and 3 in the following chapter.

[43] It is interesting to note that more and more modern physicists have come to the same conclusion. To cite only one of them, Max Planck writes: "I regard consciousness as fundamental. I regard matter as derivative from consciousness. We cannot get behind consciousness." This does not necessarily imply a metaphysical monism. On the contrary, all such *isms* are merely an escape from what really matters into idle speculation.

[44] In order to capture the precise meaning of this term, it would have to be paraphrased to read: "There exists no such thing to which the designation 'origin' applies."

point concisely in discussing them as functions of wholeness (Mahāmudrā):

> Mahāmudrā's exact delimitation is [its]
> Non-origin (*skye-med*) in view of the fact that both *dran* and
>   *dran-med* are not [yet or no longer] there;
> Beyond the intellect's [scope] (*blo-las 'das*), it does not abide as
>   some thing or other.[45]

Time and again Saraha directs our attention to an internal logic at work among these vectorial connectives, always in the attempt to describe wholeness as essentially functional. The following passages speak for themselves:

> In [one's] self-reflexive mind (*rang-sems*),[46] Mahāmudrā,
> The [possible] different[iation] between *dran* and *ma-dran*
>   [that is, *dran-med*] lies in [what is its] non-origin;
> This [feature of Mahāmudrā] goes beyond the intellect's
>   scope [restricted to the dichotomy of] errancy and non-
>   errancy;
> Inflated by divisive [tendencies and their] addictive [power][47]
>   that [are the working of] *dran-pa* it becomes the cause of
>   samsara.[48]

And again:

> By *dran-pa* as [a necessary] condition the divisive concepts [of
>   representational thought] come about in an incidental
>   manner; [*dran-pa*'s]
> Antecedent, *dran-pa med*, as well as [Being's]
> Non-origin (*skye-med*) and transcendence (*blo-'das*) are alike in
>   [their presenting Being's] wondrousness.

---

[45] *Kāyakośa-amṛta-vajragīti*, fol. 80a. Just as Saraha's *Dohākośa* Trilogy has as its theme "spontaneity," so his *Vajragīti* Trilogy takes up the theme of "Mahāmudrā fourfold." How well this topic was understood is evident from the fact that Advaya Avadhūti wrote his commentary on Saraha's "People *Dohā*" in the light of this "fourfold."

[46] As already noted in the above discussion of *rang-bzhin/svābhava*, the Tibetan term *rang* (Skt. *sva*) in its technical use denotes self-reflexivity. It does not mean that mind (*sems*) is one thing and self (*rang*) another, somehow mysteriously wielded together.

[47] *zhen-rtog*. This term is not found in the epistemology-oriented sutra literature, but is frequently used in works pertaining to the sNying-thig tradition, foremost with Vimalamitra.

[48] *Kāyakośa-amṛta-vajragīti*, fol. 83a.

Thus what comes into existence in Mahāmudrā is [and continues being] a prior non-being and
Even later on when it [seems to] have come into existence through the power of [necessary] conditions
Remains inseparable from [what is Being's] non-origin.[49]

Further:

Therefore Mahāmudrā means ultimate synthesis
[Such that] *dran-pa* enters a synthesis with *dran-med* and this with *skye-med.*
Since *dran-med* is the very non-dividedness by concepts [of Being as our spirituality] and
Since *dran-pa* comes into existence through incidental [conditions setting up a pattern of universal] connectedness, both
Have the same flavor [of Being's nothingness] in the vibrant dimension of [what is Being's] non-origin (*skye-ba med-pa'i ngang*);
Therefore the paradox[50] of there being an origin [or origination, *skye*] and [a] non-origin (*skye-med*) surpasses the scope of the intellect (*blo-las 'das*).[51]

THE CLOSURE OF SAMSARA, THE OPENNESS OF BEING

Like the sNying-thig thinkers after him, Saraha sees *dran-pa* as the captivating power of the phenomenal world in all its multiplicity and diversity (*snang-ba*), as samsara (in the narrower sense of the term) holding us fast in its grip;[52] and *dran-med* as the openness of Being (*stong-pa*) free of attachment to the merely phenomenal. These two dynamics, the closure of samsara and the openness of Being, though markedly distinct from one another, are not altogether separate, as the following passage suggests:

---

49 *Kāyakośa-amṛta-vajragīti,* fol. 82a.

50 *zung-'jug.* Loosely speaking, *zung-'jug* and *dbyer-med* are interchangeable, but there is a subtle and logical difference between the two. *Dbyer-med* refers to the indivisibility of Being in the sense that Being itself is prior to all differentiation of opposites, while *zung-'jug* refers to a dialectical synthesis of opposites that have already been constituted.

51 *Kāyakośa-amṛta-vajragīti,* fol. 81b.

52 In his *Kāyakośa-amṛta-vajragīti,* fol. 84b, Saraha explicitly speaks of *dran-pa* as "the things of samsara" (*'khor-ba'i dngos-po*).

> Although under the vectorial momentum[53] of the phenomenal *dran-pa* may come-into-being
> It does not pass beyond the vectorial momentum of [Being's] open-dimensionality that is *dran-med*.[54]

All-pervasive as it is, the cognitive side to human mind or spirituality seems to proliferate conceptual distinctions (*rtog-pa*) endlessly, each idea a closure that narrows the individual perspective. At the same time, mind is also possessed of the capacity to move into greater wholes and open up new perspectives (*rig-pa*). The form of the relationship between these two functions of mind determines how one responds to the surrounding world—fanatically pursuing the "real world" by turning it into ever more ethereal and ephemeral concepts (*dran-rtog*), or quickening one's sensitivities (*dran-rig*) in order to intensify one's feeling for wholeness.

Saraha and the sNying-thig thinkers seem to have been in agreement that the development of discursive consciousness on the one hand, with its dependence on concepts, and of intuitive awareness on the other, which dispenses with concepts in order to approach as near as possible to the ecstatic intensity of wholeness itself, share a common ground in the human individual. The common origin of discursive-representational thinking and intuitive-ecstatic awareness is circumscribed for them by the term *dran-pa*—a code name for a fundamental, organismic capacity for mentation that gives rise to both reflexive (discursive-representational) and self-reflexive (intuitive-ecstatic) modes of thought.[55]

The functional character of what we have called the four vectorial connectives is seen in their ability to "seal," which manifests itself less as a particular stage in a defined process than as a permanent feature of the interpenetrating, interacting, and interlocking of all things. In the words of Saraha:

---

[53] *rkyen* (*pratyaya*). In Buddhist thought, causality has generally been conceived of in terms of webs or networks of relationships. The idea of a chain of links, as seen in Western thought, is considered to be a secondary and rationalistic reduction of the way reality actually unfolds in experience. For a modern Western view of causality as a complex of vectors moving along in time and space, see for example Calvin O. Schrag, *Experience and Being* (Evanston: Northwestern University Press, 1969), 82–89.

[54] *Kāyakośa-amṛta-vajragīti*, fol. 78b.

[55] The complexity of *dran-pa*, which, following Erich Jantsch (*The Self-organizing Universe*, Oxford: Pergamon Press, 1980, 163, 169 *et passim*), I have translated as "organismic mentation," involves being embedded in a "field" that is as much material and non-material (i.e., mental or spiritual) as *dran-pa* itself.

Hey-ho! Wise persons who bristle with operacy[56]
Have sealed the *dran-med* with the *skye-med* [which means that]
The *skye-med* has been sealed with the *dran-med*. [The implication is that]
The phenomenal (*snang-ba*), too, is to be sealed with the noumenal (*stong-pa*) and
The noumenal is to be sealed with the phenomenal.

When [the reciprocity of] the *dran-pa* and the phenomenal rises [as having] the flavor of ecstasy
This means that it has been sealed by [the reciprocity of] the noumenal and *dran-med*.
When [the reciprocity of] the phenomenal and *dran-pa* and [the reciprocity of] the noumenal and *dran-med*
Have been sealed by the abidingness [of the *skye-med*], then,
Once [the reciprocity of] the phenomenal and *dran-pa* has risen [as having the] flavor of ecstasy,
You do not have to scrutinize it by an imagination tied to qualifying characteristics—that which has no qualifying characteristic is beyond the scope of the intellect (*blo-las 'das*).

Once [the reciprocity of] the *dran-med* and noumenal has been sealed by the *skye-med*
The *skye-med* is going to be sealed by the *blo-'das*.
By sealing [this double reciprocity of] the *dran-pa* [and the phenomenal] and the *dran-med* [and the noumenal] with [the spontaneity of] ecstasy
You will neither slip into [a one-sided and merely postulated] immateriality ["nothingness" (*stong-pa*)] nor fall into the extreme of nihility; [similarly]
By sealing the abidingness of the *skye-med* [with what is beyond the scope of the intellect]
You will neither slip into [a one-sided and merely postulated] materiality (*dngos-po*) nor fall into the extreme of eternalism.[57]

---

[56] *thabs-zin*. This rather difficult term suggests both the experiencer's "hold" on "efficacy" or "operacy" (*thabs*), as well as the "hold" of this operacy on the experiencer.

[57] These lines are directed against the widespread rationalistic and one-sided approach to a reality that is basically multifaceted and beyond conceptualization. Intellectual reductionism thinks in binary mode—immaterial/material, nihility (eternalism *a parte post*)/eternalism (eternalism *a parte ante*)—and thus abstracts from the immediacy of experience, which is of primary importance for Saraha.

All that is [turns out to be] beyond the scope of the intellect
and [to be such as] not having come into existence [as
some intellectually manipulatable thing].
All that is [turns out to have] the driving force of ecstatic experience.
By knowing [reality to be] like this you will not fall into the
extreme of some spiritual coma.[58] [59]

WHOLENESS AND THE BROKEN SYMMETRY OF BEING

We are tempted to ask why there should be four vectorial connectives and not only three, given the fact that the number three figures so prominently in Buddhist thought as a counterfoil to the binary mode of consciousness with its subject-object dichotomy. The answer lies in Saraha's insistence on the experience of wholeness as a process, a "becoming." The description of Being he offers is deliberately phenomenological and often provocative, nothing at all like the usual cut-and-dried deductive formulations of speculative reasoning. For him, wholeness is a process—"the seal than which none could be greater," "the sealing than which none could be more impressive" (*mahāmudrā*, *phyag-rgya chen-po*).

The idea of wholeness as process presupposes for Saraha a pervasive "intelligence/spirituality" (*Geistigkeit*) that keeps wholeness in any form, be it in the form of a particular human individual or of the universe itself, from stagnating. Spirituality stimulates the whole to ever-

[58] *btang-snyoms*, *upekṣā*. Translators stuck in the scientific positivism of the last century and content with the mechanics of exchanging words without a second thought for context, have translated this term as *equanimity*. By contrast, Saraha (*Kāyakośa-amṛta-vajragīti*, fols. 84b–85a) explains the term with an eye to its different usages in different belief systems within Buddhism itself and, as is to be expected, rejects any univocal definition. From his *Vākkośa-rucirasvara-vajragīti*, fol. 86a (in bsTan-'gyur, vol. *Tsi*, fols. 85a–89b) it is obvious that *btang-snyoms* is the third item in the ternary mode, the other two being *dngos-po*, "substantiality/materiality," and *dngos-med*, "insubstantiality/immateriality":

dngos-po dngos-med btang-snyoms la-sogs kun
'byed-pa med-de dran-med skye-med yul

Substantiality, insubstantiality, spiritual coma and all the rest [of
the toys with which the belief systems play]
Are without exception objectifications of the *dran-med* and *skye-med*.

To do justice to Saraha's critique would require a lengthy treatment that falls beyond the scope of the present study.

[59] *Kāyakośa-amṛta-vajragīti*, fol. 84b.

greater self-reflexivity, to ever-deeper self-consciousness, to ever more radiant ecstasy.[60] It does this by effecting a break in the symmetry of the original, undifferentiated continuum of Being, whose primordial openness (nothingness) is pure potential and sheer intensity. Without a break in symmetry, Being would have no way to encounter itself and become aware of itself. The break in symmetry is effected as a differentiation of wholeness, first into two, then into three.

The twofold differentiation sets up polar opposites, but not in the sense of a static opposition of contradictory terms. In Saraha two (*dran-pa↔dran-med*) represents rather the principle of complementarity, which is essential to all things that evolve and which takes different concrete forms as the evolution advances.

This first differentiation contains a dim memory of the original, unbroken unity. The term that Saraha uses, *dran-pa*, should not be confused with the usual associations the word *memory* carries for us today—learning one's multiplication tables by rote, storing data electronically, recollecting how I fell in love with the person who would one day become my wife, and so on. *Dran-pa* is a systemic, "organismic mentation" that is as much instinctual as it is spiritual.[61] This is why Saraha, and after him sGam-po-pa (1079–1153) and Klong-chen rab-'byams-pa (1308–1363/64), are able to use the compound *dran-rig,*[62] with *dran-(pa)* indicating the instinctual aspect and *rig(-pa)* the spiritual aspect of psychic energy. The first break in symmetry, therefore, sets up a kind of gravitational pull in the form of *dran-pa,* a longing for a lost, original unity, which in turn effects two further ruptures: *dran-rtog,* "the conceptualizing trend in the individual's overall organismic mentation," and *dran-bsam,* "the representational-discursive trend in the individual's overall organismic mentation." These two tendencies combine to produce the effect of more and more ideas with less and less insight.[63]

---

[60] I use the phrase *radiantly ecstatic* in the attempt to bring out the significance of the *lumen naturale* in experience and with it the *ek-stasis* of the experiencer from ego-centered captivity.

[61] Saraha here anticipates Jung's idea of spiritual instincts or a "religious function" that is "a principle *sui generis*, a specific and necessary form of instinctual power." *The Collected Works of C. G. Jung* (New York: Pantheon, 1957–1970), vol. 8, 58. Cf. Edward C. Whitmont, *The Symbolic Quest* (New York: Putnam, 1969), 82.

[62] See *Kāyakośa-amṛta-vajragīti*, fols. 80b, 82b. sGam-po-pa, *Collected Works*, vols. *Ca*, fols. 32b, 40a; *Tha*, fol. 34a. Klong-chen rab-'byams-pa, *mKha'-yang*, vol. 1, 355, 419; *Bla-yang* II, 81.

[63] Saraha uses *dran-rtog* in his *Dohākośa-nāma mahāmudrā-upadeśa*, fol. 96b. sGam-po-pa uses this term in vol. *Cha*, fol. 10b of his *Collected Works*; and Klong-

If we think of this first break in symmetry as a movement from "within" to "without," the idea of an evolving system turning back to its origins in order to recover a lost unity would suggest a reverse movement from "without" to "within." Taken in tandem, these two movements make it look as if nothing at all has happened. The excursus and recursus seem to turn movement and memory into non-movement and non-memory (*dran-med*). The power of instinct is drained and in its place one has a sense of renewed intensification or revitalization of a state that had never been fully lost. In the words of Saraha:

> The proposition that the phenomenal has subsided means
> That *dran-pa* has been swept away and *dran-med* has increased in vitality.[64]

But the complementarity of *dran-pa*↔*dran-med* is not so easily disposed of by assuming that the one reverts to the other. The relationship rests on an inbuilt tension whose reconciliation cries out for a third force or vectorial connective. This is where the principle of *skye-med* or "non-origin" comes into play. *Skye-med* is at the core of all creativity in that it introduces into wholeness the element of "spirituality" (*sems-nyid*) as a self-catalytic power in thought and experience. This seems to be behind Saraha's comment:

> The coming to light of our [that is, Being's] spirituality (*sems-nyid*) in its Mahāmudrā experience means that
> Non-origin (*skye-med*) comes to light as the miracle of origination in any form.[65]

Yet even this does not go far enough. The three vectorial connectives, *dran-pa*, *dran-med*, and *skye-med*, conjoin to form a synthesis of the one (*skye-med*) and the two (*dran-pa* and *dran-med*) as well as a division into unity (*skye-med*) and duality (*dran-pa* and *dran-med*). These two differentiations make wholeness accessible to reason, but still fail to account for the wholeness itself. For this a "fourth" vectorial connective is required, one which does not simply usher in the idea of an all-encompassing One that swallows up all former differentiations.[66] This

---

chen rab-'byams-pa uses it in both his *mKha'-yang*, vol. 1, 347, 351 and his *Zab-yang*, vol. 1, 363. On the whole, however, Klong-chen rab-'byams-pa prefers *dran-bsam*.

[64] *Kāyakośa-amṛta-vajragīti*, fol. 81a.

[65] *Kāyakośa-amṛta-vajragīti*, fol. 83b.

[66] In *Dohākośa-nāma mahāmudrā-upadeśa*, fol. 96b, Saraha is quite explicit about this matter:

fourth vectorial connective is *blo-las 'das*, that which points "beyond the scope of intellect." It directs our attention to a wholeness transcending the pale of the ego-centered mind that "grasps" whatever it fancies there "to be grasped,"[67] and at the same time invites us to cultivate a visionary capacity and joyful ecstasy.

MYSTICAL VISION

Saraha stands out in the history of Indian Buddhism as both traditional and unconventional. Grounded in the Buddhist commitment to the individual as the final locus for experiencing the meaningfulness of life, he directs the process of spiritual development to an intensified experience of reality itself. This experience—an invigorating, humanly enhancing vision that does not lose touch with everyday reality but sees it bathed in a supernal light of beauty—may properly be called mystical. Such vision has nothing in common with the escapism of much so-called "mystical insight" whose content is reductive and whose spiritual effects are inflationary and short-lived. Saraha strikes a splendid simile in speaking of this mystical experience of wholeness, of being *in the world but not of* the world:

> Beautiful is the color of a lotus flower, growing in the mud
> but having no passion for the mud—
> Radiant is the core intensity [of your spiritual capacity][68]

> Just as the magic wish-fulfilling gem has nothing material about it,
> So the visionary's comportment (*rnal-'byor spyod-pa*) has nothing
> material about it.
> Even if he talks nonsense by ordinary standards
> His intellect (*blo*) does not pass beyond the one.
>
> But since in this very One (*gcig-nyid*) there is no such thing as a one
> The multiplicity of the observable has lost its *raison d'être*.
> Like a madman, roaming about without any regard for anything,
> He remains in his comportment without purposefulness, like a
> small child.

[67] We should recall here that Buddhist texts do not use the subject-object distinction the way we find it in the West, but prefer to speak in terms of an "act of grasping" (*'dzin*) and the correlative that solicits that act, the "to-be-grasped" (*gzung*).

[68] For metrical reasons *snying-po* is used as a short form for *ye-shes snying-po*. This latter term appears in a subsequent stanza:

> *sna-tshogs dran phyir rjes-su 'brang-ba med*
> *gsal dang mi-mnyam ye-shes snying-po nyid*

without having had to give up the grime of the subject-
object dichotomy;
Lonely roams the deer living in a dense forest:
Without having a passion for a cause [life's] climax is Being-
in-its-beingness.[69]

Saraha's unconventionality is most conspicuous in his presentation of the process of individuation. Nothing is taboo to him; no time-worn idea is sacred. He is relentless in attacking prejudices accumulated through tradition or previous spiritual discipline. But his is not a deconstruction for deconstruction's sake. His aim is always to clear the way to our luminous Self. Guiding images have an important role to play as one makes one's way to the Mahāmudrā experience in which the complementarity-in-spontaneity of wholeness is brought to bear on daily life. Saraha singles out two such guiding images.

The first, as we have seen, is the image of the "innermost mentor" (*bla-ma*) with whom one enters into dialogue in order to discover the true inner light of one's humanness. The other is the "visionary experience of the meaning of Being in and through a gestalt" (*chos-sku*), where the gestalt is a whole experienced as inseparable and aesthetically indistinguishable from the concrete body of the one who has the vision. In other words, the *chos-sku* is the outward form of an inward meaning that guides one's thinking and acting within one's wider existential context. As Klong-chen rab-'byams-pa has already observed,[70] in disciplines that deal with experience—the rDzogs-chen, sNying-thig, and certainly also the early Mahāmudrā writings—the *chos-sku* is *not* an absolute, as speculative reductionists of the Hīnayāna and Mahāyāna persuasion seem to think, but a guiding image that accompanies one on the way. In the sense that it is something "seen,"

---

mun-sel nyi-ma sgron-me'i kha-dog ltar
rang-rig rang-la 'bar-na 'dzin-rtog zad

Since the multiplicity of the phenomenal is [co-existent with] your
organismic mentation you should not run after it[s deceptive
lure];
Rather, when [what is] the core intensity of your spiritual capacity,
radiant and unlike everything else
With the color of the sun dispelling darkness or [that of] a shining
lamp
Comes ablaze in you as the ecstatic intensity you alone can experience by yourself, your egologically divisive trend has ceased to operate.

[69] *Cittakośa-aja-vajragīti*, fol. 88a.

[70] *Theg-mchog*, vol. 2, 374.

it remains restricted to visual imagination, but beneath it throbs a wide world of archetypal energy.[71]

Since growing into one's authentic Self requires that one have some initial "vision" (*lta-ba*) of what one wants to become, the first step is to open a horizon against which this vision can become central. This is the theme of the "People *Dohā*," a work that, to judge from the many commentaries, both Indian and Tibetan,[72] that have been written about it, is Saraha's most challenging.[73]

A vision must be given form, and for this one must engage the creativity of active imagination (*sgom-pa*) and tap the wealth[74] of hidden inner potential. The meaning and function of creative imagination in all its ramifications is the theme of the "Queen *Dohā*."

Not only must the form correspond to an individual's innermost experience, it also must be grounded in our common humanity. In other words, it must be made available to others so that they, too, can mold their life by it (*spyod-pa*). This is the theme of the "King *Dohā*."[75]

Wholeness is not something to which we have direct access. Our only recourse is to open ourselves to its dynamism by learning to *see* what we have hitherto only *looked at,* to give the imagination free rein to develop what has been seen, and finally to mold our lives in the light of

---

[71] In his *Chos-dbyings,* 330, Klong-chen rab-'byams-pa states succinctly that in the *chos-sku* the *longs-sku* (the gestalt through which one experiences oneself as part of a social nexus) and the *sprul-sku* (the gestalt through which each individual acts as a guiding image) are embedded.

[72] In the translation contained in this book, as many of these commentaries as are available have been consulted. There is no agreement among the commentators about how to combine the various *dohās*, or rhymed two-line stanzas, into sections with a specific theme. To facilitate things for the reader I have adopted Karma 'Phrin-la's enumeration and subheadings.

[73] See chapter 1, note 12.

[74] Significantly the first part of the Tibetan title of this work, lost in its original Apabhraṃśa version, reads *Mi-zad-pa'i gter-mdzod,* "An inexhaustible treasure," and the second part contains the word *man-ngag,* an instruction that is more in the nature of an "inner voice" than a verbal teaching or injunction (*gdams-ngag*).

[75] With a few minor changes the translation given here is the same as the one in my *The Royal Song of Saraha* (Seattle: University of Washington Press, 1969; Berkeley: Shambhala Publications, 1973), now out of print. In that work one can also find a translation of the commentaries by sKye-med bde-chen and Karma 'Phrin-las, whose section headings have been adopted here.

what imagination has wrought. In the end, wholeness is to be found nowhere but in ourselves.

In seeing oneself as the locus of wholeness, we must not slip into the error of positing some kind of interior receptacle that needs to be unlocked. Our habitual way of conceiving of ourselves as composed of body and mind precludes the idea of wholeness that we have been speaking of here. As Gabriel Marcel has said, and many have repeated since him, it is not that we *have* a body but that we *are* our body. It is no less true that our mind or spirit are not something we possess but something that we are.

The idea of approaching the human being as a physical-psychical whole is still something of a novel experiment for Western science and intellectual history. For the Buddhist mystics, however, this idea has been at the core of their idea of the human. Simply put, the human individual is always seen as located in a wider field, as a center that organizes, constellates, and intensifies the forces that surround and act through it. It is to this image and its complex "energies" that we turn in the following chapter.

Chapter 3

The Body

TRADITIONAL INDIAN THINKING shared with non-Indian ways of thinking the idea that the human being is made up of both physical-material and psychic-spiritual properties. Behind this view of the human lay a static and rigidly deterministic view of the world. Various attempts were made to resolve this body-mind dualism by metaphysically reducing matter to mind or vice-versa. With the advent of Mahāyāna Buddhism, and its rDzogs-chen development, a new perspective opened up that enabled this dualism to be resolved in a dynamic view of human nature, without recourse to metaphysical reductionism. From this perspective – or more properly, participatory vision – one experiences oneself as the outcome of numerous, hierarchically interlaced processes, not unlike a standing wave generated on a field of intersecting energies. That is, one experiences oneself, living and embodied, as the innermost center of a constellation of surrounding, interacting forces. This is what Saraha has in mind in the following image:

> In the stalk of a lotus flower with [many] leaves there lies in the midst of its pistils
> A very subtle stillness, both fragrant and color-saturated.[1]

As a complex, living ensemble, both the essential structure and the ongoing evolution of the human individual depend on symmetry-breaking processes and their interaction with each other and with the surrounding world. The abiding structure that persists through the course of the individual's development is what is called the "fourfold centers of energy" (*'khor-lo bzhi-po*),[2] which Saraha is fully aware of and

---

[1] See stanza 54 in the "People *Dohā*."

[2] *Theg-mchog*, vol. 1, 357; *Bla-yang*, vol. 1, 112.

which is basic to the tuning-in process (*rnal-'byor, yoga*). One may imagine a great vortex in which energy nodes pulsate and interconnect in such a way that an intricate, multidimensional pattern is set up, as shown in figure 1.

FIGURE 1

The dimension of a self-organizing dynamics

↑

The linguistic/symbolic dimension

↑

The mental/spiritual dimension

↑

The physical/physiological dimension

The idea of energy-centers sees the individual as a kind of "multilevel autopoiesis."[3] These levels are not to be seen as mere strata stacked up one atop the other so that the individual can only inhabit one at a time—a metaphor still common among Westerners and Indians alike—but as the dimensions and levels of an integrated whole.

THE SYMMETRY OF BODY-ENERGIES

There were, of course, numerous other models at least outwardly similar to Saraha's. The major difference between them was the name and number of energy-centers in the body (*cakra, 'khor-lo*). The Buddhists, for example, recognized six such centers, one "located" in the region of the sexual organs (*gsang*), and another above the crown of the head (*gtsug-tor*), bracketing, as it were, the ones "located" in the regions of the navel, the heart, the throat, and the forehead, and setting up dimensions as shown in figure 1. The Hindus recognized seven such

[3] This is a term coined by Erich Jantsch in *The Self-organizing Universe*, drawing on Humberto R. Maturana's and Francisco Varela's suggestive notion of "autopoiesis."

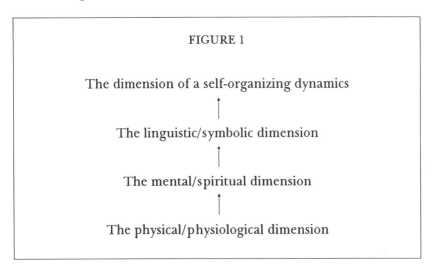

centers of energy, two of which were located in the genital and abdominal region, the other five corresponding to the locations assigned them by the Buddhists. Although the Buddhist schema is hardly known in the West, the Hindu schema has attracted considerable attention.[4]

The three basic patterns that energy follows as it flows through the body are known as *rtsa* (*nāḍī*). This highly technical term, difficult to find a single English equivalent for, may be characterized variously as "conduits," "conductors," "channels," "canalizations," or, to borrow a term coined by C. H. Waddington, "chreods" traversing the "epigenetic landscape." (It is misleading, however, to think of them as "veins" or "arteries."[5]) As lines of force they both indicate where the potential energy of the body lies and give a sense of direction to the system's self-organization.

Two of these lines of force set up a bilateral symmetry around a central axis: the *ro-ma* to the right and the *rkyang-ma*[6] to the left. Inasmuch as these lines of force do not simply cancel each other out in a static balance of opposites but initiate a dynamic process, the symmetry has constantly to be broken down and reinstated. This process may therefore be thought to rely on two underlying principles: complementarity and hierarchy.

The principle of complementarity means that the functions of the

---

[4] There is a vast literature on this topic, some of it popular, some very serious. Of those in the latter category, we may single out four: Hiroshi Motoyama, *Theories of the Chakras: Bridge to Higher Consciousness* (Wheaton: The Theosophical Publishing House, 1981), Harish Johari, *Chakras: Energy Centers of Transformation* (Rochester, VT: Destiny Books, 1987), Fritz Frederick Smith, *Inner Bridges: A Guide to Energy Movement and Body Structure* (Atlanta: Humanics New Age, 1986), and Arnold Mindell, *Dreambody: The Body's Role in Revealing the Self* (Santa Monica: Sigo Press, 1982).

[5] A sharp critique of this reductionist identification, already found in Klong-chen rab-'byams-pa's *mKha'-yang*, vol. 1, 61, is offered by 'Jigs-med gling-pa (1729-1798) in the *rNam-mkhyen shing-rta*, a commentary he composed on his own *Yon-tan mdzod*, 324. As Klong-chen rab-'byams-pa informs us (*Theg-mchog*, vol. 1, 355), these conduits or lines of force are not in substances in themselves but are suffused with pristine awareness of Being that shines through them like rays of sunlight shining through a window. In other words, the pristine awareness of Being contains within it a dynamic process that constitutes these conduits as occasions for the individual to come to vision, to cultivate this vision, and to appropriate the vision into the individual's way of life.

[6] See *Theg-mchog*, vol. 1, 360–61; *Tshig-don*, 251–52; *rNam-mkhyen shing-rta*, 317–18; Yon-tan rgya-mtsho, *Nyi-zla'i sgron-ma*, 223. With some qualification, these two lines may be likened to the *iḍā* and *piṅgalā* channels in Hindu presentations.

right and left sides are distinct but correlative. In this connection, the *ro-ma* line of force is associated with the *thabs*, the "operacy" and actual material manifestation of energy in the system; and the *rkyang-ma* line of force with the *shes-rab*, the appreciative insight generated by the system that propels it to spiritual renewal.

The principle of hierarchy rests on a characterization of the *thabs* dynamics as referring to a lower, ordinary view of reality (*kun-rdzob, saṃvṛtisatya*) that sees the world as an impersonal "it," while the *shes-rab* dynamics points to a higher view of reality (*don-dam*)[7] that focuses on the meanings imparted by the individual to the lower order.

Together these two complementarily and hierarchically ordered lines of force have their common origin in a kind of central vertical axis known as the *kun-'dar-ma* line of force. Seen as branchings of the central axis, the *rkyang-ma* sets up symmetrical approximations to the whole field while the *ro-ma* insures the continued rupture of the symmetry so that the whole can evolve further.

The above description views the structure of the body in spatial metaphors with energy flowing horizontally and vertically. The actual "currents" (*rlung*[8]) that flow through these channels and animate the system as a whole require the introduction of a temporal metaphor. Apart from performing metabolic functions, the *rlung* are primarily carriers and processors of information. They do this in two ways, characterized respectively as the *las-kyi rlung*, or "action current," and *ye-shes-kyi rlung*, or "pristine-awareness current." Each of these currents refers to a distinct context with its own function and semantic content.

The action current stimulates a state of increasing frustration brought about by mindless, instinctual activity (*las, karman*)—the realm of samsara. The pristine-awareness current stimulates a deepening awareness of the meaningfulness of life (*ye-shes, jñāna*)—the realm of Being's openness. The indissoluble connection that Buddhism sets up between the *rtsa* lines of force and the vital currents of

---

[7] *Tshig-don*, 256. The differentiation between two levels of reality does not imply a rigid separation nor does it bear any resemblance to the Platonic notion of a higher reality of Ideas over against the lower reality of actual things. Rather, this differentiation points to a symbiotic organization of parts that remain coordinated within the system as a whole. Because of the system's pervasively cognitive character, the two levels present degrees of intensity in insight.

[8] Literally, the term *rlung* means "wind" and refers to a kind of spontaneous "motility." Used in the above context, *rlung* is a metaphorical expression for the system's "aliveness."

rlung shows clear affinities to the modern notion of living organisms (including human beings) as space-time structures.

The semantic content or information that is carried along the intricate network of the system is called *thig-le*, a term notoriously difficult to translate into Western languages.[9] Its hierarchical organization, in reference to the body, contains three levels.

On the first and "lowest" level, represented by the *ro-ma* lines of force and the *las-kyi rlung* currents, the information serves to ensure biological normalcy of such things as sexual differentiation, and sets limits to the organismic and ecological activity or "operacy" (*thabs*) of the system. The information on this lower level lays the ground for the ordinary world of reality with its cause-and-effect mode of understanding and its short-lived pleasures.

A second, "higher" level, represented by the *rkyang-ma* line of force and the *ye-shes-kyi rlung* current, carries information about the pristine awareness of the system as a whole and manifests itself in discerning insight (*shes-rab*). This information conveys a new order of reality whose pleasures are more enduring.

The third and still "higher" level is represented by the axial *kun-'dar-ma* line of force, where the living body (*lus*) is raised to a new cog-

---

[9] On this term, see my *Matrix of Mystery*, 53–54, 240 n. 47. In the present context, according to *Tshig-don*, 256, *thig-le* suffuses the whole nexus of conduits with its light. As both light and the emission of light, *thig-le* is a dynamic concept, a conjunction of movement and rest. Thus as movement, or the causal momentum that gives rise to the ordinary world of reality, it passes along the *ro-ma* line of force; as rest, it remains in the *rkyang-ma* as pristine awareness at the higher order of reality; and as the semantic content of the meaningfulness of Being that undergirds rest and movement, as the pure fact of *Da-sein* or "being-there," it operates from the *kun-'dar-ma* line of force. As an information scheme, this process contains a starting point, a way, and a goal, each with its own organizational dynamic. As starting point, it is represented as the *Da-sein* of five colors, indicating virtual patterns of pristine awareness modes (*'od-lnga lhun-grub-kyi thig-le*). These colors light up to form haloes, thus providing the semantic content to the "ownmostness" of Being as the *lumen naturale* (*'od-lnga'i mu-khyud-du snang-bas rang-bzhin 'od-kyi thig-le*) of the whole. As way, it is the information of both the "causal momentum" of ordinary reality (*kun-rdzob rgyu'i thig-le*) and the "rest" of higher reality (*gnas-pa don-dam-gyi thig-le*). And as goal or culmination, it represents the self-maturation of the total potential of the system (*rang-smin-gyi thig-le*) into a trinity of light (*'od*), pristine awareness (*ye-shes*), and ecstatic intensity (*rig-pa*). See also *Theg-mchog*, vol. 2, 79.

In order to avoid any possible misunderstanding, let me point out that "information," as here used, does not mean a transfer of knowledge, but a reporting of how it goes with the system as a whole.

FIGURE 2

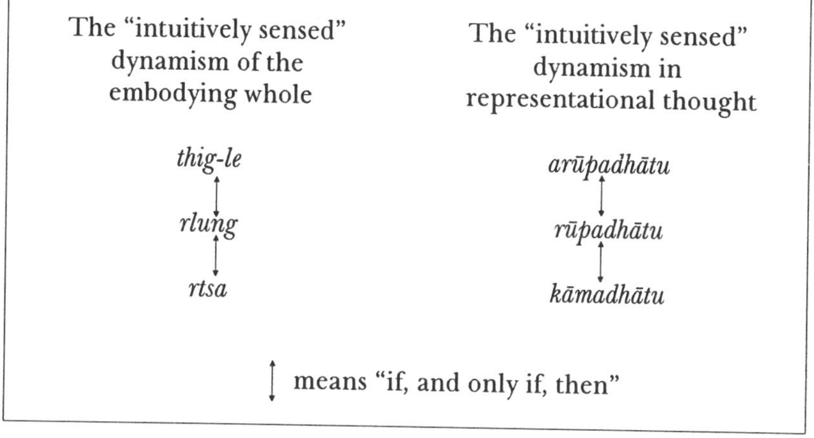

nitive intensity and takes on the character of a gestalt experience (*sku*). The information contained on this level is what we may call the *lumen naturale* of Being itself (*'od-gsal*). The diaphanous, utterly symbolical (*ka-dag*), open (*stong-pa*), energy-intensity "stuff" (*ngo-bo*) of Being is transfigured into a radiant (*gsal-ba*), spontaneously and holistically present (*lhun-grub*) "ownmostness" (*rang-bzhin*), no less a spiritual reality (*thugs-rje*) for all its supracognitive, self-regulatory, and ecstatic intensity (*rig-pa*).

As a carrier of information, the *lumen naturale* is called *rang-bzhin chos-nyid-kyi thig-le*, where *rang-bzhin* indicates that Being has been transformed from a virtual wholeness into an actual one, and that the finite individual is both the whole and yet no more than a part of the whole. The dynamic by which the *lumen naturale* creates "meanings in material concreteness" (*chos*) and dissolves them into a nothingness of its own making (*nyid*) is summed up in the term *thig-le* . As Klong-chen rab-'byams-pa says, when wholeness as pure potential is embodied in the wholeness that we are as individuals, the three lines of force interlace to form a structured process.[10]

This may be summarized with the help of diagrams. Figure 2 shows the structural aspect of the evolving corporeal schema as intuitively sensed and as anthropologically projected onto the world of sensuous engagements (*kāmadhātu/kāmaloka*), the world of imaginative-aesthetic

[10] *mKha'-yang*, vol. 2, 154–55. In becoming embodied, wholeness loses its ecstatic intensity (*rig-pa*) and becomes *ma-rig-pa* "not-quite-*rig-pa*," often wrongly translated as "ignorance."

FIGURE 3

THE STARTING POINT (*gzhi*)

The commonly accepted lower-order reality (*kun-rdzob*)

right *ro-ma*	center *kun-'dar-ma*	left *rkyang-ma*

[The organismic "feeling" tones:]

irritation (*zhe-sdang*)	dullness (*gti-mug*)	desire (*'dod-chags*)

The higher-order reality (*don-dam*)

"operacy" (*thabs*)	non-duality (*gnyis-su med-pa*)	appreciation (*shes-rab*)

THE WAY (*lam*)

radiance (*gsal*)	non-dividedness by concepts (*mi-rtog*)	pleasure (*bde*)

THE CULMINATION/GOAL (*'bras-bu*)

the gestaltism context (*longs-sku*) and cultural norms (*sprul-sku*)	the gestalt of meaning (*chos-sku*)	the site of the all-encompassing *lumen naturale* as ecstatic intensity (*bde-ba chen-po 'od-gsal nam-mkha'i mtha' khyab-pa'i rten*)

forms (*rūpadhātu/rūpaloka*), and the transcendent world where all forms are held in abeyance (*arūpadhātu/arūpaloka*).

Figure 3 shows the complex functional aspect of the body-image structure. The above description of how the image of body comes to take shape through the interaction of the two lines of force (*ro-ma*, *rkyang-ma*) with the axial line of force (*kun-'dar-ma*), represents the prevailing view of the sNying-thig tradition. This has much in common with the bKa'-brgyud tradition, in which Saraha plays an important role, but it puts more stress on the "branching" than on the "self-balancing" or "centering" of the life process as it evolves into body.

Elsewhere[11] the dynamic quality of the centering process is

---

[11] *mKha'-snying*, vol. 1, 61–62. Clearly this position reflects a different interpretative tradition. Yon-tan rgya-mtsho, in his *Nyi-ma'i 'od-zer*, 233, provides additional information about this central line of force that is not without interest. He says:

> [This central (*dbu-ma*) line of force] is so called because from the viewpoint of its position it is located between the two other lines of force; and from the viewpoint of its virtual presence [in any living system] it is [the system's] energy/intensity-"stuff" as its non-duality of ecstasy and nothingness (*bde-stong*), divested of the limiting categories of existence and nonexistence. Its upper end abides as the gnosemic *haṃ*, presenting [the system's] *thabs* dynamics, which is white in color and information through and through (*thig-le dkar*) and stems from the father's [contribution to embryogenesis]; its lower end abides as the gnosemic *a*, presenting [the system's] *shes-rab* dynamics, which is red in color and information through and through (*thig-le dmar*) and stems from the mother's [contribution to embryogenesis]. Being of a non-dual nature [even if paradoxically] its upper end extends into the head region, specifically the fontanelle, and its lower end extends below the navel [as the body's center] into the sex region; it serves as the site for [the system's] genus-specific and species-specific potential (*kun-gzhi*) in its function as [the individual's] life-force (*srog-rlung*), itself a space/sky-like openness (*nam-mkha'*).

Together the gnosemes *haṃ* and *a* combine to form the Sanskrit word *ahaṃ*, "I," indicating that the "I" is already contained in what we have termed the body image as an experience of the world. Though distinct as *a* and *haṃ*, and though both are informational through and through (*thig-le*), of itself each component is incomplete. The implication is that the ego or "I" has no privileged status whatsoever. The "location" of these gnosemes is also of great significance, indicating clearly that the human being is from the start sexually spiritual and spiritually sexual. In other words, the sexual and the spiritual dimensions interpenetrate at the core of the individual's existence in such a way that the functions of activity (*thabs, thig-le*), which aims at materialization and fixation, and

indicated by the term *dbu-ma,* "center." To the extent that it is the center of a "higher order" (*don-dam-pa'i dbu-ma*), it relies on what we have been calling the principle of complementarity, or what the original texts calls "the center in which *thabs* and *shes-rab* form an inseparable unity" (*thabs-shes dbyer-med-kyi dbu-ma*).

Since complementarity means that the opposites in it both define each other and exclude each other, one can speak of a *shes-rab-kyi dbu-ma* (or *kun-'dar-ma*), and a *thabs-kyi dbu-ma* (*avadhūti*) as different representations of one and the same reality—in this case, *dbu-ma.*

A definite color symbolism is attached to the three lines that form this center. The basic complementarity line of force is said to be white on the outside and red on the inside, while the *kun-'dar-ma* line of force is all red and the *avadhūti* line of force all white. The use of colors here clearly depicts the rupture in symmetry whose importance we stressed above. Moreover, the threefold pattern that forms on the higher level polarizes on the lower level as the white *ro-ma* and the red *rkyang-ma.* The transposition of color—and perhaps also of right and left sides—takes place because the *ro-ma* to the right of the central axis remains linked with *thabs,* and the *rkyang-ma* to the left, with *shes-rab.*

BEYOND THE BODY-MIND DICHOTOMY

From what has been said thus far, it should be clear that the lines of force that interact to form the body image belong to a thoroughly dynamic process. Bearing in mind that the traditional Western static view of the world and human beings has had little relevance for our attempt to understand life processes, and that we still lack an adequate conceptual model for describing these processes, it is obvious that any attempt to view the living body in terms of a body-mind dualism is bound to fail. There is good reason to claim, with some qualification, that the energic model of the lines of force we have been describing corresponds to what contemporary life sciences call the physiological and the biological. Furthermore, the stress on the cognitive element

---

discerning insight (*shes-rab, thig-le*), which aims at openness and freedom from the material entrapments of activity, are both conjoined existentially and yet are objectively distinct. The "I" is thus not a specific object but an index pointing to this unity of the spiritual and the sexual. Because this unity is manifest in the body image, the experiencing individual cannot but project sexuality and spirituality into the surrounding world.

in this model shows striking similarities to what Erich Jantsch has called "organismic mentation."[12]

But there is more. The reference to Being as a *lumen naturale* points to a still higher stage in the evolution of the body. The term I have chosen to translate as *lumen naturale* (*'od-gsal*) assumes that there is in us a supraluminous intensity (*'od*)[13] that constitutes us in our ownmostness (*rang-bzhin*) as luminous (*gsal*) beings. This supraluminous light is like an effulgence (*gdangs*) of the whole system that illuminates the pristine awareness (*ye-shes*) that opens our eyes to the structure of the lower level. The structure of the supraluminous itself is composed of four *'od-rtsa,*[14] that is, four intermeshing dimensions of lines of force (*rtsa*) glistening in the supraluminous hues (*'od*) of pristine awareness.

Words have a way of hardening into bias and eclipsing the experience or reality they purport to describe. The term *rtsa,* applied as it is to the structure of the body image, tends to obscure the sense of the dynamic process that is crucial to the body. The rDzogs-chen/sNying-thig thinkers sought to make up for this lack by speaking of *rtsa-chen,*[15] that is, "superchannels" or "superchreods." Like any process, the transformation of Being into body tends to organize itself structurally, which the term *rtsa* communicates. But insofar as Being is embodied in our ownmost *lumen naturale,* it requires the additional connotation of a current flowing through a pipeline attached to the inexhaustible reservoir of the original fullness of Being. Only insofar as we are "fed"

---

[12] *The Self-organizing Universe,* 169. According to Klong-chen rab-'byams-pa (*Theg-mchog,* vol 2, 52), modified by 'Jigs-med gling-pa (*rNam-mkhyen shing-rta,* 315), the three lines of force are like a network of roads, motility is like a blind horse, and the information system is like a lame rider. Each needs the other in order to advance towards growth and self-realization.

[13] The sNying-thig distinction between *'od* and *'od-gsal* calls to mind the words of one of Jung's disciples, Marie-Louise von Franz, *On Dreams and Death* (Boston: Shambhala, 1986), 146: "Jung has expressed the assumption that psychic reality might lie on a supraluminous level of frequency, that is, it could exceed the speed of light. 'Light,' in this case, would appropriately enough be the last transitional phenomenon of the process of becoming unobservable, before the psyche 'irrealizes' the body, as Jung puts it, and its first appearance after it incarnates itself in the space-time continuum by shifting its energy to a lower gear."

[14] *Tshig-don,* 250; *Theg-mchog,* vol. 2, 67, 79, 220; *mKha'-yang,* vol. 1, 420; vol. 3, 94, 120, 181.

[15] *Tshig-don,* 251f.

by this reservoir does Being give life to our concrete experience of being a body.

If we think of embodiment as quantifiable "matter," the process by which this embodiment takes place is rather like a nonquantifiable, qualitative "radiation." To designate this shift, one needs images that appeal to one's aesthetic sense and capture the feeling-toned aspect of insight. This is the role of the images of purest gold (*ka-ti gser*), the crystal tube (*shel-gyi sbubs-ma*), and the tightly woven white silk thread (*dar dkar snal-ma phra-la 'khyil-ba*)—all of which aim at communicating a sense of emancipation (*stong-pa rang-grol*).[16] The purest gold highlights the flow of Being in its supraluminous intensity. The crystal tube, in contrast, points to the withdrawal of this supraluminosity back into itself in order to recapture its full measure of intensity, like a light focused through a shutter. The crystal tube is thus also referred to as the "way" of the *chos-sku*, the system's (i.e., the "whole" human being's) experience of itself as a meaning-rich gestalt, and the "locus" at which the whole attains optimal intensity. Together the purest gold and crystal tube form vertical superchreods that channel the energy of the whole.

The third image, that of a tightly woven white silk thread, indicates the emergence of a cognitive domain composed of two horizontally related superchreods. The one tends towards representational thinking about reified "objects"; the other, towards an open horizon of Being into which everything is dissolved in order to emerge again with new meaning. It is worth noting here that the images of the crystal tube and while silk thread are reported to have appeared to people with near-death experiences. The latter image is of particular interest, since the white thread indicates the "way" that information travels through the system: aided by four "lamps" (*sgron-ma*),[17] bearers of pristine awareness, that form a kind of relay system for the flow of discerning insight (*shes-rab*). The tightly woven nature of this superchreod symbolizes the intensity with which the inner landscape is felt prior to its externalization.

---

[16] *Theg-mchog*, vol. 1, 375; *Tshig-don*, 250, 257; *Grub-mtha'*, 376–77. The term *ka-ti shel-gyi sbu-gu-can* is used synonymously with *ka-ti gser (ka-ti gser-gyi rtsa-chen)*. See *mKha'-yang*, vol. 2, 141; vol. 3, 84, 119, 167. The most difficult of these four images is *stong-pa rang-grol*. The word is composed of two adjectives—*stong-pa*, which indicates the nothingness of Being that is also a fullness, and *rang-grol*, which points to a process that is self-actualizing (*rang*) and finds its proper home in being dissolved (*grol*) into the fullness/nothingness of Being.

[17] For a detailed discussion of these "lamps," see my *Meditation Differently* (Delhi: Motilal Banarsidass, 1992).

From what has been said so far, it should be clear that in rDzogs-chen thought the body is not viewed as a static structure but as a process of continued structuralization. So, too, the meaning of the whole does not display itself as a disconnected series of insights but as an emerging system. The following passage expresses this multilevel autopoiesis in poetic form, well suited to Saraha's way of thinking:

> Within the physical body (*lus*) of each and every sentient being
> There resides Being's pristine awareness with its lighting-up as the possibility for its self-renewal,[18]
> Just as the trap of a womb or an egg
> [Does not let the child or the bird] be visible but keeps them covered up.
> As soon, however, as their capabilities have fully matured, they will come forth, [so also]
> As soon as the body [as it exists as a mere] representation [of objectifying thought] has been discarded,
> There comes the encounter with Being's auto-manifesting domain [such that]
> Being's ecstatic [supracognitive] intensity that can only be experienced by itself [that is, your very being], having been there since time before time,

---

[18] *dag-pa'i snang-ba*. This term occurs frequently in the *Rig-pa rang-shar*, 444, 456, 462, 466, and 813, and as *dag-snang* on 688, 721, 744, and 769, as well as in the *Seng-ge rtsal-rdzogs*, 310 and 356. The rendition cited in the text attempts to convey the sense of a coming-to-presence, a lighting-up (*snang-ba*) of the whole's pure and symbol-rich (*dag-pa*) possibility with no thematic, subjectifying, or objectifying demands to compromise its purity. Note, for example, the following passages:

> Being's lighting-up as pure possibility occurs as a cognitive domain without any subjective demands (*Rig-pa rang-shar*, 813).

> When the presencing of Being's errancy mode with its mistaken identifications (*'khrul-snang*) has ceased to be operative, its lighting-up as pure possibility (*dag-snang*) occurs (*Rig-pa rang-shar*, 721).

> Therefore, the lighting-up as pure possibility is Being's pristine awareness operation (*Rig-pa rang-shar*, 744).

> In the palace of Being's openness/nothingness its lighting-up lies hidden as its treasure (*Rig-pa rang-shar*, 466).

Lastly,

> It is in the wake of Being's lighting-up as pure possibility that one may fall into samsara (*Seng-ge rtsal-rdzogs*, 356).

Sees the energy/intensity-stuff Being [and by implication it itself] is made of without divisive concepts [that are the hallmark of representational thought].
Being's pristine awareness with its lighting-up as the possibility of its self-renewal and
The reality of the "Buddha"-experience are seen [as tautologous].
The energy/intensity-"stuff" this auto-manifesting of Being's pristine awareness is made of
Is without the notions that one's subjective mind entertains;
The past and the future
Have become suspended in the immediacy of this lighting-up.
The auto-manifesting of Being's superb pristine awareness
May not be an object of direct perception [that is restricted to the level of representational thought],
Yet it can be shown [by means of] the endogenous lamp.[19]
Being's pristine awareness [shining through] this very lamp
Lies beyond the reach of the visible and the invisible.
A yogi who deeply feels and understands Being's empowering dynamics
Does not look for its openness/nothingness—
He never moves away from what is [Being's and his] ownmostness.[20]

Similarly, the idea of the human body (*lus*) as a multilevel or multilayered self-organizing process is contained in a lengthy essay[21] ascribed to a certain Vimalamitra (of unknown date). Without attempting here to reproduce the intricacy of its argument, we may single out the four levels distinguished in this process:

1. The body as a precious mystery (*rin-po-che gsang-ba'i lus*): the triune gestalt dynamics (*sku*) of Being individually referred to as *chos-sku*, *longs-sku*, and *sprul-sku*;

2. The body as an enchantment of Being's pristine awareness (*ye-shes sgyu-ma'i lus*);

3. The body as a complex of drives and discursive ventures (*rnam-rtog bag-chags-kyi lus*); and

---

[19] *Rang-byung sgron-ma* is an abbreviation of the *lengthy* name of this "lamp": *shes-rab rang-byung sgron-ma*. For details see my *Meditation Differently*.

[20] *Seng-ge rtsal-rdzogs*, 308–10.

[21] *Sems-kyi dmigs-drug-gi rnam-par bshad-pa*, preserved in Klong-chen rab-'byams-pa's *sNying-thig ya-bzhi*, vol. 8 (*Bi-ma snying-thig*, part 2), 387–570.

4. The body as the energy in what modern psychology calls the detection threshold (*rnam-par rig-tsam-gyi lus*).[22]

The idea of the body as a process structure—a modern scientific term that attempts to fuse contrary notions into a single dynamic one—may be considered a tacit assumption in the writings of Saraha. His aim, as should now be clear, was to wean the experiencing individual gradually away from the deadening constructs of the ordinary world by showing these constructs to be products of one's own making. This disengagement begins with a "tuning in" (*rnal-'byor, yoga*) to life-forces that surround and penetrate one's being. This "tuning in" relies on felt images (or imagined feelings). It begins with the most intimate image—one's own body. Unlike "meditation" (*bsam-gtan, dhyāna*), which is basically an exchange of one fixation (physical reality) for another (imaginal reality), culminating in a state of quasi-comatose absorption (*ting-nge-'dzin, samādhi*), such "tuning in" rejects a static view of the world and its accompanying subject-object dichotomy. Its aim is to transport the individual into a realm, as Saraha says, "beyond the scope of the intellect." As soon as we set out to describe this realm we land ourselves in a web of enormous complexity. To understand this complexity—so important for tuning in to the dynamics of life through creative, participatory imagination—we now turn to the sNying-thig literature.

---

[22] *Sems-kyi dmigs-drug-gi rnam-par bshad-pa,* preserved in Klong-chen rab-'byams-pa's *sNying-thig ya-bzhi,* vol. 8 (*Bi-ma snying-thig,* part 2), 444.

Chapter 4

Complexity

A RECOGNITION OF THE CENTRALITY of the human individual in the universe and of the ubiquitousness of the body in all human experience lies at the heart of what has come to be known as the sNying-thig teaching, probably the most profound examination of wholeness to be found in non-Western intellectual history.

The perennial quest for origins – still present today in humanistic cosmologies[1] – also marks the treatment of *hominization* by the thinkers of the sNying-thig tradition. For them, the "beginning" contains the code for all human becoming, and decoding it gives us understanding of the human individual. The key to this work of decoding lies in *Kun-tu bzang-po*, or what we may call the principle of complementarity.

Kun-tu bzang-po – anthropomorphically envisioned as the union of the masculine and the feminine principle – not only expresses the universal "abstract" principle of complementarity, but also the equally universal "ethical" principle of reciprocity. According to this latter principle, every intentional act performed by a "subject" (mind, soul, spirit, wholeness, Being) and directed at an "object" (body, entity) elicits a response in the object that transforms that object itself into a subject for whom the original subject is the object. Intentional activity is, therefore, never "at rest" in a simple subject-object relationship. Its very creativity lies in the "restlessness" of the terms, thus generating a

[1] Notably B. J. Carr and M. J. Rees, "The Anthropic Principle and the Structure of the Physical World" (*Nature* 278, 1979). One may also mention here the evolutionary theory of Teilhard de Chardin as laid out in his *L'Apparition de l'Homme* and *L'Energie Humaine* and summed up in his posthumously published *The Phenomenon of Man* (New York: Harper & Row, 1959).

host of possibilities that are continually combined into a structured whole.

Kun-tu bzang-po is compared to a king (never without his queen) who oversees and coordinates a federation of autonomous principalities. Similarly, it is said to be like the "mind" that serves as an organizing principle for the "body," in the sense that the complex of sense organs that make up the body are coordinated by the omnipresent mind, which, despite our usual misrepresentations of it, can be experienced as one's *lumen naturale*.

Crucial to understanding how Tibetan Buddhism views the complexity of the human individual, we need to examine in some detail the notion of the "five resonance domains."

THE FIVE RESONANCE DOMAINS

The following stanza from Klong-chen rab-'byams-pa contains the core of the notion of the resonance domains in condensed form:

> Homage to the luster (*gdangs*) in the five resonance domains
> (*rigs*) as their pristine awareness modes (*ye-shes*) giving rise
> to the varied ideas [that constitute our experienceable
> world, *sna-tshogs 'char-sgo*] such that
> Having manifested itself by itself (*rang-shar*) [as some
> distinctly structured light] by itself dissolves into its
> legitimate dwelling [that is the nothingness of Being's
> dynamic freedom, *rang-sar grol*], because this luster
> Stems from the very reach (*ngang*) that is Being's self-
> sameness (*mnyam-nyid*), inexpressible by word of mouth
> and beyond the scope of representational thought:
> Uncontrived since time before time, the supercompleteness of
> Being's ownmost dynamics (*rang-bzhin*).[2]

The allusion to "luster" in the opening line is important. It refers to the radiant glow (*gdangs*) of the *lumen naturale* (*'od-gsal*) at work (*rang-bzhin*). Its pure spontaneity (*lhun-grub*) orders the energy-intensity "stuff" (*ngo-bo*) of Being into a symmetricality.[3] The unrefracted, purely symbolical (*ka-dag*) openness/nothingness (*stong-pa*) of Being is a veritable matrix of both its own radiant intensity (*gsal-ba*) and that of the *lumen naturale* of the human individual (*rang-bzhin*). This matrix resonates with the surrounding world by radiating outwards into five

---

[2] *Nam-mkha' rab-'byams* (in *mKha'-yang*, vol. 1, 397–410), 397.

[3] On this idea see my *Matrix of Mystery*.

"resonance domains" that provide the energy for the individual's psychophysical life[4] and serve as a prereflective horizon for life in space and time.

Each of the five resonance domains is suffused with five modes of pristine awareness (*ye-shes*), one or the other of which is always in the ascendancy. Together they form a spectacular display of color. Strictly speaking, these modes of pristine awareness are the manner in which Being resonates with itself and with everything it touches. In human terms, pristine awareness takes the form of an ultimate spiritual concern (*thugs-rje*)[5] that is experienced as immanent to the whole and intensely ecstatic (*rig-pa*) for the individual. It is this intensity that adds the "luster" of pure dynamism to one's *lumen naturale* and, by implication, makes up the "stuff" of one's living body.

Each of the resonance domains is governed by a principle of complementarity, symbolized as the union of a man and a woman (*yab-yum*), indicating the "analytic-operational" (masculine) aspect (*thabs*) and the "intuitive-appreciative" (feminine) aspect (*shes-rab*) of concrete human existence.[6] The male partner in each domain is conceived of

---

[4] In *mKha'-yang*, vol. 1, 182 Klong-chen rab-'byams-pa states:

> Since all those who have become spiritually awake [*sangs-rgyas*] in the past and [will do so] in the future or in the present are enfolded in the five resonance domains, and since all that comes-to-presence as samsara and nirvana, from the highest level of the world, the heavens, down to the lowest level, the hells, has "fanned out" from and becomes enfolded again in the five resonance domains, [the fact remains that] the five resonance domains [as] pristine awareness modes do not exist apart from one's body-mind; the very origin of one's body from out of the five fundamental forces is the intrinsic luster (*rang-gdangs*) of the five pristine awareness modes [pertaining to] the male-female complementarity/togetherness/union in the five resonance domains.

[5] It is important to distinguish between "concern" (*thugs-rje*) as an expression of a higher-order level and "compassion" (*snying-rje*) as a lower-order expression that only too often turns into mere sentimentality.

[6] The *Rig-pa rang-shar*, 447, explicitly states that the male stands for the operational in the widest sense of the word—including what we would call vibrations, oscillations, and rhythms—and is characterized as a "ceaselessly on-going process" (*'gag-pa med-pa*), tying itself up, as it were, in materiality; the female stands for what we would call "appreciation," "insight," and "intuition" and is characterized as "invariant" (*'gyur-ba med-pa*), because Being-in-its-beingness is apprehended through it.

These two complementary forces have little in common with Plato's two "fundamental principles": the rational, mathematical, formal principle, called *logos*, which he arbitrarily labels as good; and the intuitive, emotional, aesthetic principle, or *eros*, which he brands as evil. It seems to me that this distinction has had devastating consequences for Western intellectual history.

as a regent (*rgyal-ba*) of one of the principalities that combine to make up the federated kingdom of the overseeing king (*rgyal-po*).

The *lumen naturale* or pristine awareness of Being that shines on human beings and suffuses them with light is envisioned as passing through a "gate" or "outlet" to be refracted into the multiplicity of the world of experience (*sna-tshogs 'char-sgo*). The passage from Klong-chen rab-'byams-pa suggests a distinction between two gates, an entry and an exit, leading to and from a common reality. On the one hand, the human being represents Being closed in on itself by entering the world of lived experience. On the other hand, as the *lumen naturale* that illumines human experience, Being is seen to open itself up to its own dynamic "nothingness." From the point of view of the experiencing individual, one and the same Being holds out two options for living: the ecstatic intensity (*rig-pa'i rtsal*)[7] of the *lumen naturale* and the ordinary world of things and ideas (*'char-gzhi*).

The first to formulate this idea of two gates to a common reality seems to have been Śrīsimha (also of unknown date, perhaps of Chinese origin):

> From a common source untouched by names
> Two gates [for things and ideas] to come-to-presence have evolved:
> A low-level intensity as the gate for the coming-to-presence of errancy and
> An ecstatic intensity as the gate for the coming-to-presence of a [multifunctional] pristine awareness;
> These [two gates] have evolved from a common plane.[8]

And in another context:

> From the pure field-like expanse [of Being] untouched by names
> Two gates [for things and ideas] to come-to-presence have evolved;
> They are a low-level intensity and a [multifunctional] pristine awareness;
> These are not different entities,
> They are merely individualized aspects [of one and the same reality)].

---

[7] The term *rtsal* is rich in connotations, "creativity" and "elegance" being the most prominent. Significantly, the term occurs only in connection with high-intensity operations of the psyche (as is the case here) and with *ye-shes* and *thugs*.

[8] *Rin-po-che 'khor-lo'i rgyud* (in *rNying-rgyud*, vol. 4, 24–35), 24.

For those who do not understand, (this one and the same reality) becomes the way to samsara,
For those who understand, it becomes the way to supra-spiritual wakefulness.[9]

THE MANDALA OF THE FIVE RESONANCE DOMAINS

The five resonance domains are like a mandala of intersecting vectors, four lines centered on a common zero-point and each capable of functioning as its own zero-point for specific functions.[10] Conceiving of these resonance domains as higher-order probability structures[11] leads us to expect them to influence the lower-level probability structures by modifying the probability of probabilistic events. There seems no *a priori* reason not to conceive of our psychophysical existence as a probabilistic event.

Whether viewed as probability structures of the *lumen naturale*[12] or as experiences of the ecstatic intensity of Being,[13] these resonance domains were assigned names according to the role they play in the process of the self-realization of Being in human existence and the way in which they touch the individual. For the interplay among the various domains affects the individual growth into the fullness of Being. Basically this interplay follows the pattern of symmetry, rup-

---

[9] *rDzogs-pa-chen-po Kun-tu bzang-po ye-shes gsal-bar ston-pa'i rgyud* (in *rNying-rgyud*, vol. 8, 101–12), 104.

[10] R. M. Zaner, *The Problem of Embodiment* (The Hague: Martinus Nijhoff 1964), 253–54, states:

> . . . my animate organism functions as this single Null-point only as the consequence of a continuously on-going series of automatic syntheses in virtue of which it is continuously experienced as a corporeal *system* of body-members, -components and -organs, each of which can also function as a relative null-point for specific purposes and with regard to specific objects. My hand, with which I grasp and feel within my "manipulatory sphere" is itself an orientational point relative to that which is grasped and handled. Similarly, my eyes are experienced by me as the zero-point for the visual field. My head itself functions as a zero-point, not only for the visual, but for auditory and gustatory data as well (I turn my head "in order to" hear the music more clearly), and so forth.

[11] The term *probability structure* was coined and explained by Rupert Sheldrake. Similarities between Sheldrake's idea of "morphic fields as probability structures" and the Buddhist idea of *rigs* (R. Sheldrake, *The Presence of the Past*, 119) are too obvious to be ignored.

[12] *mKha'-yang*, vol. 2, 380.

[13] *Tshig-don*, 225.

tured symmetry, and renewed wholeness that we discussed in chapter 3. As we say, this process combines opposing energies into a dynamic vertical axis that ensures continuity through time and a static horizontal plane that provides continuity in space. That is, as concrete, living organisms, we experience ourselves as a "continuously on-going act" and as the "primary condition for the objective physico-cultural world."[14]

Central to the process of the growth of the individual into the fullness of Being, both literally and figuratively, is the movement of the "resonance domain towards the beingness-of-Being" (*tathāgatakula, de-bzhin gshegs-pa'i rigs*).[15] Next comes the more static "diamond-scepter" resonance domain (*vajrakula, rdo-rje'i rigs*), immune to transition and change.[16] This is followed by the "gem" resonance domain (*ratnakula, rin-chen rigs*), which comprises the wealth of qualities found both in the experiencer and in the surrounding world. The fourth is the "lotus flower" resonance domain (*padmakula, padma'i rigs*), which suggests someone inwardly unaffected by the outer vicissitudes of the world, like a lotus flower growing in the water but not held fast by the water. Fifth and finally is the "action" resonance domain (*karmakula, las-kyi rigs*), which indicates that actions performed on this higher-order level of being leave no loose ends.[17]

---

[14] R. M. Zaner, *The Problem of Embodiment,* 249, 250.

[15] Whether this resonance domain is conceived of as a manifestation of the *lumen naturale* or as the ecstatic intensity of the whole, its description remains practically the same. Thus, in *Tshig-don,* 225, Klong-chen rab-'byams-pa states:

> Even those who have become spiritually awake (*sangs-rgyas*) in the past have become so by having "seen" Being's ecstatic intensity and so (*de-bzhin-du*) have gone (*gshegs*) to the level of being spiritually awake.

and in *mKha'-yang,* vol. 2, 380, he says:

> *De-bzhin gshegs-pa'i rigs* is called so because the *lumen naturale,* [this paradox of being] both a coming-to-presence and a [passing into Being's] openness/nothingness in an absolute sense (*snang-stong chen-po*), is the road travelled by all those who become spiritually awake.

[16] *'pho-'gyur med-pa* in the words of Klong-chen rab-'byams-pa. See *mKha'-yang,* vol. 2, 380. Literally translated, this phrase means that "there is neither a stepping out of itself into a 'past' or a 'future' nor a remaining unchanged in a congealed 'now'." It is a critique of the Brahmanical *ātman* idea as propounded in the *Bṛhadāraṇyaka-Upaniṣad* IV 10, 1–7, and the *Chāndogya-Upaniṣad* VI 1. Padma las-'brel-rtsal defines this resonance domain in his *Rin-po-che dbang-gi phreng-ba,* 186, to the effect that "once [the experiencer] has understood [the meaning of Being's] ecstatic intensity there is [for him] no longer any change [in him] nor a reversal [to non-ecstatic levels]."

[17] Usually these actions are referred to by the term *'phrin-las,* not by *las,*

These five domains, each a reflection of the *lumen naturale* of Being and each a locus for the creation of meaning, provide an environment or "playground" for the ecstatic intensity of Being. Despite the concrete imagery associated with the domains, there is nothing static or rigid about them. They are rather dynamic regimes whose multiplicity reflects a series of fluidly structured psychic processes that change as the individual develops.[18] The anthropomorphic representation of each domain is determined by the nature of the experience to which it refers. In figure 4 five pairs of male and female figures (or syzygies as they were called in Gnosticism and medieval alchemy)[19] are arranged geometrically to form a circular or spherical mandala whose center "informs" the four cardinal points, moving clockwise from east to south to west to north and back again to the east. It represents the complex pattern of the conscious embodiment of human being in both its mundane and divine aspects.

The central resonance domain serves as a "zero-point" to orient the whole. It is symbolized by the regent Vairocana (*rNam-par snang-mdzad*) in union with his consort Dharmadhātvīśvarī (*Chos-kyi dbyings-kyi dbang-phyug-ma*). Their indissoluble union may be likened to what

---

which is used in connection with our habitual blundering through life. For this reason Padma las-'brel-rtsal, *Rin-po-che dbang-gi phreng-ba*, 186, says that this resonance domain bears its name "because one does not become spiritually awake due to one's non-understanding (*ma-rtogs-pa*) the ecstatic intensity of Being." This definition is taken over into the *Bla-ma dgongs-'dus*, vol. 10, 719.

18 The idea of a gestalt as a process-structure is clearly stated in *mKha'-snying*, vol. 1, 448–49 and in *mKha'-yang*, vol. 2, 578–79. These two passages, though different in wording, are identical in content. They state that each of the five gestalts is a formulation of the outwardly radiating glow (*gdangs*) of the intrinsic luminosity of Being (*mdangs*), transforming the *lumen naturale* (our own and that of Being itself) from a "virtual" state into an "actual" presence. The dynamic at work in the constellation of these gestalts belongs to the ecstatic intensity of Being that lives and works within us (*dngos-po gshis-kyi gnas-lugs*) as the five modes of pristine awareness. Recognizing the structure of this dynamic as consisting of a starting point, a way, and a goal, one becomes aware of an efficiency principle manifesting itself ("lighting up") in the form of five gestalts, each of which presents a three-phase process. The starting point, pristine awareness of the ecstatic intensity of Being (*gzhi rig-pa'i ye-shes*), lights up (*snang*) as a totality of observable qualities (*rnam*) and becomes the "Vairocana" (*rnam-snang* = *rnam-par snang-ba*) gestalt. The goal is a non-ego-centered (and hence non-reifying, *'dzin-med*) insight into this lighting-up. The same process applies to the other gestalts that form as Being projects itself out of its initial nongeometric field into an array of geometric patterns.

19 On the term *syzygy* see note 37 in chapter 2.

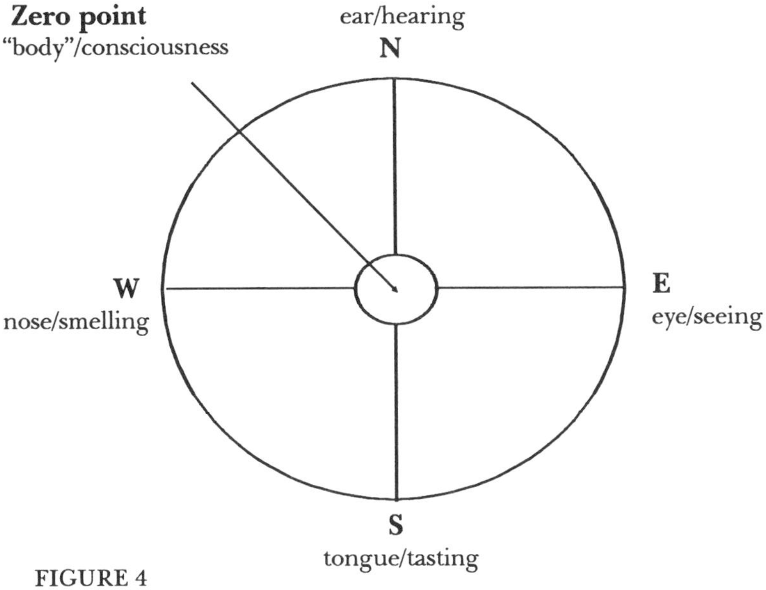

FIGURE 4

modern science calls the "excitation of a field," the excitation being the masculine principle and the field the feminine principle. Basically cognitive in character, this central domain reflects the spirituality of the whole (here, the human system) as a dynamic, evolving system. Its color is deep blue.

The resonance domain to the east is represented by the regent Vajrasattva (*rDo-rje sems-dpa'*) in union with his consort Māmakī (*Mi-bskyod-pa*). It indicates the mode of seeing peculiar to ego-consciousness, setting up a gap between the perceiver and the perceived, then bridging this gap by appropriating as "mine" what has been perceived. Its color is white, indicating its sensitivity to the slightest disturbance.

To the south lies the domain of feeling, whose regent is Ratnasambhava (*Rin-chen 'byung-ldan*) in union with his consort Buddhalocanā (*Sangs-rgyas spyan-ma*). Its color is yellow, the color of gold, indicating value.

The regent of the domain in the west is Amitābha (*sNang-ba mtha'-yas*) in union with his consort Pāṇḍaravāsinī (*Gos dkar-mo*). It indicates the world of ideas that one builds up through experience of the world that is seen and felt. Its color is red, suggestive of the passion with which we cling to our ideas.

The final resonance domain lies to the north. Its regent is Amoghasiddhi (*Don-yod grub-pa*) in union with his consort Samaya

Tārā (*Dam-tshig sgrol-ma*). It reflects the world of actions as *fait accompli*. Its color is green, suggestive of an abiding restfulness in the midst of life's turmoils.

The five resonance domains are also related to the psychophysical makeup of the individual. At first sight there seems to be a twofold dualism here: between the resonance domains and the psychophysical configuration, and between body and mind. But on closer examination, the opposition is seen to indicate degrees of intensity or "density."

Insofar as intensity and density mark a process of growth, they imply a tension of opposites. Abstractly we may speak of a principle of complementarity at work, but concrete images like the union of man and woman bring the point closer to experience—namely, the inseparability[20] of the fact that "action" expresses purpose (*thabs*) and "discerning insight" expresses an awareness of value (*shes-rab*) and a sense of what is worth doing.

In the realm of "low-intensity energy," which to us who inhabit it is of paramount importance, the overall principle of complementarity is expressed concretely in what I would call "self-materializing intensities" and "self-spiritualizing intensities." In the case of the former, a

---

[20] *dbyer-med.* There are two aspects to consider here. The inseparability symbolized as a man and woman in intimate union is to be understood ontologically. Experientially, it is meant to designate a necessary unity, without implying a necessity that determines how it is to be applied (see Gregory Bateson, *Mind and Nature,* 38)—in other words, a kind of probability structure. Bateson's idea of necessary unity has been anticipated by Klong-chen rab-'byams-pa, who, in discussing the unity of "action" (*thabs*) and "discerning insight" (*shes-rab*), states in his *Yid-bzhin rin-po-che'i mdzod,* chapter 20, stanza 2 (665):

> Since in the absence of "action" "appreciation" will not arise
> You have first of all to look for the foundation of your thinking
> (*bsam-gtan*) by various "actions."

The term *bsam-gtan,* here rendered as "foundation of thinking" is usually translated as "meditation" in texts of the epistemology-oriented (Hīnayāna) schools of Buddhism. There it describes the process of an analytical concentration (*dhyāna*) passing through the phases of attention (to an arbitrarily selected "object" of concentration), discursive thinking, joyfulness and pleasurable feeling, climaxing in a disinterested absorption in the object of fixation. According to Klong-chen rab-'byams-pa these phases represent the very defects of *bsam-gtan/dhyāna* that need to be rectified by replacing reifying, dichotimizing thought with the clarity (*dvangs*) and brilliance (*gsal*) of the *lumen naturale*. In a word, rDzogs-chen (sNying-thig) thinking marks a radical break from the older mechanistic determinism. See also my *From Reductionism to Creativity,* chapter 5. As noted above, in typical blunt fashion, Saraha rejects *bsam-gtan/dhyāna* outright.

further complementarity is set up between an individual's pycho-physical makeup and its supporting cosmic forces; and in the case of the latter, between the instinctive and the spiritual. The feedback between complementary elements may be either positive or negative. An overview of the whole scheme is given in two diagrams. Figure 5 uses a linear model to show the principle of complementarity within each particular domain. Figure 6 depicts an "evolutionary" process that may be envisioned as spiralling upwards or downwards.

THE EVOLUTIONARY CENTER

The idea of the human individual as first and foremost a spiritual and visionary being was instrumental in bringing about a shift from the more or less static and materially oriented view of the early Buddhist teaching to a more dynamic and mentally oriented standpoint. This transformation of perspective is immediately noticeable in what I have called the self-materializing intensities of Being. From this standpoint the sNying-thig tradition rearranged the traditional sequence of five aggregates or "sets" that go into the makeup of the human person (*skandha, phung-po*) by placing perceptual processes (*vijñāna, rnam-shes*, short for *rnam-par shes-pa*)—usually rendered inexactly as "consciousness"—first and locating these processes as a center around which the other four revolve. The perceptual processes, each representing a particular form of sense experience, combine to "localize" the individual in time and space.

This central aggregate of perceptual processes is linked in turn to a "cosmic" correlate, itself the central force in a "set" (*khams*)[21] of five forces. These cosmic forces all belong to the realm of "matter" as a form of "frozen" energy or as a self-geometrizing low-level intensity. The central cosmic force is termed *nam-mkha'* (*ākāśa*) and corresponds to the notions of "sky," "space," and "ether." It is at once an outer immensity that engulfs all things and an inner immensity that fills us from within.

The sNying-thig thinkers also keep the Mahāyānist idea of two regimes or sets as constitutive of the individual. The first regime, or "dark" side of the individual, is the instinctive (*nyon-mongs*), the emotionality that is always at work in deciding which ideas or perceptions

[21] I have deliberately avoided the Sanskrit equivalent of this Tibetan word. The Tibetan language clearly distinguishes between *khams*, the "material" aspect of what we call reality, and *dbyings*, the "immaterial" aspect of reality. The Sanskrit language has only one term for both aspects—*dhātu*.

FIGURE 5

RESONANCE DOMAINS	THE REGENTS		THE INDIVIDUAL'S SENSIBILITIES	
rigs	male *yab*	female *yum*	instinctive *nyon-mongs*	intuitive *ye-shes*
de-bzhin gshegs-pa'i rigs "evolutionary growth"	*rNam-par snang-mdzad* Vairocana	*Chos-kyi dbyings-kyi dbang-phyug-ma* Dharma-dhātvīśvarī	*gti-mug* dullness	*chos-dbyings* "meaning field" awareness
rdo-rje'i rigs "diamond-scepter"	*rDo-rje sems-dpa'* Vajrasattva	*Mi-bskyod-pa* Māmakī	*zhe-sdang* irritation	*me-long lta-bu'i* "mirror-like" awareness
Rin-chen rigs "gem"	*Rin-chen 'byung-ldan* Ratna-sambhava	*Sangs-rgyas spyan-ma* Buddha-locanā	*nga-rgyal* arrogance	*mnyam-nyid* "consistency/ co-equality" awareness
Padma'i rigs "lotus flower"	*sNang-ba mtha'-yas* Amitābha	*Gos dkar-mo* Pāṇḍa-ravāsinī	*'dod-chags* desire	*sor-rtogs* "individuating understanding" awareness
Las-kyi rigs "deeds"	*Don-yod grub-pa* Amogha-siddhi	*Dam-tshig sgrol-ma* Samaya Tārā	*phrag-dog* jealousy	*bya-grub* "tasks-posed-and-accomplished" awareness

The Individual's Biological Constituents		The Individual's		Color
local aggregates *phung-po*	supportive cosmic forces *khams*	sensory apparatus *dbang-po*	its empowerments *dbang-bskur*	*kha-dog*
rnam-shes perception	*nam-mkha'* sky-space	*lus* body	*thugs* spirit	*mthing-ga* blue
gzugs color-shape	*chu* water	*mig* eye	*sku* gestalt	*dkar-po* white
tshor-ba feeling	*sa* earth	*lce* tongue	*yon-tan* qualities	*ser-po* yellow
'du-shes ideas	*me* fire	*sna* nose	*gsung* announce-ment	*dmar-po* red
'du-byed model building	*rlung* wind	*rna* ear	*'phrin-las* concerned action	*ljang-gu* green

FIGURE 6

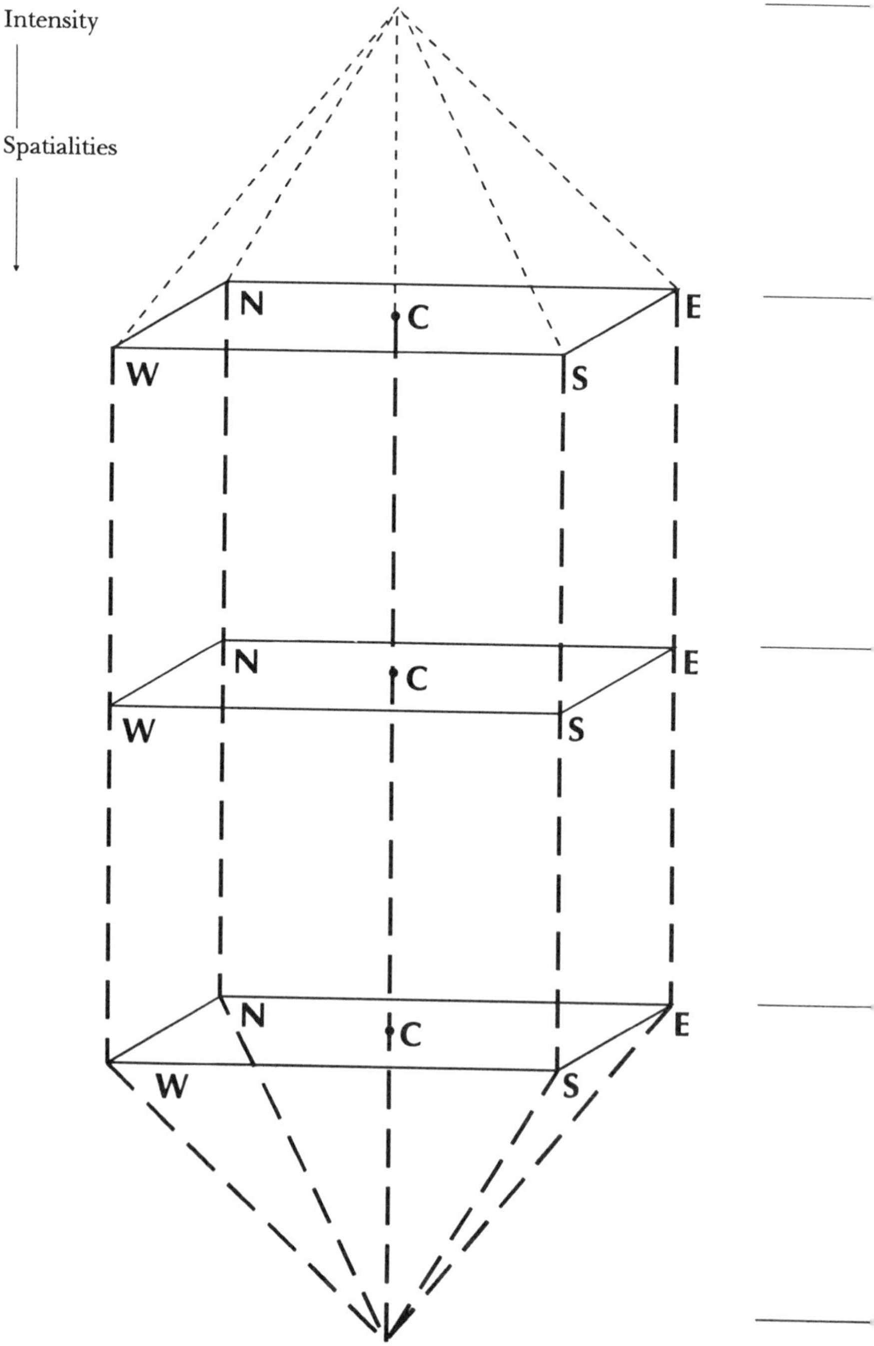

Kun-tu bzang-po – Kun-tu bzang-mo

Resonance domains (spatialities) with their male-female regents (intensities) "The spirit plane"

"The psychic plane" (the complementarity of the instinctive and mental)

C center: *de-bzhin gshegs-pa'i rigs*:
rNam-par snang-mdzad –
Chos-kyi dbyings-kyi
dbang-phyug-ma
E east: *rdo-rje rigs*:
rDo-rje sems-dpa' –
Mi-bskyod-pa
S south: *rin-chen rigs*:
Rin-chen 'byung-ldan –
Sangs-rgyas spyan-ma
W west: *padma'i rigs*:
sNang-ba mtha'-yas –
Gos dkar-mo
N north: *las-kyi rigs:*
Don-yod grub-pa
Dam-tshig sgrol-ma

* for further correspondence, see figure 5

- - - - - - "primary" projections

— — — "secondary" projections

"The material plane" (the complementarity of the local and cosmic

"The concrete individual" (physico-mental function complex)

it wants to attend to, and among these which it will turn into an *idée fixe*. The second or "bright" side – for want of a better term, I call it the "spiritual" regime – comprises the five modes of pristine awareness referred to earlier (*ye-shes*). In the present context the outstanding emotion on the dark side is "dullness" (*gti-mug*), and the outstanding mode of awareness on the bright side is that of Being itself as an open horizon against which meanings emerge (*chos-kyi dbyings-kyi ye-shes*).

Just as the localizing forces (the closure into what Heidegger has called *das Ge-stell*) and the cosmic forces (an opening that is also a closing-in-on-itself) are complementary, so do the realms of the instinctive and the spiritual complement one another. Moreover, there is a looping or "feedback" between these two complementarities that functions in both a positive and a negative sense. Positively, openness and brightness reinforce each other, so that the more I am able to open up, the brighter does my perception become and the more aware I am of the meaningfulness of life. Negatively, the more I get bogged down in particular objects of perception, the greater is my sense of dullness; and as this feeling grows the less able I am to perceive clearly, so that in the end "nothing makes sense" any more.

The body (*lus*) is of pivotal importance for these complementarities and intensities, not as an object for *thought* but as an organ of perception, a living instrument for knowledge through which the various senses give us access to the surrounding world. Just as we may speak of the primacy and centrality of perception[22] as the "intelligent" functioning of an organism, so we may speak of the primacy and centrality of the body as an organism's most concrete means of recourse to the world, since it is of the same texture as the perceptions that occur "in" and "in relation to" the body and its environment. This "texture" is what we have called the self-materializing intensity of Being into a state of "frozen" energy or, because of the marked decline of supracognitive intensity (*rig-pa*), a state of dull cognitive intensity that is not

---

[22] The "primacy of perception" suggests, of course, the work of Merleau-Ponty. However, as Calvin Schrag has pointed out, it is important not to misunderstand Merleau-Ponty's thesis as a claim that perception is primary because it is "an exclusive source of knowledge and truth." It might have been better in this regard to speak of the "primacy of experience." Schrag continues: "Each of the emergent fields of experience can be thematized and rendered explicit through an elucidation of their peculiar figures and backgrounds and their intentional structure, and this explication and elucidation is able to proceed without reductivism only if the primordial reciprocity of perception, conception, and valuation is held in attention and acknowledged" (*Experience and Being*, 20).

quite what it could or should be (*ma-rig-pa*). In other words, the idea of the body as something reified and static is a misconception—or, in Whitehead's apt phrase, a good example of "misplaced concreteness."

But how have we come so to misunderstand the body? The answer lies within the very dynamics of Being itself. The reifying intellect, itself an expression of the drop in the original intensity of Being, introduces a division between process and structure, downplaying the former and imposing on the latter an objective metaphysic that makes it more manageable.

> Who would understand and describe something alive
> Seeks first to expel the spirit within,
> Then he holds the parts in his hand,
> Except, alas! the spirit that bound them together.
>
> Goethe, *Faust*, I:1936–39

By contrast, sNying-thig thought never lost sight of the process, as the following terse passage from Klong-chen rab-'byams-pa shows:

> Since the [beginningless] beginning [of the universe, *thog-ma-nas*] the pristine awareness that is Being's incipience [to unfold, *gzhi'i ye-shes*] sets itself up as our body through a drop in its ecstatic intensity (*ma-rig-pa*).[23]

He elaborates further:

> The "stuff" of which [Being's and our own] pristine awareness [as a function of Being's] ecstatic intensity [is made of, *gzhi'i rig-pa ye-shes-kyi ngo-bo*] goes astray into [a state of] unawareness[24] in [what is] its interim phase [between beginning and end] and ascribes [to it itself what it fails to recognize as its] body . . . That is to say, in the interim phase [Being's] lowered ecstatic intensity does not recognize the pristine awareness [as being a function of Being's ecstatic intensity] so that through the emergence of an egological "grasping" (*'dzin-pa*) of [Being's] lighting-up as a pristine awareness, this lighting-up [as the end-phase of the process] is ascribed [to itself as its] body.[25]

However low its level of intensity, however misconceived and misguided our idea of it, the body is crucial to our awareness of human

---

[23] *mKha'-yang*, vol. 1, 444.

[24] *ma-shes-pa*. According to the *Rig-pa rang-shar*, 680, "unawareness" is a form of "dullness" (*gti-mug*), one of the basic emotions that make up our instinctuality.

[25] *mKha'-yang*, vol. 1, 445.

existence and needs therefore to be *re-intensified* by seeing it for what it actually is—intense energy. Again, Klong-chen rab-'byams-pa:

> Although the body has been set up from out of [Being's] lowered intensity (*gzhi ma-rig-pa*), once it is recognized [as Being's ecstatic intensity] one [will find] that it has never passed beyond [Being's] triune pristine awareness modes (*ye-shes gsum*) in its passage from a beginning through an interim phase to an end.[26] [27]

This re-intensification of the body, which restores our bond to an original intensity that resists traditional static notions of the cosmos and the human, of man and the universe, can best be called "spirit" or "spirituality" (*thugs*). Though the German words *Geist* and *Geistigkeit* are admittedly better than their English equivalents, even they are not entirely free of substantialist and idealist nuance. To render *thugs* as "mind" or "consciousness" would only make matters worse. Not only do these terms miss out on the range of meanings that attach to "spirit" and "spirituality," they perpetuate the fallacy of reducing to a "thing" what is really a dynamic center that radiates in all directions, animates the whole of our life, and "touches" us in its every activity and manifestation.

The consequences of seeing corporeality and spirituality as degrees of intensity are far-reaching. At one stroke, this standpoint demolishes the naive dualism that has inflicted upon us an obsession with things—material and immaterial—and opens us to the liberating idea of pure process in which all opposites are ultimately dissolved. Note the following passage in the *sGra-thal-'gyur-ba* (137):

> Since anyone endowed with a body (*lus-can*) is pervaded by
> mind/mentation (*sems*)
> There does not exist anyone endowed with mind/mentation
> (*sems-can*) who does not [exemplify the process of the]
> dissipation [of old and worn-out structures, *sangs*] and the
> unfolding [of new dynamic regimes, *rgyas*][28]

---

[26] Scrupulous attention should be given to the wording in sNying-thig texts. Klong-chen rab-'byams-pa does not speak of this process in terms of "the three aspects of time" (exteriorized "structures" reified into a past, present, and future, *'das—da-lta—ma-'ongs*), but of experienceable "intrapsychic" phases (*thog—bar—mtha'*).

[27] *mKha'-snying*, vol. 1, 444.

[28] In rendering the terms as I have in the text, I am trying to bring out the Tibetan connotations, which differ markedly from the Indian (Sanskrit) terms whose translations, or rather interpretations, they are. In particular, the Sanskrit word *sattva* stresses the idea of something "existing" (*sat*) and not the idea

Translating the passage into modern language, the living body is "matter" occupying space according to its degree of intensity. Insofar as this intensity is not perverted by the conceptualizing-reifying intellect, it is what we have called "spirituality" (*thugs*).[29] Put in more experiential terms, our very corporeality *is* our spirituality in the sense that both are an expression of a single supraordinate potentiality that has become real in our *Befindlichkeit*[30] and attunement to a wholeness into whose fullness we must grow.

VISION

The four remaining resonance domains, corresponding to the points of the compass in the mandala (see figure 4) may be examined in terms of their internal relationships. We begin with the domain of vision.

In a sense, our general corporeal-spiritual *Befindlichkeit* already affirms our spiritual nature, but the intrinsic luminosity of our human condition also points to our "visionary" capacity, that is, to our capacity to actualize meaning. Mythopoetically, this inner light is referred to as Vairocana (*rNam-par snang-mdzad*), the "Illuminer" whose consort is Dharmadhātvīśvarī (Tib. *Chos-kyi dbyings-kyi dbang-phyug-ma*), "Mistress of the Dimension of Meanings."

Given their longstanding and wide-ranging interest in the cognitive process, it is hardly surprising that Buddhist thinkers should have come to see the basic intentional character of thinking, namely that an idea is always directed at an object, real or imaginary. The importance of the sense of sight in the human world no doubt contributed to vision

---

of this something as "being endowed with mind/mentation" (*sems*); so, too, *sangs-rgyas* is used to render the canonically attested description of the process of spiritual awakening—darkness dissipating and light expanding—and is not a mechanical rendering of the past participle *buddha*.

29 *Chos-dbyings*, 218. We may note here the tremendous difference of the sNying-thig approach to the problem of being and becoming human. When the sNying-thig thinkers speak of *lus*, the individual's corporeality or "body," they do not primarily speak of it in terms of sexuality. The Westerner's preoccupation with the sexual—exaggerated in the pansexual theory of Freud—may be traced to the influences of Plato (see note 6 above), Gnostic thought, and Christian doctrine. In basing itself on the principle of complementarity, sNying-thig thinking avoids the reductionism endemic to much Western thinking about the body.

30 Heidegger's German word means something like "situatedness" or "contextuality."

being assigned first place among the forms of sense knowledge. The intentional object of vision is referred to generically as *rūpa* (*gzugs*), a term that entails both color and shape and is defined as perishable and ephemeral.[31]

In its concrete transitoriness, vision points beyond itself to a background of supporting cosmic forces of which it is but a fleeting manifestation. These fundamental forces all interpenetrate, forming a continual symmetry in the original unity of Being that is experienced as the limitation of finite location in "space."[32] Actually, the cosmic forces in the background are ambivalent: they "radiate" (*dangs-ma*) the pristine awareness of Being[33] to form a link with the *lumen naturale*, and at the same time they "materialize" (*snyigs-ma*) into the physical universe, which can thus never be "nothing-but matter." The visible is related foremost to the fundamental force called "water" (*chu*). Like the observable effect after which it is named, water's function is to sustain life by "moistening" (*rlan*), "gathering," and "holding together" (*sdud*).[34] As such, "water" is used interchangeably with "pristine awareness." Thus, the *Rig-pa rang-shar* (812) states:

> Being's pristine awareness [as] water (*ye-shes chu*) gathers everything that comes-to-presence.

Or again, the *sGra-thal-'gyur-ba*(110) states graphically:

> The body is engulfed and permeated by [Being's] supreme pristine awareness (*ye-shes chen-pos khyab*).[35]
> Like oil in sesame seed.

---

[31] This definition is already found in the Pali *Saṃyutta-nikāya* III, 86, and is discussed at length by Vasubandhu in his *Vyākhyā* and *Abhidharmakośa* I, 13.

[32] See above.

[33] *ye-shes-kyi rtsal.* See *mKha'-snying*, vol. 1, 436.

[34] The *Mu-tig phreng-ba*, 449, states summarily that "water is a gathering and moistening"; and the *sGra-thal-'gyur-ba*, 130, is still more explicit in declaring that "the matter-dominated aspect of water moistens and gathers."

[35] This line renders Klong-chen rab-'byams-pa's version of the above quotation (*mKha'-snying*, vol. 1, 440), which he attributes, incorrectly, to the *Rig-pa rang-shar*. The *A-'dzom* blocks read: "Pristine awareness as a function of an ecstatic supracognitive intensity that can be known and felt only by Being as experiencer itself (*rang-rig ye-shes*) resides (*gnas*) in the experiencer's body." These two versions highlight the difference between structure-oriented thinking and process-oriented thinking. The *A-'dzom* version of the text under consideration reflects a static view, as intimated by the intransitive verb "resides," and is reminiscent of *Hevajratantra* I, i.12. Klong-chen rab-'byams-pa's version reflects a dynamic view, though he may well have changed the original text to suit his

The moisture (*rlan*) of this pristine awareness makes
Brightness and brilliance engulf and permeate the body.

Besides being perishable and ephemeral, the visible—which serves as a class name for the representations of all five traditional senses—also represents material resistance[36] to the perceptual act, thus effecting a relationship between the experiencing individual and the physical world. The material resistance of the object of vision produces in us an instinctive emotional response, an "irritation" (*zhe-sdang*) that symbolizes the general human condition of "existentiality in turmoil." This can be seen in the following exegesis of the term:

zhe means the profoundness of mind in its pellucidity and consummation,
sdang means the irritation with the things of samsara;
Hence, understand mind to be both *zhe* and *sdang*.[37]

Just as the spatially limited visible world is correlated with the irritation it causes in the seeing individual, so do the cosmic forces—the materializing force of water and the spiritualizing force of pristine awareness—relate to and reinforce one another. While irritation pits the seer and the seen against each other, the mirror-like pristine awareness lights up "things" as mere presence, so that the everyday things of life glow with the nothingness of original Being, like an image in a concave mirror that recedes into an infinite background only to reappear close to view. This aesthetically moving experience is frequently likened to the reflection of the moon in water.

In the diaphaneity of Being, without any foundation to support it, dissolving into the freedom [of Being's nothingness], complete in its wholeness,
Whatever comes-to-presence [as the phenomenal] is in its thereness a brilliance that yet is nothing, similar to the moon's [reflection] in water.[38]

The section continues:

---

purposes. The transitive verb *khyab*, frequently used in logical treatises, implies a milieu that engulfs and quickens an organism from within.

[36] See Vasubandhu's *Vyākhyā* and *Abhidharmakośa* I, 13.

[37] *Man-ngag thams-cad-kyi sdom* (in *rNying-rgyud*, vol. 2, 28–226), 210.

[38] *mKha'-yang*, vol. 2, 506.

> In whichever manner [something] comes-to-presence, it is nothing as such,
> It is like the water and the moon's reflection in it that cannot be split into two [separate entities].
> To speak of this [phenomenon] as a non-dual reality is metaphorical diction.[39]

If corporeality is both the fundamental condition for the emergence of the psychophysical-cultural world and the zero-point around which the world is organized, the eye (*mig*) represents the zero-point for the visual field. In marked contrast to older, mechanistic views of visual perception in which the eye was a mere mechanism for "taking in" and processing data from the world, rDzogs-chen (sNying-thig) thinkers conceived of it as an "outlet" (*'char-sgo*)[40] for pristine awareness. The dynamic nature of pristine awareness crytallizes into a particular gestalt (*sku*)[41] that transmits to the beholder the meaningfulness of Being and resonates the fullness of the greater whole.

The eye, as focal center of the visual field, forms part of a wider field whose focal center is the body, which in turn becomes the locus for spirituality. As an outlet for the manifestation of Being, the eye stimulates this spiritual dynamic. It is, we might say, the *Gestaltung* of meaning and the supraordinate value of Being, symbolized in the figure of Vajrasattva (Akṣobhya).[42] The field against which the gestalt takes shape, symbolized as Vajrasattva's consort, is termed Māmakī[43]—a noun derived from the pronoun *mama*, "mine." Despite the obvious

---

[39] *mKha'-yang*, vol. 2, 506.

[40] See page 61 in the text above, and *dGongs-pa zang-thal*, vol. 2, 401.

[41] The technical term for this gestalt as the expression and the expressed of life's meaningfulness is *chos-sku*. The participation of the experiencing individual in a meaningful world by "seeing with fresh eyes" is termed *longs-(spyod rdzogs-pa'i) sku*: the *Gestaltung* of a total (*rdzogs*) engagement (*spyod*) in this world outlined (*longs*) by the dynamics of the whole. Since the experiencing individual is always situated in a context, engagement with the world of meaning "turns" one into a guiding image (*sprul-[pa'i] sku*). For further details concerning these three gestalts (*sku gsum*), see my *From Reductionism to Creativity*, 221–43.

[42] Of these two interchangeable terms, Vajrasattva is the more dynamic and Akṣobhya the more static. The Tibetan interpretation of the Sanskrit Vajrasattva, *rdo-rje sems-dpa'*, makes this clear. As the texts repeatedly state, the Diamond (*vajra, rdo-rje*) owes its "value" to the fact that it cuts through everything but cannot itself be broken. This makes it a suitable symbol for the "valiant mind" (*sems-dpa'*), indicating the courage needed to "cut through" time-worn notions. Akṣobhya, like the Tibetan term *Mi-bskyod-pa*, merely indicates the "unshakeability" of the figure bearing this name.

[43] This word has remained untranslated in Tibetan works.

association with personal ego, the expression is purely symbolic, referring to the dynamic *Gestaltung* which re-creates the world, and us, through pristine awareness. Both the image we project on the world and the world that limits our projection combine in the formation of the visual gestalt. The "intimacy" (if we may use the word) of the individual's role in the *Gestaltung* dictates its qualification as "mine." For in reflecting the world, I (Vajrasattva) project onto it and so reveal what is most truly mine (Māmakī).

In more mundane terms, we may speak of this process of reflection-projection as an individual's "operacy" (Skt. *upāya,* Tib. *thabs*) aimed at materializing stable but ephemeral structures out of the colored bits of matter carried along by the water. This operative role of the individual is symbolized by the diamond (*vajra, rdo-rje*), thus reaffirming its existential rather than ego-centered nature. On the strictly organismic level this symbol is used for the penis.

SIGNS AND SYMBOLS

Complementing this complex process located geometrically in the east is another complex process located on the west end of the mandala. The feedback between the outer, material world and the inner world of sense perception brings to light another dimension of experience—the symbolic. The use of signs, symbols, and ideas (*'du-shes*)[44] both belongs to the world of matter and yet clearly transcends the physical. As we noted in the simile of the lotus flower (*padma*) in the pond, the water envelops the leaves but does not discolor them or hold them captive. So, too, the resonance domain of the symbolic reaches deeply into the realm of samsara but is not polluted by it.

It is also not without significance that the regent of this domain, more than the regent of any other domain, is associated with light. Thus the rDzogs-chen (sNying-thig) thinkers render his Indian name, Amitābha, in Tibetan as "The lighting-up that exceeds all bounds" (*sNang-ba mtha'-yas*).[45]

---

[44] Regarding the distinction between sign, symbol, and idea see, for example, *The Collected Works of C. G. Jung*, vol. 6, 473–79. On the corresponding Sanskrit term *saṃjñā,* which covers all three meanings, see my *From Reductionism to Creativity*, 28.

[45] There are two Tibetan versions of this Indian name: *sNang-ba mtha'-yas*, and the more widely used *'Od dpag-med*. The former stresses the dynamic aspect of lighting-up (*snang-ba*), as is evident from *mKha'-snying*, vol. 1, 449; the latter refers to the presence of this light (*'od*).

The cosmic force in the background of this material constellation of signs, symbols, and ideas is called "fire" (*me*). More than any other cosmic force, fire carries the sense of shining brilliance and is therefore most suited to represent the spiritualizing dynamic of Being.[46] Thus, the *Rig-pa rang-shar* speaks of the supracognitive intensity of Being (*rig-pa*) as an all-consuming fire, and of our critical acumen (*shes-rab*) as a fire that consumes all dichotomies.[47] Similarly, the *Mu-tig phreng-ba* speaks of the fire of critical acumen as burning away one's emotion-pollutants (491), and the *Seng-ge rtsal-rdzogs* speaks of one's critical acumen as reducing one's unknowing (that is, one's low-level cognitive capacity or intensity, *ma-rig-pa*) to ashes (295).

The "set" (*phung-po*) of signs, symbols and ideas by means of which we construct our sociocultural world and communicate with it is related to the instinctive-emotional dimension of human existence, or *'dod-chags*. The term is used to cover desire, passionate longing, sexuality, and the like. Here, however, it is restricted to the sense of an inordinate preoccupation with a self (*bdag*). The "self" here should be understood in the sense of the Brahmanical *ātman* that was posited as one entity among others, and in the course of the history of Indian philosophy tended towards a reductive monism:

> *'dod-pa* is the claim that [any] entity [among the] entities that constitute our reality is a self;
> *chags-pa* is the clinging to this claim of [something being] a self.[48]

The complementarity between the material (the signs and symbols) and the instinctive (desire, passionate longing, and wishful thinking) shows the close bond between what we *conceive* and what we *want*, which in turn leads to what we *can do*.

Behind this rationalized interpretation of desire, the older associ-

---

[46] A penetrating study of fire in the Western context has been made by Gaston Bachelard, *The Psychoanalysis of Fire* (Boston: Beacon Press, 1964).

[47] *Rig-pa rang-shar*, 682, 812. This passage is highly suggestive in that it lists all the fundamental forces with the exception of "space":

> The fire (*me*) of one's critical acumen consumes all dichotomies;
> The wind (*rlung*) of [Being's] ecstatic supraconscious intensity [in us] disperses every subjectivity;
> The water (*chu*) of [our] pristine awareness [modes] gathers all of the phenomenal;
> From the soil (*sa*) of the gestalt [we present] the play of [the world's] multiplicity comes about.

[48] *Kun-byed rgyal-po* (in *rNying-rgyud*, vol, 1, 1–219), 11.

ations with the sexual drive are still discernible, as the very name of this resonance domain, "fire," suggests. From ancient times in India, the lotus flower, particularly the red lotus (*padma*), has been a symbol for the vulva. Indeed, the range of flowering blossoms that have served this symbolic function, right down to women artists in our own day,[49] is so wide as to suggest that we are dealing with something archetypal here. This symbol, with the idea and passion it represents, is also associated with the nose (*sna*). The olfactory system, already present in the reptilian brain,[50] plays a very important role in genital functions related to mating.

The image of "fire" as an all-consuming force is well known.[51] By burning away emotional pollution, fire purifies and in so doing allows us to gain a deeper, "pristine" awareness of reality in all its manifold complexity, free of distortion and oversimplification. In the process fire also deodorizes.[52] The term *odor of sanctity* has a somewhat archaic ring to the modern ear, but there is good evidence that it described an actual experience. To judge from the accounts about those who emitted it, the stench was unbearable—which was why, in ancient Indian tradition, gods would not come near human beings.

In its "material" aspect, the purgative function of fire is to clean the organism of the pollution of instinct. But it is in its "radiation"

---

[49] Especially worthy of note is the Chinese pen-and-ink porcelain work of Judy Chicago entitled *The Cunt as Temple, Tomb, Cave and Flower*, reproduced by Elinor W. Gadon, *The Once and Future Goddess* (San Francisco: Harper & Row, 1989), pl. 30. There she observes, "Chicago resacralizes a woman's body and female sexuality as the source of life and creativity." On Suzanne Santoro's photograph *Flower and Clitoris*, Gadon comments (317): "When the photograph of the clitoris is placed next to a half-opened flower, we are confronted with the structural beauty of our organic selves. The multiple layering and deep unfolding is not unlike that of the flower revealing its reproductive heart, the pistil and stamen." This same symbolic fusion is subtly intimated in many of Georgia O'Keefe's flower paintings as well.

[50] The reptilian brain is the most primitive structure in the functional hierarchy of the nervous system, which Paul D. MacLean ("A Triune Concept of the Brain and Behavior") has divided into three evolutionary strata: the reptilian, the paleomammalian or limbic, and the neomammalian. A good summary is given by Erich Jantsch, *The Self-organizing Universe*, 165–69, and Charles D. Laughlin, Jr., John McManus, and Eugene G. d'Aquili, *Brain, Symbol and Experience* (Boston: Shambhala, 1990).

[51] See especially Gaston Bachelard, *The Psychoanalysis of Fire*, chapter 4, "Sexualized Fire," 43–58.

[52] Gaston Bachelard, *The Psychoanalysis of Fire*, 103.

aspect that fire has its greatest effect, on the one hand joining itself to the *lumen naturale* of Being in order to intensify its light, and directing the light of Being out of itself and towards the world. This dual orientation of the light of Being is represented symbolically in the figures of Amitābha and his consort Pāṇḍaravāsinī (*Gos dkar-mo*), "She who is dressed in white." As influenced by him, she takes on the same fiery red color as he. But as a purifying influence on him, she is depicted as dressed in white—or, as the Sanskrit word *pāṇḍara* suggests, in fair or pale hues—which carries the sense of a purity that is *felt* rather than merely *observed.* The symbolism of Amitābha and Pāṇḍaravāsinī in intimate union restores a balance all too often overlooked: not only are we spiritual and visionary beings, we are also passionate beings who enhance and complete each other. In actual practice (*thabs*), vision tends to separate and distinguish. Insight (*shes-rab*) preserves the element of passion that erases distinctions and reunites, bathing everything in a single warm light.

In place of all nauseous odors, fire suffuses the preternatural light of Being with a delicate fragrance that prevails in announcing (*gsung*) a pure, primordial presence. Thus the *lumen naturale* of Being is described ontologically as *byang-chub(-kyi) sems*, "mind suffused with and moving in the direction of the clarity and completeness of Being."[53] Its visible form (*sku*) speaks (*gsung*) in luminous and melodious tones—and does so playfully.

The image of the "play of light" can be seen in the term *'od-zer,* "ray of light," usually occurring in the phrase "the sun (*nyi-ma*), its light (*'od*), and its rays (*zer*)."[54] For example:

> Having taking up its abode in light as its gestalt (*sku'i 'od*), it frolics in its rays [as its] announcement [of itself, *gsung-gi zer*].[55]

FEELING AND ACTION

The three resonance domains considered so far are manifest as ener-

[53] In terms of the overall dynamic, this term is used synonymously with *de-bzhin gshegs-pa'i snying-po*, "the energy that propels the individual in the direction of the beingness of Being." Insofar as it makes Being present to the individual directly, and not through representation, it is called one's "evolutionary resonance domain" (*de-bzhin gshegs-pa'i rigs*). See also above.

[54] *rDo-rje sems-dpa' snying-gi me-long*, 371.

[55] This phrase occurs verbatim in the *Chos-chen-po rmad-du byung-ba* (in *rNying-rgyud*, vol. 2, 487–531), 505.

gies manifesting themselves in the spiritual realm—as spirit (*thugs*), form (*sku*), and speech (*gsung*); and in the material realm—as body (*lus*), vision (*mig*), and smell (*sna*). Together they account for the symbolic recreation of and communication with the sociocultural world.

The importance of the triune dynamic in Buddhist thought seems to be reflected in human experience itself. But there is another primordial archetype of equal importance in Buddhist thought: the mandala as fourfold. The mandala allows us to introduce two further resonance domains.

The first of these is the "gem resonance domain," whose regent is Ratnasambhava (*Rin-chen 'byung-ldan*) and whose consort is Buddhalocanā (*Sangs-rgyas spyan-ma*).[56] The energy of this domain defines the constitutive element of "feeling." Its corresponding cosmic force is "earth," in whose depths lie buried gems and treasures that only an "eye fully awake" can see—namely, the enormous wealth of qualities that one can "savor" as one's own potential (*yon-tan*, thence the association with the *lce*, the tongue). The intensity of sensitivity here is markedly diminished. At its lowest point, it is experienced as the emotion-pollutant of arrogance (*nga-rgyal*), an utter insensitivity to everything that pertains to feelings (*tshor-ba*). And yet it is feeling more than any other human function that opens the way to the inner landscape (*sa*) so rich in precious (*rin-chen*) qualities (*yon-tan*). Only by being roused to pristine awareness can one realize one's co-equality (*mnyam-nyid*) with Being and savor those qualities. Only then can the arrogance of ego be transformed into the pride of the authentic Self, the supreme guiding image and "epiphany" of wholeness. It is in this sense that *nga-rgyal* is interpreted as the voice of the authentic Self:

> I (*nga*) am the thrust into an unerring clarity and completeness and
> Since time before time I have ruled (*rgyal*) over Being-in-its-beingness.[57]

Finally there is the resonance domain of "action," whose regent is Amoghasiddhi (*Don-yod grub-pa*), "He whose success is assured," and whose consort is Samaya Tārā (*Dam-tshig sgrol-ma*), "She who through

---

[56] Literally, these names mean "Source of Gems" and "Buddha-Eye." Both the Sanskrit *locanā* and the Tibetan *spyan* emphasize the "seeing," not the physical organ of the "eye." This means that *buddha* and *sangs-rgyas* need to be understood adverbially, as seeing "in a spiritually awake manner." The whole context points in this direction, as does the pairing of Buddhalocanā—rather than Māmakī, as in other traditions—with Ratnasambhava.

[57] *Kun-byed rgyal-po*, 11.

her commitment [to wholeness] frees [the whole from everything that might limit its scope]." As archetypal images, the regent and his consort "inform" the existential limits of human life. At the biological, instinctive level they operate in activities (*las*)—hence the name of this resonance domain—that consist basically of model building (*'du-byed*).[58] Through the interplay and mutual feedback between the inner and outer world, we build a model of ourselves and our world, a model we safeguard jealously (*phrag-dog*), only to discover one day that all these artificial constructs have been blown away by the "wind" (*rlung*), the very cosmic force that permits us to build models in the first place but never intends for them to be immobile.

The idea of a wealth of inner qualities (*yon-tan*) flowing from a supraordinate dimension closed off to the rationalizing intellect, and of concerned action (*'phrin-las*) flowing back to this transcendent dimension sets up a complementarity: the gem resonance domain provides the resources, and the action domain puts them to use for the sake of wholeness. In other words, we see a sensitivity to what is interacting with a sensitivity to what is to be done (*bya-grub*). Concerned activity is associated with the auditory sense, the ear (*rna*), calling to mind the old adage about actions speaking louder than words.

THE COLORS OF THE RESONANCE DOMAINS

In conclusion, a brief word about the association of the resonance domains, their regents, and their respective modes of pristine awareness modes with particular colors.[59] The choice of colors here is not a mere function of specific physical properties but rather a way of highlighting the "feeling-toned" nature of the various modes of pristine awareness. Coloration is meant both to appeal to one's sensitivities and to draw one beyond the sway of the concrete.[60]

The association of the particular cosmic forces with these colors is, therefore, not accidental, but deliberately functional. The blueness of a bright sky, as Goethe has already noted,[61] draws us a great distance

---

[58] Skt. *saṃskārāḥ*. This term is synonymous with *karman* (Tib. *las*). On model-building as a continuously ongoing activity with the individual and in social and cultural systems see Erich Jantsch, *Design for Evolution*, 191ff.

[59] See figure 5.

[60] See Khrag-thung Rol-pa'i rdo-rje, *Dag-snang ye-shes dra-ba-las gNas-lugs rang-byung-gi rgyud rdo-rje'i snying-po*, 269–74.

[61] *Theory of Colors*, para. 781.

from ourselves and ultimately into the infinity of Being itself. The sparkling whiteness of flowing water enhances the sense of transparency and clarity. The redness of fire helps one feel the force of an all-consuming yet purifying passion. The yellowness of earth suggests gold and hence reminds us of hidden value. The greenness in the freshness of a gentle breeze creates a sense of relief from agony and despair through concerned and compassionate, not blunderingly sentimental, actions. In all of this, it is clear that the rDzogs-chen (sNying-thig) conception of the relationship between light and color is free of the limitations that the Aristotelian categories imposed on Western scholastic views.[62]

The general tenor of Saraha's Songs, both his *Dohās* and his *Vajragītis*, are basically poetic representations of lived experience, despite obvious didactic elements. Unlike our usual mode of experience as experience *of* something re-presented to us, the *lived* experience retains its original spontaneity, wholeness, and presence. This is what Saraha attempts to capture in his Songs.

However spontaneous and holistic an experience, for the human individual it is always an *embodied* experience. It puts us "in touch with" the world which, from the Buddhist perspective, is always a world of our own making. This explains the strong attachment we feel to our world and our tendency to forget the role that ego-consciousness plays in constructing it. Saraha attempts to keep this insight to the fore by presenting the body as something living and dynamic, not as a mere mechanism for perception.

The spontaneity that marks lived experience, which in turn is inseparable from the living body, is felt as an ecstasy—an *ek-stasis* that draws us beyond the confines of the mental and the material and into the complexity and wholeness of which we are a part. In Saraha, this sense of ecstasy bursts forth in jubilant song. The pity is that only the text of the Songs has come down to us; their melodies have been lost. When we add to this the fact that the natural rhythms of Saraha's language also disappear for the most part in their Tibetan translation, the loss is still more keen. In their place, we must rely heavily on the notions of wholeness, body, and complexity to capture the flavor of Saraha's work.

---

[62] Umberto Eco, *Art and Beauty in the Middle Ages* (New Haven: Yale University Press, 1986) 50, states: "Light in its pure state was substantial form, and thus a creative force in the neo-Platonic sense. Light as the color or splendor of an opaque body was accidental form."

Saraha's
Three Cycles of Dohā

A Treasure of *Dohā* in the Form of a Song

(People *Dohā*)

> *A brief presentation of non-Buddhist sociocultural practices and their critique*

1 Not knowing Being-in-its-beingness the Brahmins
Vainly recite the four Vedas;[1]
[Undergoing a symbolic] purification [of body, speech, and mind] with earth, water, and kusa grass
They stay in their homes and perform burnt offerings.
The performance of such worthless and meaningless offerings has
Only succeeded in hurting the eyes by the smoke.

2 [Among them] there are those who dress themselves up as Śiva carrying a one-pronged or three-pronged staff,[2] as well as
Those who insist on difference[3] [between Śiva and themselves] and those who [attempt to live up to and promulgate] the teaching of the *Paramahaṃsa*[4] and
[Finally] those who do not know what is proper and what is not but think of the one to be as good as the other;[5]
They [all] mislead the living beings into falsehood.

3 [Still others] smear their bodies with ashes from burnt human bones
And tie their hair on their heads into a knot.
Inside their homes they kindle lamps and
Seating themselves in the corners [of a mandala] they tinkle bells.
Then sitting cross-legged, they close their eyes and
Fool people by whispering into their ears.
To any female that comes,
Be she a widow or one who has her menses as indicated by their clothing,[6]
They impart initiations and charge the disciple a fee.

4 With long nails, the body covered with dirt,
Running around naked and tearing out their hair [on the head and other parts of the body]
The [Digambara] Jains[7] by following a way that is a noxious farce
Deceive themselves in [assuming that their] materiality-Self is going in for a state of emancipation.
If by nakedness freedom is realized
Why have dogs and jackals not realized freedom?
If by plucking out one's hair freedom is realized
A woman's depilated private parts[8] should have realized freedom.
If by lifting a tail[9] freedom is realized
Peacocks and yaks and other animals should have realized freedom.
If by eating what one happens to pick up freedom is realized
Why have horses and elephants not realized freedom?
Saraha says: For the Jains
There never exists a chance of emancipation.

> *A brief presentation of Buddhist sociocultural practices and their critique*

5 Then there are the worthy ones such as
The novices, the monks, and the elders who, dissociated from the beingness of ecstasy,[10]

Exclusively subject their bodies to austerities.
In their renunciation of worldliness
Some sit there and explain the Sutras,
Others one sees as claiming that [the experience of] one-flavoredness[11] is the mind's [natural] state,
And still others run after the Mahāyāna.[12]
They [all] deal with the treatises that explain the basic texts.

6 Furthermore, some imagine [elaborate] mandalas and [concentrate on] all the energy vortices;[13]
Others explain the meaning of the fourth empowerment;[14]
Some intellectualize [Being's nothingness] as the fundamental force of space;
And still others visualize [Being's] nothingness as [some] nothingness-[thing].

7 On the whole, these people entertain contradictory propositions.
Anyone who, without [comprehending what] complementarity-in-spontaneity [means],[15]
Imagines nirvana [as something apart from samsara]
Will never realize the unitary knowledge of
What is ultimately real.
How is anyone who [one-sidedly] concentrates on what he fancies
Ever to find release?

8 What is the point of kindling lamps? What is the point of making offerings?
What is to be effected by it? What is the point of uttering mantras?
There is no point in going on pilgrimages or undergoing austerities;
Will release be found by stepping into water?

> *The proper way of practice*

9 He who immerses himself in nothingness as apart from compassion
Will not gain the supreme way;

And he who in active imagination deals with compassion exclusively
Stays on here in samsara and does not find release.
He who can combine both
Will not stay in samsara and also will not stay in nirvana.

10 Hey! Whatever is being spoken is a pack of lies and a perversion;[16] in getting rid of [any such verbiage]
Also dismiss whatever craving for anything whatsoever there may be.

11 Once a deeply felt understanding has come about, everything turns out to be This;
Nobody is going to know anything but This.
Reading [the texts] is This, thinking [about them] is This, dealing with them in active imagination is This.
Explaining the treatises and legends[17] also is This.
There is no visionary experience that does not reveal This.[18]

12 To put the matter in a nutshell, this means that one has seen the innermost mentor's face, [so that]
He into whose heart the innermost mentor's words have sunk
Is like a person who sees a treasure in the palm of his hand.

➤ *The elimination of incidental limit-factors of inner experience*

13 Being's genuineness as an uncontrived presence[19] is not something that can be directly perceived[20] by a fool [and hence]
A fool is deceived by his mistaken ideas about it[21]—thus Saraha says.

14 If, without meditative concentration and also without [its resulting] renunciations,[22] but
By staying at home in the company of his womenfolk[23]
A person will not become free from the fetters of his delighting in the sensuous and sensual objects, then
I, Saraha say: "He does not know Being-in-its-beingness."

15 If [Being's genuineness] is directly visible, what is the point in concentrating on it?
If it is hidden, [it is like] looking for something in the dark.
Being's complementarity-in-spontaneity is Being-in-its-beingness [in action] and
This is neither a substance nor a non-substance.
Saraha tearfully and constantly proclaims [this fact].

16 "[By means of that very body] you have taken up [in becoming an embodied being], bound to be born, to die, and to stay on for a while,
By that very body most excellent ecstasy is realized"—
Although Saraha [openly] speaks this secret and profound word
The brutish world does not comprehend it—what can one do?

17 Since [complementarity-in-spontaneity] is not an object for meditative concentration, what is there to concentrate upon?
What is inexpressible by word of mouth, what is there to talk about?

18 By the grip the state of being enworlded has on us, all living beings are deceived; [and so]
Being's ownmostness, [its] genuineness,[24] is not something that can be taken up [that is, appropriated] by anyone.

19 [In it] there are no Tantras [to explain it], no mantras [to conjure it up], no meditative concentrations on something to be concentrated upon.
All [assumptions to the contrary] are the cause that your egologically predisposed awareness (*yid*)[25] goes astray.
Your mental-spiritual disposition (*sems*) that by presenting Being's ownmostness is pure, should not be ruined by meditative concentrations.
Do not harass your authentic Self (*bdag-nyid*)[26] abiding in and as ecstasy.

> *Experiencing the way of one's spiritual growth without flaws*
> *Involving procedures that have specifiable aspects*

20 "By such activities as eating, drinking, copulating, and [relishing] the four joys [that are being built up thereby],
For ever, over and again, replenishing the energy vortices,
The other side of worldliness is reached"—
Humble the deluded [literalists] by putting your foot on their heads and go away.[27]

21 Where the biotic currents (*rlung*), [evolving into patterns of thought (*rnam-rtog*) and neural-metabolic mentation (*sems*), evolving into instinctual-spiritual assessment (*dran-rig*)] no longer stir and
The sun (*nyi-ma*) [a symbol of the phenomenal (*snang-ba*)], and the moon (*zla-ba*) [a symbol of the noumenal], have ceased to enter upon the scene,
There you should take a breather.[28]—Oh, you ignorant people!
Saraha has given all the instructions[29] and gone away.[30]

22 Do not create duality; create unity.[31]
Rather than introducing differentiations into the fabric [that is your being][32]
Turn the totality of the three realms of [your] enworldedness[33]
Into the single color of a passion of which there could be none greater.

23 There is in it neither beginning, nor middle, nor end;
It is neither worldliness nor nirvana.
In this superb ecstasy
There is neither an I nor a Thou.
Whatever you see in front, behind, or in the ten regions [of the compass]
Is This.
Since from now on errancy has stopped
You do not have to ask anyone any longer.[34]

24 Where the [dualing activity of the] senses has subsided

There also the stuff your [mind] is made of[35] dissipates.
Friends! This is Being's complementarity-in-spontaneity having become your body.[36]
[If you have any doubts] ask the innermost mentor [and he will] clearly [confirm this].

> *Involving appreciative intuitions without specifiable aspects*

25 There where your egologically predisposed awareness (*yid*) is about to be fettered and where the biotic currents (*rlung*) are about to dissipate, [a "place" that]
Here on earth is [in between the supraordinate fundamental forces and their materialized] branches,
There, in between[37] [these opposites] you should come to fully know [this bliss], you fools!
He who knows to make an end of the ocean of delusion
Is [in this knowledge] this very superb ecstasy which
Saraha has shown and passed away [into it].

26 Hey-ho! This is what only you yourself can know in ecstatic experience.[38]
Do not turn it into errancy.
Substance and non-substance are [notions that would even] fetter him who has passed into ecstasy. Therefore,
Without differentiating between samsara and nirvana
Let your egological mind whose reifying tendencies have been deconstructed by Being's genuineness in it[39] stay with this unitary experience, oh yogi.
Know it to be like water poured into water.[40]

> *Annulling the chances of slipping into either extreme*

27 Since meditative concentration is falsehood, release is not gained [by it];
It is like a magic net [cast over you] or like the embrace by a phantom woman.
Putting my trust in the words of the reliable innermost mentor as [ultimate] truth
I, Saraha, say: I have nothing to talk about.

➤ *How to avoid slipping into pitfalls*

28 Whilst looking and looking at the sky that has been clear since its very beginning,
The seeing it [as some thing] ceases.
And even this in time will cease.

29 The fool is deceived by the flaws [in his discursive] thinking about [what his egologically predisposed awareness is] when its reifying tendencies have been deconstructed by Being's genuineness in it.[41]
Even more so, reviling all other people,
He is, because of the flaw of arrogance [about what he believes to be experience and practice], unable to understand [Being's nondemonstrable] beingness.
The whole world is deluded by meditative concentration.
Being's intrinsic genuineness cannot demonstrably be understood by anyone [as being some thing].

30 The root of your mental-spiritual disposition cannot demonstrably be understood because
[As Being's] complementarity-in-spontaneity [manifesting itself] in a triple manner[42]
It is not known from where its [manifestations] have originated, where they end,
And where they stay.
For him who thinks about Being-in-its-beingness that has no root
It suffices to obtain the innermost mentor's instruction.[43]

31 "Samsara is just the mind's energy/intensity-'stuff' "[44]—
You fools! Know these words to have been over and again spoken by Saraha.
Although Being's intrinsic genuineness cannot be spoken of in words [that come from one's mouth],
It can be seen by the eye of the instruction [that is given by Being itself and to which your human] teacher[45] [can open your eyes].
I have tasted samsara and nirvana and eaten [both]:
There is not the slightest evil in either.

32 When your egologically predisposed awareness whose reifying tendencies have been deconstructed by Being's genuineness in it (*gnyug-ma'i yid*) has been cleansed [of its egocentricity] and refined,
Your innermost mentor's qualities enter your heart.
Having understood this, Saraha has broken out in song.
Not a single mantra or Tantra has he seen [in this experience].

➤ *The criteria for bondage and freedom*

33 The living beings are individually fettered by their karmic blundering;
If and when they are freed of their karmic blundering their egological awareness becomes [their state of] release.
If and when what constitutes your existentiality[46] is freed, then and there nothing else exists for sure—
Superb nirvana has been won.

34 Mind as a dynamic principle (*sems-nyid*) is the seed of the universe:
Homage to the mind (*sems*) that is like the wish-granting gem
From which samsara and nirvana come forth and
Which bestows as its gift whatever we desire.[47]

35 By this mind, when fettered, one's whole being becomes fettered,
If [this mind] is free there is no doubt [about one's whole being being free, too].
By what the stupid are fettered
The wise are quickly set free.

➤ *The liberating operation*
The Mahāmudrā imagination
A. The initiation of this process as its own incentive to proceed

36 One's psychic background [mind, *sems*) must be understood to be like the sky (*nam-mkha'*) and

The sky must similarly be understood [to be like] one's psychic background.[48]

If and when one's egologically predisposed awareness (*yid*) has been turned into a not-so-predisposed awareness

The unsurpassable experience of being spiritually awake is won by it.

37 Once [this egologically predisposed awareness] has been made to resemble the sky, the wind [of conceptualizations] is prevented from blowing [and]

By thoroughly knowing what [its] identity [with Being] means, [the unsettling storm of conceptualizations] wholly subsides [in the gentle breeze of pristine awareness modes].

If you should have the capacity [to experience] what Saraha has just said

Transitoriness and instability [so characteristic of samsara] are quickly discarded.

38 When the forces [named after their cosmic counterparts and constituting you as a living being, felt and imaged by you as] wind and fire and earth and

Ambrosial water [cease moving in an outward direction and this very ambrosial water as pristine awareness modes starts] flowing, the wind [of your divisive thought constructions] recedes into the mind-"stuff" [of which you and Being are made][49]

When through a four-phased process of a linking backward[50] the unitary source [of all Being] is entered,

The superb ecstasy [experienced is such that it] cannot be contained in the dimension of [physical] space.[51]

> *Intellectual discussions miss the point*

39 Although in every home people talk about it

They absolutely do not know where ecstasy abides.

All living beings demean themselves with their representational mode of thinking. Saraha says:

What cannot be encompassed by representational

thought can never be set up [as a content of such thinking].

> *The dichotomic thinking shared by worldly people is of no avail*

40 Although in each and every living being
Being-in-its-beingness exists, it is not understood [and felt as what it is].

> *Coming to grips with the liberating pristine awareness*

41 Since everything [particular] shares in the flavor [that is the flavor of wholeness]
[Its] pristine awareness surpassing representational thinking is unsurpassed.[52]

> *The reason for not understanding this awareness*

42 Yesterday and today, tomorrow and the days after
People have claimed [and continue claiming] that the things [of this world] are the best [of all possible things].
Hey-ho, my lovely friends, this is like your not noticing how
The water you hold in the palms of your hands, whilst sipping it, is used up.

> *In real understanding you go beyond bondage and freedom*[53]

43 If with certainty you understand what "doing what is to be done" and "not-doing what is to be done"[54] mean,
Then there is neither bondage nor freedom.

> *Such understanding may be made possible by the use of propositions*

44 Since [such understanding] has no linguistic devices about it, from among the yogis who claim that it exists [as something] to be explained [by words]
Only one among a hundred may be able to [really] understand.

> *How to relax the mind*

45 If in the manner of tangled threads this mind is fettered,
Becomes disentangled and relaxed, there is no doubt about its becoming free.[55]

By what the deluded are fettered
The wise are becoming free.

46 Fettered, it attempts to run off into the ten directions of the compass,
Let loose, it stays unswerving and stable.
This reversal of one's ordinary comprehension I have understood to be like a camel's behavior.[56]
My dear child, you, too, should look at yourself with due attention.

47 Hey-ho, look with your senses[, still in the throes of your organismic thinking, at your mind in its relaxed state]:
I have seen nothing but the latter.[57]

> *To cut the mind's attachment to objects*

48 At the feet of a person who has done his [home]work
Cut your mind's ties [to an objective world].

> *Supplementary instructions*
> *Getting rid of the Haṭha-yoga practices*

49 Do not think that in the [feeling of pleasure that comes] when the [biotic current called] wind [as the carrier of concepts] is stopped [in its traversing the structural pathways in the body] you have become your very [freedom].
[What you do is like bending] a tree [with whatever force you can muster]; you should not be such a "tree-trunk" yogi [who attempts to keep his life-force] at the tip of his nose.
Oh no! This is not [a feasible] shortcut. Cling to Being's spontaneity itself and
Completely sever the bond that holds you to what is [merely] the highest point in the realm of enworldedness,[58] [because]
From here, where your egologically predisposed awareness (*yid*) has become concentrated [in what is its detection threshold], the gusts of the wind [of conceptualizations], once

They start to blow and spread, will become ever more violent.

50 If Being's complementarity-in-spontaneity is deeply felt and understood
Your authentic Self has become stable through it [without your resorting to artificial means].

> *The freedom experienced by him who understands*

51 When your egologically predisposed awareness is about to cease operating
The bondage that your body provides is cut and
When [everything is felt as having] the same flavor as Being's complementarity-in-spontaneity
There are no [longer such fictions as] low-caste persons or [high-caste] Brahmins.

> *The pointlessness of going from one place to another*

52 This [your body] is the Jamna,
This [your body] is the Ganges, and so also
It is Varanasi and Prayag.
This [your body] is the moon and the sun.

53 He who, having visited the primary and secondary places of pilgrimage,
Says that [this running around] is the deeply felt understanding [of Being-in-its-beingness], does not really see Being's abidingness.
There is no other sacred place that can compare with your body.
I have properly and with certainty seen its dignity.[59]

54 In the stalk of a lotus flower with [many] leaves there lies in the midst of its pistils
A very subtle stillness, both fragrant and color-saturated.
By introducing differentiations [that destroy its unity] the deluded are plagued by suffering.
Do not bring to nought what is the fruition of your being.[60]

> *B. The visionary experience as initiating a deeply felt understanding*
> *A critical assessment*
> *The necessity to cut the fetters of emotional beliefs*

55 There are people who claim Brahma or Viṣṇu or Śiva to be the ground and reason for the whole world.[61]
[Only] if one worships [Being's genuineness] where this [triadic] pattern does not exist, the host of karmic limitations comes to its end.

> *The necessity to cut the fetters of verbiage*

56 Hey-ho, my children, listen. Those who in their delight in the piquancy of disputations [claim] to know where Being's beingness abides,
[Merely] continue making pronouncements in [their attempt to] explain it, but are unable to really know it.[62]

> *Words cannot point out Being's abidingness*

57 Hey-ho, my children, listen. By [resorting to] various [propositions and symbol terms]
The flavor of Being-in-its-beingness cannot be demonstrated.
The superbness of ecstasy's abiding presence lies in the fact that all divisive concepts are [and finally] have been discarded;
A person's growing up [into the fullness of his being] is precisely this.[63]

> *The necessity to cut the fetters of concentration*

58 [Here] the intellect [with its mistaken notions (*blo*)] has stopped [functioning] and the [emotionally toned] egologically predisposed awareness (*yid*) has been vanquished and [when and]
Where the arrogance [concerning Being's misplaced concreteness] has been destroyed
There is the deeply felt understanding that all this has just been some magic.
What is the point in fettering it by meditative concentration [on it]?

> *The substance of this deeply felt understanding*
> *Its coming from the innermost mentor*

59 What comes into existence as concrete sense objects dissipates [in the beingness of Being like clouds] in the sky:

Once these concrete sense objects have so been dispersed, why should they come up again?

Since their [beginningless] beginning they have been [Being's] dynamics in its unoriginatedness.

This I have today understood by [trusting] the teaching of the bounteous innermost mentor.

> *The totality of our entitative reality is [our] mentation*

60 If you know what has become seeing and hearing and touching and thinking[64] and

Eating, smelling, walking and going and sitting and

Small talk and dialogue

Is [your] mentation, [you will have realized that] there is nothing that has not sprung from it.

> *C. The unification of vision and imagination*[65]
> *I. The primacy of the innermost mentor in the process*
> *The flaw in disregarding him*

61 He who does not drink to the last drop the nectar-like water of the innermost mentor's instruction

That with its coolness removes all pain,

Will painfully die of thirst in the desert of

Frustrations [forced upon him by] meaningless treatises.[66]

> *The necessity of attending him*[67]
> *Question*

62 If the innermost mentor does not speak

The disciple has no chance of comprehending.

Who is to demonstrate the flavor in the nectar [that is Being's] complementarity-in-spontaneity

And how [is he going to do so]?

> *Answer*

63 When the stupid, through the power of their belief in [what the logicians claim to be] the means of valid cognitions,[68]
Come up with differentiations [concerning Being's unitary pristine awareness],[69]
[The wise] amuse themselves in the home of [an] untouchable;
They are not soiled by its [alleged] dirt.[70]

> *II. The presentation of the topics of vision, imagination, conduct, and goal*
> *Non-possessive conduct*

64 When you are a beggar you have to make the rounds with your bowl [which you have picked up from the street and which you may throw away once you have eaten from it]; and
If you were a king what would you do with it anyway?[71]

> *Imagination is not concerned with acceptance and rejection*

65 Once you have dismissed the distinction [between samsara and nirvana] and [once without accepting or rejecting the one or the other] you abide in [what is] Being-in-its-beingness
An intrinsically unshakable equipoise has become [for you] a given fact.[72]
Whilst abiding in nirvana you are samsara's beauty.[73]
You do not have to apply to diseases medicines meant for different diseases.
Once you have thoroughly dismissed [the dichotomy of] thinking and what is being thought
You should stay [in the world] like a small child;

> *The deeply felt understanding of abidingness*
> *A short presentation*
> *Deriving [inner] certainty from the innermost mentor's vitalization*

66 By earnestly applying yourself to the innermost mentor's message

Being's complementarity-in-spontaneity will doubtlessly come to life in you.

> *This understanding is without compare*

67 Dissociated from colors, qualities, linguistic devices and beyond compare
It cannot be expressed by words of mouth; in vain I would try to demonstrate it:
Just like a young woman's innermost yearning for the pleasures of sex[74]—
Can this overwhelming power be shown to anyone?[75]

> *Its freedom from defining characteristics*

68 Where the notions of substance and non-substance have been thoroughly eradicated
There the whole world[76] completely comes to rest.

> *To settle oneself firmly in Being's genuineness*

69 When your egologically predisposed awareness is no longer stirring and has steadied itself in [what is its] legitimate abode,
Then by itself it has become free of notions [constituting] samsara.
When there is no longer [any differentiation between] the I and the other
Then you have won your unsurpassable embodied[77] beingness.

> *A detailed presentation*
> *Being beyond the belief systems and discursive reasoning*
> *Being beyond belief systems*

70 Once, without slipping into errancy because of the certainty concerning what has been shown [to you by your innermost mentor],
You have come to know that this [experience] has come about in you by itself,[78] [you realize that]
[Being's abidingness] since its [beginningless] beginning

has not been interested in [any of the claims of] it being a substance:
Atomistic,[79] non-atomistic,[80] or mentalistic.[81]
This is all Saraha has had to say.[82]

> *Beyond discursive reasoning*

71 Hey-ho, know all the above to be a single flawless reality.
[Though this reality as the master of the house] resides at home, it [forsakes this knowledge and] goes outside to search for it.
[It's like your] having seen the master of the house and then asking the neighbors about his whereabouts.
Saraha says: Know your authentic Self.

> *Beyond the exercises of the stupid*

72 [This knowing] is not meditative concentration, not the concentrated-on, and not the recitation of mantras, [as believed by] the stupid.[83]

> *Beyond the practices recommended by the Sutras and Tantras*

73 Even if I should have learned everything the innermost mentor has pointed out,
By labelling [it as this or that] would I win release?
By going over these objective domains of cognition and being tortured and tormented by [what they offer]
I would not win Being's
complementarity-in-spontaneity, instead I would hold fast to evil.

> *The substance of understanding Being's abidingness*

74 Rather, [let me] enjoy the sensory objects without being soiled by them:
Like a lotus flower that remains untouched by water.

> *Understanding the emotions to be friends*[84]
> *The main point*

75 A yogi who takes refuge in what is the root [of his being]—
Does poison affect a person who has a charm against it?

> *The futility of other means*

76 Even if I were to make a hundred thousand offerings to the gods [of popular belief systems]
I would remain fettered, so what am I to do with them?
By such [performances] samsara is not abolished and
Without understanding Being's genuineness as an uncontrived presence, [none] can cross [the ocean of samsara].

> *Understanding the meaning of deathlessness*

77 The bounteous innermost mentor, without ever closing his eyes, has understood what the cessation of the [conceptualizing activity by the] mind (*sems*) and
The cessation of [the movement of] the biotic forces (*rlung*) [sustaining the mind's activity] mean.[85]
Even while the biotic forces may stir, the innermost mentor remains unshakable.[86]
At the time of your dying what can The Lady of Enchantment (*rnal-'byor-ma*) do?[87]

> *The necessity to link this understanding with one's self*

78 [Know that] for the length of time the senses [let themselves be] trapped in the city of the sense objects,
They have sallied from no other place than [what is Being's genuineness] itself.
Think about what you are doing now![88]
With [the help of Being's] higher intelligence so difficult [to understand] enter [its abidingness] right now.

> *Propositions about abidingness obscure it*

79 What [Being's complementarity-in-spontaneity] is and where it resides
Is not seen there.
All the pandits explain the treatises, but
They do not understand that the "Buddha" is in their body.[89]

> *Cutting the rope of one's mind*

80 Once the [owner of] an [unruly][90] elephant is satisfied with having got rid of it [by having sold it]
[He is no longer bothered by its] coming and going.[91]
If you understand in this way, there is no further room for questions.[92]
Only the shameless pandits do not understand.

> *The fruition of whatever is needed*
> *Freedom from old age and death*

81 While alive, any [person with this understanding] is not [affected and] changed [by karmic blunders and emotional vagaries],
And when he grows old and is going to die, what does that [mean to him]?

> *Winning the finest treasure*

82 The flawless intellect [that comes about by] the innermost mentor's pointing it out
Is the [inexhaustible] treasure; what else deserves this name?

> *Letting the whole of the phenomenal reality find its freedom in the one overarching reality*

83 Its domain is the purity [of Being's abidingness], but this is not to be indulged in as [something concrete],
It is to be enjoyed from [the perspective of Being's] nothingness only;
Just as a pilot crow flies from the ship
And again returns to it after having circled and circled [the ocean].[93]

> *III. Getting rid of one's obsession with the mind's projections*
> *Cutting the tie of the belief in duality*

84 By the mere sight of a black rope as a poisonous snake
People get terrified.
Friends, [similarly] respectable persons

Are fettered by the dilemma [of there being] two
realities.[94]

> *To resolve the phenomenal into Being's possibilizing dynamics*

85 Hey-ho, you fools, Saraha has said:
Do not fetter yourself with your obsession with [any of the two] projections [of your mind].
Look [what happens to] fish, moths, elephants, bees,
And deer.[95]

> *Preserving the above as Being's uncontrived abidingness*
> *Everything is mind/mentation*

86 Whatever [notions] proceed from the mind
They are just the [intimations of the] guardian-lord.[96]
Are the water and its ripples different [things]?[97]
Samsara and nirvana are [Being's] sky-like open-dimensionality.

> *Mind/mentation is not something literally existent*

87 If [the disciple] hears in serving [his teacher] and
Firmly relies on what he hears as [being the innermost mentor's] supermind,[98] [all concretistic notions]
Will subside in his heart
Just like dust particles are no longer visible when the rays of the sun no longer shine [through the window].[99]

> *The fusion of what does not literally exist with the mind's projected domain*

88 Just as when water is poured into water
It takes on the same taste as the water [into which it is poured],
So the mind in which defects and qualities are equally present,
[And as such] the guardian-lord, is not seen by anyone.[100]

> *To resolve the mind's projections in the sphere where even Being's possibilizing dynamics has ended*

89 For the fools there is no chance [to get rid of their

dichotomic thought processes, unless they recognize themselves for what they really are],
[This recognition is] like flames spreading through the forest [of unknowing].
Know the whole phenomenal [world] that confronts your senses
To be Being's complementarity-in-spontaneity [that in its] nothingness is the root of your being.[101]

> *IV. The differences in epistemologically oriented belief systems*
> *A general statement*
> *Doing away with what is thought to be good*

90 If you hold dear [and become obsessed with] the sentimental feeling
Into which your mind thinks [of the above as something] pleasing,[102]
It will create more pain
Than the husk of a sesame seed.

> *Differences in feeling about and understanding it*

91 "It is like this, but it is not so" –
Friends, look at a pig and an ox.[103]

> *Self-fulfilment and other-enrichment are realized when errancy into duality has ended*

92 Like the granting of what is needed by the wish-fulfilling gem
Is [the beneficence of] the wise in whom errancy has been destroyed – oh what miracle!
When the ecstasy [of an awareness that can only be experienced by you] is within yourself [and coming about] by itself, all the tendencies [to give it concrete] shape
Are made to become like the open sky.

> *Being's abidingness is beyond belief systems*
> *It is not a domain for words*

93 You should never mention [the word] *kālakūṭa* poison[104] –

[If you did, this would be like] grasping Being's ownmostness, as vast as the sky, with your egologically predisposed awareness [as if it were some object].

If and when this awareness is being turned into what is no longer an egologically predisposed awareness

Being's ownmostness, [its] complementarity-in-spontaneity, comes as the most beautiful [realization].

➢ *By talking about it the real meaning of ecstasy is not seen*

94 In each and every house people talk about it,

But the abidingness of ecstasy is not at all known.

Saraha says: All living beings are confused about it.[105]

➢ *Methods of making the mind stay in its place*
The inseparability of ecstasy and nothingness
A non-referential assessment

95 Having fully discarded the particularization [of Being's unitary character] into ecstasy [as its feeling tone] and mystery [as its understanding]

I have seen the inseparability of [active] imagination and [passive] imagination.[106]

➢ *A referential assessment*

96 Other people [emphasizing its referential character] concentrate on it by objectifying it.

But even by thinking about it [in this way] dichotomic thought will [eventually] cease.[107]

➢ *Settling the mind in the possibilizing dynamics of Being*

97 When [the restless surface] mind is shown [and understands its source or all-ground] mind,[108]

Its conceptualizations and [with it its egocentricity] are no longer stirring and it stays firmly [rooted].

In the same manner as salt dissolves in water[109]

So the mind submerges in its [and Being's] ownmostness.

> *Self and other as presences of Being's identity with itself*

98 At that time I have seen myself and the other as alike [in being Being's identity with itself],[110]
What is there to be done with it by having laboriously turned it into a concentration [on something other than what it is]?

> *Discussing the differences in epistemologically oriented statements*
> *Being's possibilizing dynamics as the source of such claims*

99 In this singularity one sees many directives
That present themselves clearly as one's many personal likings.[111]
The guardian-lord, the authentic Self, alone and at odds with all other [arguments]
Presents himself in different houses as different arguments.[112]

> *Real understanding is beyond any arguments and belief systems*

100 By eating this one [authenticity] everything else is coming ablaze.[113]
[Yet this authentic Self mistaken about his real status] goes outside his house and looks for the master of the house.
Even if [this master] should come [the searcher] does not see him, neither does he see him if he should go and
He does not recognize him if he were to sit there.

> *Saraha's own presentation*
> *Limpid concentration*

101 [Once] this supreme powerful lord [who is like the ocean] without waves
Has become [pure] concentration [that is like water] without mud,[114]
Let the water stay clear and the lamp shine alone in its luster!
[Here] I do not accept or reject [anything that may] come or go [in its passing through it].[115]

> *The fruition of understanding Being's possibilizing dynamics*

102 Rather,[116] your mind that in its sleep meets [and enjoys] a dancing-girl never seen before
Rests on what has no grounding.[117]
Do not look at her as different from your mind of which she is its sensuous form.[118]
Thus, you have the "Buddha"-experience in your hand.

> *The fusion of composure and post-composure experiences*
> *The composure experience*

103 When your body, speech, and mind have become inseparable [in what is Being's beingness]
Complementarity-in-spontaneity is there in all its beauty.[119]

> *The post-composure experience*

104 When the master of the house[120] has been devoured the mistress of the house has a good time;
Whatever sensory objects [and regions] she sees are to be enjoyed [by her].[121]

> *V. The patterning of the ways and their goals*[122]
> *The five gestalt experiences as process structures*[123]
> *chos-sku*
> *Its essence*

105 With the play I have staged
The children have become tired and exhausted.[124]
[But] these children have not been born by another mother [than me].
Therefore the ways of the Lady are without compare,[125] and so

> *The method of getting to [the Lady]*
> *Putting an end to dichotomic thinking*

106 By eating the master [of the house] your ownmostness [will shine in its] beauty;
Let this mind that is [otherwise] clogged with images to which it is strongly attached,

Enter [and reside in] Being's immanent wholeness in you, once it has discarded this attachment and [its] attachment-free phase.

In this deterioration of the mind's [dichotomic thinking] I have come to see the Lady.[126]

> *The continuity of this experience*

107 Do not think [of the "objective" and the "subjective" as different] when eating [the "objective"] and drinking [the "subjective"].

My sweetheart! I have seen [with my own eyes] that [this differentiation between the subjective and objective] that comes to the fore in my mind

Cannot be demonstrated as something external apart from my mind.[127]

> *Summing it all up*

108 The Lady of enchantment is without compare.

> *longs-sku*[128]
> *Analogies to illustrate it*

109 While [Being's] flawlessness does not reside [as some thing] anywhere in the three levels [that constitute an individual's hierarchical organization] and also does not derive from it,[129]

Under suitable circumstances [it will manifest itself similar to] the fire coming ablaze in tinder or

The moonstone that cannot but let water flow when the rays of the moon touch it.

> *The meaning of the above*

110 Through its operacy (*thabs*) it rules over all the spiritual realms,

[Through its appreciative awareness, *shes-rab*] this spirituality is the all-accomplishing Lady,

Know them [in their ecstasy, *bde-ba*] to be the bonding of Being's complementarity-in-spontaneity.[130]

> *ngo-bo-nyid-kyi sku*[131]
> *An investigation of its dimension*
> *It is not understood by resorting to linguistic symbols*

111 Not one among all the living beings [who are trapped in their use of] linguistic symbols
[Is able to understand] that which has nothing to do with linguistic symbols.
As soon, however, as that which has nothing to do with linguistic symbols [dawns upon him]
He will know what linguistic symbols mean.[132]
[It is like this,] he who delights in ink[, that is, a calligrapher, does not necessarily know how to] read, and
He who[, posing as a Brahmin,] recites the Vedas will utter nonsense and be exposed [for what he is, a non-Brahmin].

> *By understanding its meaning one is able to travel one's road*
> *If one does not yet understand one should attempt to understand*

112 My honorable friends, if you do not know the partner[133] [of the commonly accepted reality], think about [this problem]:
From where have your ideas come and whereto do they return?

> *The number of levels and on which one this understanding resides*

113 As without, so within,
It continuously resides on the fourteenth level.[134]

> *The necessity and implication of its understanding*

114 That which has no body resides hidden in your body,
By its knowledge you become free.

> *Recognizing the method for its understanding*
> *Explaining the four opening words*
> *Understanding Being's abidingness through these four opening words in a manner that will not go wrong*

115 First I [was shown and] recited the four opening words [of life's lesson],[135]

But when I had imbibed the nectar[136] [of their message]
I became oblivious [to the words]. He who knows the one [resounding] letter
No longer knows [or bothers about] words.[137]

> *Comprehending what is meant by the above*[138]

116 [By understanding] this single [resounding] letter as dissociated from the three conditions [that constitute the concreteness of the individual's body, speech, and mind]
It [turns out to be] the divine in the midst of the [individual's] triune [hierarchical organization] that does not go wrong.[139]

> *The triunely organized hierarchy gone wrong*

117 He in whom the triune hierarchical organization has gone wrong
Is like a low-caste person [posing as a] Brahmin.

> *Real understanding does not come from having sex with a woman as a mere object, referred to as the Karmamudrā*
> *Illustrating by analogies the error a person commits by desiring to gain true understanding from her*

118 Each and everyone who does not know Being,
But expects the realization of ecstasy in the sexual act,
Is like a thirsty person who chases the water in a mirage.
He may die of thirst before he will reach the water of the sky.

> *The orgasmic experience does not lead to other-enrichment*

119 He who enjoys the pleasure that
Resides in between the diamond and the lotus –
So what! since there is no capacity [to effect anything] in this pleasure
With what will he fulfil the expectations people have in the triple universe of theirs?

> *The possibility of understanding Being-in-its-beingness by stamping it with the seal of [its] unoriginatedness*

120 [This understanding of] ecstasy [may come] at the

moment [of its being sealed with the unoriginatedness of its nothingness as in the third empowerment[140] in the wake of its own] operacy
Or [be experienced] in both [its aspects of the one just referred to] and as what it is in itself.
Anyhow, be it through the vitalizing presence of the innermost mentor [or the vitalizing instruction he gives],
Maybe only one among the many will know it.

> *The essence of what it is about*

121 Friends, profound and vast,
It is not something other [than itself] but it also is not a Self.
Know it as Being's genuineness relished [by you]
At the time of the fourth joy [expressing Being's] complementarity-in-spontaneity.[141]

> *bde-ba-chen-po'i sku*

122 Like the jewel of the moon in the darkness of the night
With its rising [dispelling the darkness],
So in the single moment of [experiencing] this sublime ecstasy
All the evils of [ordinary] thinking are vanquished.

> *sprul-sku*

123 When the harbinger of misery[142] sets
The lord of the stars together[143] with the planets rises.
In this panorama [the *chos-sku*) wondrously manifests itself in wondrous manifestations (*sprul-pa*).
This is what is really [meant by] the vortices of energy[144] in the overall pattern.[145]

> *A summary of the above by pointing out what it means to abide in self-emancipating ecstasy*

124 Hey-ho, if a deluded person's mind [caught in its fictions] should come to understand [what this his] mind is,
It [and by implication he himself] would through this

self-reflexive move become emancipated[146] from all noxious views;
If, through the power of sublime ecstasy,
It should abide in this ecstasy this would be [that person's] real achievement.[147]

> *A summary of what has to be made a deeply felt experience*
> *How, for the time being, to deal with one's way by active imagination*
> *Letting one's conceptual thinking idle*

125 Let the elephant of your mind (*sems*) ramble idly [over its territory of sense objects]
And let it ask itself [about itself][148]

> *How to let it idle*

126 Let it drink the [lake's] water in which the mountain-like sky [is reflected] and let it
Happily [spend its time] at [the lake's] shore.[149]

> *Through such an experience you will come to know how the phenomenal world regains its freedom in its legitimate place that is Being-in-its-beingness*
> *An analogy*

127 Once the elephant, the sensuous object, has been seized by its trunk
It may look as if it had been killed.[150]

> *Applying this analogy to a real person*

128 A yogi, rather like an elephant warden,
Lets the elephant roam and come back [of its own].

> *Demolishing the limitations set by the imaginable and the imagination*
> *Demolishing the limitations set by acceptance and rejection*

129 When you are certain that that which is samsara is also nirvana,
Do not think of [making] a distinction between the one and the other.

Having discarded these distinctions through [the realization of] the unitary character of Being
I have deeply understood its stainlessness.

> *Demolishing the limitations set by the assumption that a cognitive situation either has an objective reference or is without an objective reference*
> *The recognition of what is to be demolished and its demolition*[151]

130 The egologically predisposed awareness operates with having an external [objectifiable] reference
And without having an external [objectifiable] reference that is [its] nothingness.[152]
Both [claims] are faulty and
He who is a real yogi will not deal with either of them in active imagination.

> *The impossibility of establishing an objective reference is ecstasy*

131 Imagination [that pertains to one's egologically predisposed awareness] operates with having an objective reference[153] and without having an objective reference,
[In either case] it is an aspect of ecstasy.

> *The real understanding comes through the innermost mentor's vitalizing influence*

132 Know its intensity, unsurpassability, and self-originatedness [to come from]
The innermost mentor's [knowing when] the time [is ripe][154] and [from your] serving [him].[155]

> *Demolishing the limitations set by searching for its location*
> *There is no need to look for special places*

133 If without going into the [solitude of] forests or without staying at home
You [can get this fact into] your egologically predisposed awareness and so come to know thoroughly that whatever there is, is this [ecstasy],
Then, because of your understanding that everything continually presents Being's intelligence,[156]

What is samsara is also nirvana.

➤ *If your egologically predisposed awareness has regained its original purity no disharmony is found*

134 If the stains in your egologically predisposed awareness have disappeared, [the pristine awareness of Being's] complementarity-in-spontaneity [shines forth] and [this means that]
Then [and there] nothing disharmonious can enter.

➤ *Demolishing the limitations set by assuming that Being is something static*

135 When the ocean has become transparently clear
The waves, because of their being its water, subside in it;
Similarly Being's intelligence (*byang-chub*) does not reside [as a static entity] in forests or in homes.

➤ *A summary of the above*

136 Thus, once you have come to know thoroughly [what the] difference [between samsara and nirvana means]
You should with what is your flawless mind (*sems*)[157]
Attend to all and everything as [being the presence of Being's] undividedness [by concepts].
This is as much the "I" as it is the "Thou."

➤ *The certainty that from the perspective of ultimacy there is nothing that could be said to be an object for active imagination*

137 The very distinction between what is to be imagined and what is the thorough imaginative process
Is a fetter from which you have to be free.
As a matter of fact, do not allow that [which is referred to by the statement that] the authentic self is free,
Go astray into an "I" or a "Thou."

➤ *The climax*
The individual's natural affinity with Being-in-its-beingness

138 All living beings [present] the continuously flowing

abidingness [of Being as] "Buddhahood"[158] [which means that]
Since the mind's "stuff" (*sems-kyi ngo-bo*) is by virtue of the "stuff" [the universe is made of, *ngo-bo-nyid-kyis*] pure,[159]
This is its stainless and superb status.

> *The nonduality of samsara and nirvana*
> *Self-fulfilment as a gestalt experience of meaningfulness*

139 The solid tree of the mind (*sems*) that is without duality
Has grown to encompass the whole of the triple world of ours.

> *Other-enrichment as the gestalt experience of context and guidance*

140 Its flower of compassionate concern holds [within it] the fruit of being helpful to others,
Its name is "Superb helpfulness to others."

> *The synthesis of the phenomenal and the noumenal*

141 On the solid tree of [Being's] nothingness a flower has opened
With many varied [petals expressive of Being's] genuinely compassionate concern.
[Though being Being's] complementarity-in-spontaneity it later bears a fruit that is
Ecstasy. This [ecstasy] is not some other mind.

> *A mean attitude on the part of him who expects only a little from it*

142 If in someone this solid tree of [Being's] nothingness is such as not to show compassionate concern
It will not even have roots, leaves, and flowers.
Anyone who makes this [barren tree] the object of his concentration
Will fall into [the extreme of nihilism] and become one who is without the tools [to extricate himself from it].[160]

> *Release as the final goal*

143 One seed grows two trees.

For this reason the fruits they bear are the same.
He who thinks about them as being inseparable [and indistinguishable]
Is released from both samsara and nirvana.

> *The ultimate goal [as dynamic being] is to act in a concerned manner*
> *An analogy*

144 If a person who is in need should come [to you], but
Would have to go away without his expectation fulfilled,
He had better live by picking up the remnants in an alms bowl thrown out of the door
Than running the risk of [himself] being thrown out by the master of the house.

> *The meaning of this analogy*

145 Not to be helpful to others and
Not to make gifts to those who are needy
Is what samsara comes about to be.
Therefore it is all the more necessary to throw out [the belief in] a self.[161]

Dohākośa-upadeśa-gīti

A Treasure of *Dohā*: An Instructional Essay in the Form of a Song

(Queen *Dohā*)

> *I. Abidingness*[1]
> *The opening invocation and the statement of intent*
> *E-ma — The mystical language of the Ḍāka/Ḍākinīs*

1 Having bowed with folded hands

To the Lord of Ecstasy, the valiant mind [expressing Being's] pellucidity and consummation[2]

Whose ownmost dynamics[3] [expresses itself as the triad] of Buddha, Dharma, Sangha,

I will explain the Mahāmudrā abidingness that just is non-duality.[4]

> *Abidingness as starting-point*
> *As samsara*

2 People, ensnared [by their inconsiderate actions and emotional vagaries] like a tree by creepers,

Dry up in the miserable desert of the belief in a self.

Since, like a young prince without his country and separated from his father,

They have no chance for feeling happy, their mind has become distressed.

> *As Being-in-its-beingness*
> *The gist of the matter*

3 When Saraha, who knows from his experience of it, declares that

Of this pristine awareness of Being's beingness [which is this beingness][5] one cannot have enough, however much one may indulge in it, and that

[Being's beingness] is [furthermore] dissociated from [all that] has been constructed [by the mind] and is not some accumulated karma,

All the learned people [become frightened as if] their hearts had been filled with poison.

> *The specific aspects of this matter*
> *The difficulty of understanding abidingness discursively*

4 [Being's] still-point, Mind as a dynamic principle (*sems-nyid*),[6] is difficult to understand discursively [and as Being's]

> *Its transcending the limits set by the intellect*

Flawless energy,[7] undefiled by [rationalistic] extremes,

It has since its beginning remained such that [as] Being's ownmost dynamics it is not something that can be discursively dealt with.

> *The danger of dealing with it discursively*

If it is discursively dealt with it just becomes a poisonous snake's bite.

> *Its transcending the limits set by dichotomic thinking*
> *The objective domain*

5 All these entities [of our "reality"][8] set up by the intellect are in themselves devoid [of any substance]; and,

Dissociated from this [necessary] condition, all the postulates [we make concerning them] are not existents.

> *The subjective domain*

If one knows their beingness to be such that it is a process that [exercises its] freedom in dissolving in the abidingness of Being's ownmostness,[9]

There is neither [reifying] seeing nor hearing nor any other [perceptual activity] and thereby [one is] dissociated from what is incompatible [with Being's beingness].

> *Abidingness as way*

6 All those who entertain the notion of "existence" (*dngos-po*)[10] talk like cattle,

But those who entertain the notion of "non-existence" (*dngos-med*) are even more stupid.[11]

The two parties who speak [of existence and non-existence] by using the metaphors of a lamp shining and of a lamp being extinguished,

Abide in the Mahāmudrā that just is non-duality.

> *Abidingness as goal*
> *The gist of the matter*

7 What has become "existence" comes to rest in "non-existence" and

When this very knowledge that is dissociated from either alternative

[Though already present even] in the intellect of stupid people, is investigated by itself [in its emerging],

The moment [the external and internal] dissolves [in the immediacy of Being's] dynamic freedom, is said to be Being's meaning-rich gestalt.[12]

> *Allaying apprehensions*

8 Although foolish people declare that

There exists a level of ecstasy other than this dissolution [of the external and internal in Being's] dynamic freedom, [their statement] is similar to the water in a mirage.

> *Abidingness as universal single-flavoredness*
> *Its presence in the spiritual levels and the approaches to Being*

Ask your [usually] egologically predisposed awareness (*yid*)[13] that [actually] is this very pristine awareness heightened in its sensibility by Being's genuineness (*gnyug-ma'i ye-shes*),[14]
In which the spiritual levels and the paths and those who have become spiritually awake[15] are all of one and the same flavor.

> *Its presence in that which has to be discarded and in that which aids the discarding as its counteragent*[16]

9 For a person who understands [Being] in this way there are no fetters:
Without having wiped away any dust, [he] is not in the least defiled by dust.
Where is the dividing line between the emotion-pollutants and their counteragents to be drawn?
A person who attempts to draw such a line is fettered in samsara.

> *The single-flavoredness of samsara and nirvana*

10 Earth and water and fire and wind and the sky
Are not something other than [Being's] complementarity-in-spontaneity (*lhan-cig skyes-pa*)[17] that has only one flavor.
Not to introduce into this the conceptual duality of samsara and nirvana
Is said to be Being's abidingness as a meaning-rich expanse.[18]

> *II. Obliterating pitfalls*[19]
> *Connecting what has been said before with what follows*
> *E-ma — The mystical language of the Ḍāka/Ḍākinī*
> *The presentation of the subject-matter*

11 Alas! Look how [your mind] by itself points to Being's beingness in itself:
You have to look with an undistracted mind, otherwise

A distracted mind will not understand Being's beingness;
The jewel of Being's beingness is flung away into the dense jungle of [the categories of] substance [and quality].

> *Its detailed explanation*
> *Obliterating one's obsession with the sensual*

12 Alas! Do not become attached to any object of your desires:
If your egologically predisposed awareness (*yid*) is attached to a realm to which it can become attached
This [situation] is a severe disease that torments the superb mind in its character of being ecstasy, [which means that]
The flawless mind has been hurt by the sword of desire.

> *Obliterating one's obsession with causal explications*
> *The inseparability of cause and effect*

13 Alas! Do not look at cause and effect as a duality:
A cause that has become "existence" and an effect [that becomes "non-existence"] are not existent entities.

> *The harmfulness of the belief in cause and effect being different entities*

If a yogi's mind is intoxicated with the poison of expectation and fear,
[His mind as Being's] abidingness as complementarity-in-spontaneity is fettered.

> *Getting rid of one's obsession with egological imagination*

14 Alas! I do not say that beingness as [something] dissociated from Being's ownmost dynamics[20] [as postulated by the logicians] is what is to be imaged and imaginatively developed.
If a duality between the imaginable and the imager is introduced,
The egologically predisposed awareness (*yid*),[21] believing in this duality [of its own making], has discarded [Being's ownmost dynamics] that is [one's] mind [as

expressing Being's] pellucidity and consummation (*byang-chub sems*).
Such a person by himself commits a crime against himself.

> *Obliterating the pitfalls of one's unknowing*
> *The flaw in not heeding the advice of one's innermost mentor*

15 Alas! You have to drink as many drops of nectar[22] [that flow] from your innermost mentor's mouth [as you can],
By [observing] the preliminaries [leading up to] certain knowledge.
If a person, knowing the right time and the right means, does not heed the right time,
He is like a blind person attempting to rob the king's treasure vault.

> *The flaw in not getting the necessary empowerments*

16 Alas! A person who does not have the empowerments that are like precious gems
Is like a lowly servant aspiring to become a king.
Beguiled by [those who do not heed what] the teachings of those who know by experience[23] [have to say],
They have been condemned by the Ḍākas and fall into the deepest hell.

> *The flaw in not letting the innermost mentor's advice become your experienced certainty*

17 Alas! Anyone having received from spiritual friends that which is of the highest value [for his life],
But discarding it with a lowly attitude of mind instead of holding firmly to it,
Is [like] a person, suffering from cataracts of the eyes, being carried away [into dangerous places]:
For a great aeon he will only inflict misery on himself.

> *Obliterating the pitfalls that need special extermination efforts*
> *The flaw in not keeping one's commitments*

18 Alas! If a person who has arrived at the destination

pointed out to him does not live up to his commitments, he
Is like a person who has been condemned by the king and is taken away by the executioner.
Once the volatile life-force has been captured by the iron hook of one's actions having matured into their consequences,
[The pain caused by] bubbling molten metal poured into one's mouth[24] is hard to bear.

➤ *The flaw in resorting to evil ways of life*

19 Alas! Even if one understands Being's abidingness but resorts to lowly ways in one's conduct
One is like a king who, having been dethroned, continues giving orders.
Having renounced the bliss supreme that is inexhaustible
One is fettered by one's trifling with the [paltry] pleasures of samsara.

➤ *The flaw in indulging again in conceptual model building*

20 Alas! A yogi who has seen his own mind dissociated from conceptual proliferations,
[Yet] purposively strives for these proliferations,
Is like a person who has found a precious jewel but looks for a trinket.
However much he may exert himself, [the trinket] will never be the plane of Being's vitalizing energy.

➤ *III. Imagination*[25]
Connecting what has been said before with what follows
E-ma — The mystical language of the Ḍāka/Ḍākinīs
The abidingness of the twofold spiritual core that is being imaged

21 This pristine awareness that [involves] efforts [on our part] in taking hold of [it in its inner calm as one aspect of] our spiritual core (*byang-chub-sems zin-pa*), and that [acts]
Effortlessly in our understanding [it in its wider scope as

the other aspect of] our spiritual core (*byang-chub-sems rtogs*),[26]
[Must,] in its coming forth from the nectar [that flows] out of the mouth of superior persons,[27] [be understood as]
Shining brilliantly in the center of [the conjunction of] sun and moon.[28]

22 Sensuously understand [this pristine awareness] as rising from the vector movement[29] in the "masculine" intensification of the preconditions leading to new dynamic regimes (*tshad dang ldan-pa' i skyes-bu*) and
From the "feminine" confirmations with their bringing quality into focus (*mtshan dang ldan-pa'i phyag-rgya*).[30]
When through this [pristine unitary awareness] the whole of your ordinary reality has been turned into a different color,[31]
You will know it [to have come about] through an instruction that is fourfold.[32]

> *A detailed presentation of the imaginative process*
> *The traditional Sutra conception*

23 When, by having seen the possibilizing dynamics in the brilliant light [of your *lumen naturale*],
You will still more deeply understand [how the emergence of this unitary awareness] depends on the time and the means [determined by] your innermost mentor—
You will have to cultivate your [luminous] mind [as taught] in the [*Aṣṭasāhasrikā*] *prajñāpāramitā* and other Sutras
And how it links back to all that has been said in them.[33]

> *Non-dichotomic imagination*
> *The gist of the subject-matter*

24 This mind, that is neither to be seen in the outside [world] nor inside [one's self],
Has not been [a content of someone's] thought nor [can it be made] into [someone's] thought of it.
From the highest peak of [his] adamantine being, the

abiding presence of Being's ownmostness [Saraha] has uttered this song:
Imagine this bliss supreme, that has nothing limiting about it, to be like a stream.

➤ *Its application to everything "objective"*

25 This mind, that gets upset by all the happenings in places where many people gather,
Is stable in its ownmostness where there is neither extraversion nor introversion.
Let this mind's energy[34] run its course as it likes and be
Like a drunken person's mind that has no worries.

26 This pristine awareness, that is not defiled by the extremes [postulated by the intellect], is [imaginatively] to be cultivated.

➤ *To take everything as being consistent with itself and everything else*

The mind (*sems*) that is without [the triadic pattern of] an imagining act, [an imagining agent], and some object to be imagined, [is still] dissociated from Being's ownmost dynamic, [yet to the extent that it]
Has reached the end of expectations and fears, it is [your] adamantine mind[35] [that],
Even if it were to descend into [the deepest] hell, would not [find] any torment [as an objective fact], and

27 Even if it were to abide with [what is considered to be] the supreme goal[36] would not find [anything objective] over and above [its own blissfulness in its self-reflexive understanding], and hence
Having left behind the benefit or harm that [accrues from] happiness and misery [respectively],
[This adamantine mind] is not made to expand nor to shrink by [what is deemed to be] good or evil ways of conducting yourself.
Consider anyone who claims that the experience of being spiritually awake is [something] still greater

28 Than this pristine awareness, dissociated from the [above mentioned] duality, to be a deluded person.[37]

> *The necessity of imagination*

If none of the above extremes is looked for by your [otherwise] egologically predisposed awareness (*yid*), that [now is no longer preoccupied with the notion of]
Having to do something, [Being's] qualities[38] need not be looked for since there is nothing that is not in harmony with [this mind that is Being itself].
Since these [qualities] are not gained from the Tantras and Śāstras,

29 By not looking into them for eliminating the grime that is the cause factor [for the pollution] in his psychic disposition (*sems*) that [in itself] has no vested interest,
But by relishing [Being's] superb pristine awareness in its superbness,
A yogi who [through it] is able to neutralize the poisons of samsara
[Whether] he be [straight] like a monk or [bent] like a bow, will hold sway over all the realms in the world.

> *A summary of the above*

30 Without having to close his eyes, and without imaginatively cultivating [some preconceived content], a yogi should,
In solitude and places offering no comfort,
Imaginatively cultivate his [otherwise] egologically predisposed awareness (*yid*) that [now] is without the grime of [its egological concern with having to] renounce attachment or aversion
As the "stuff" his real mind (*don-dam sems*) is made of.

> *IV. Encounter*[39]
> *Connecting what has been said before with what follows*
> *E-ma – The mystical language of the Ḍāka/Ḍākinīs*
> *Being's abidingness in the individual's concrete reality*

31 With nothing in it of [what might be said to be] the

arranging of a mandala or the performance of a burnt offering, and
Having nothing to do with [the chanting of] mantras, [moving one's hands in certain] gestures, consecration of images and other ceremonies,
This adamantine pristine awareness that cannot be proved by any Tantra and Śāstra whatsoever, is [Being's] Beauty in its presence as its ownmost dynamics.

> *The detailed explanation of what encounter involves*
> *Using a single symbol*

32 The superb symbol[40] [for it], most precious, that enables [you] to understand [Being's abidingness] with one stroke,
Is like a snake in a thicket, beautiful [in the hand of a snake-charmer], but not so with others.
The energy [in this symbol] that reveals the energy [in our being] is [activated] by the innermost mentor:[41]
Through his [own] understanding he points it out to others and thereby points to himself.

> *The multiplicity of objects that may serve as symbols*

33 You may enjoy any of [the "material" and "immaterial"[42] entities of reality], such as sounds and so on, [inasmuch as they present]
The connectedness of your egologically predisposed awareness (*yid*), its mnemic (*dran-pa*) and non-mnemic (*dran-med*) functions with the three dynamic forces of Being (*thig-le gsum*),[43] that have
A strength similar to the sky, the wish-granting jewel, and the sun:
All these entities will become alike in piquancy, like [metal] that is touched by the philosopher's stone.

> *Encountering whatever appears before the senses in its unoriginatedness*

34 In him who has refined himself by following the way, there arises a unique pristine awareness heightened in its sensibility by Being's genuineness [in it].

Since the one who points out this very way by symbols [expressive of wholeness] is one's innermost mentor,[44]
You should rely on the [concrete] data of form, sound, fragrance, flavor, touch and the [abstract] ideas [as symbolic expressions of him].
All these entities of your reality are in the absence of conditions [to the contrary], not [something that] is being born.

35 Fortunate persons who have grown wise concerning the "unborn"
Because of it become wise concerning that which is "born."[45]

> *Encountering ecstasy without being obsessed with its experience*

This pristine awareness, that does not admit of any difference [in itself] as the sole reality,
Becomes engulfed [in ecstasy] through your mind consigned to Being's ownmost dynamics.

36 Knowing that whatever comes-to-presence as the I and Thou is this single [reality],
You should take hold of this "reality" unswervingly.
But inasmuch as [this taking hold of it] is your mind's tribulation, you have to give this up, too.
When there is no longer any yearning for anything—this [is what is meant by] taking up ecstasy.

> *Encountering whatever comes-to-presence as Being's play*

37 Your [real] mind is devoid of any actions that harm your [ordinary] mind and
Is not shrouded by whatever you do [through your mistaken ideas of] gaining and possessing [something].
Dissociated from [such] efforts and in the absence of any conditions for fortuitous circumstances,
The multiplicity of the phenomenal [world] is the marking [by Being's beingness, *phyag-rgya*] as [Being's] grandiose spectacle.

➤ *Encountering the whole of reality in its actuality and probability as one's innermost mentor*

38 Once you have had a close look at all that is, without exception, at the time [assigned by] your innermost mentor,
[You will find that] there does not exist a single entity [of reality] that has not become [this] innermost mentor.
The finger that points to the sky is not the seeing of the sky—
So it is with the innermost mentor who points to the innermost mentor.

➤ *Encounter in one's sociocultural interactions*
Solitary interaction

39 An eccentric (*brtul-zhugs spyod-pa*)[46] yogi whose mind [has been roaming about in] the world, and [somehow]
Has entered the king's palace [where it] has dallied with the king's daughter,
Will henceforth be aware of all the sensuous objects in the world as [so many symbol presences of] Being—
Like a person who has previously eaten sour food recognizes it to be sour when he sees it again.

➤ *Group interaction*

40 Having seen [and experienced] the bliss supreme in the act of copulation
In this very place so richly adorned by sacred gatherings (*tshogs-kyi 'khor-lo*),[47]
With the yogis [and yoginīs] responding to each other's use of symbols,[48] and having observed their commitment[49] [to appreciation],
He will well [understand the] co-equality of worldliness and quiescence—Mahāmudrā.

➤ *V. Sociocultural/spiritual interactions*[50]
Connecting what has been said before with what follows
E-ma—The mystical language of the Ḍāka/Ḍākinīs
Interaction with a companion in one's spiritual quest

41 A [Śaivite] yogi in whom a [pseudoexistential] pristine

awareness [allegedly imparted to him by Śiva himself]
has come about, [and hence] in whom there is no fear,
Will, whilst wearing the insignia of Śiva [as a charm]
look for a woman born in the outskirts.

[Or, a Buddhist yogi in whom the pristine awareness of the unity of masculine and feminine forces (that are working in and through him) has come about, should look for an anima-figure (*rig-ma*)[51] born in the border region (of his consciousness and the unconscious), who will impart lasting bliss and who has the excellent indications of inner spiritual wealth.]

➤ *How to find a suitable companion*

Having gone into the settlement of low-caste people,[52]
either searcher will, to the extent that [some such woman seems] suitable,
Little by little importune her and [finally] give her the ultimate [by]

42 Bestowing on her, in an unselfish and non-possessive manner,
Whatever he has of [material] goods[53] [as tokens of his] worship.

➤ *Finding out the companion's suitability*

[But before that], having roamed all over the country [to find a consort], he should have meticulously examined her features [as to what they augur], so that
Step by step he has come to know all about the nexus[54] [that exists between her and himself], her aura,[55] and her sex appeal and prowess.

➤ *Her social status*

43 His own daughter, mother, sister, and niece,
An outcaste woman, a washerwoman, a harlot, and a woman living by [gathering] rags;[56]

➤ *Her "aura"*

Blackish, whitish, honey-colored, purplish, and

➤ *Her birthmarks*

With moles [on her body]—

➤ *The "upgrading" of the personality disposition*
Purity of body and speech

such a consort/*anima*-figure whose personality disposition [allows itself easily] to be "upgraded"[57]

44 [Should be] sixteen years of age, very beautiful, have brownish [curly] hair,
Exude the fragrance of the [blue] lotus flower, have firm and strong breasts, a slim waist,
A broad abdomen, and a *bhaga*[58] whose vivid glow in its closing in [on itself] and reaching passionate [intensity]
Fervidly quickens her [partner's] *gsang-thub* with its luminous potency.

➤ *Purity of mind*

45 [From a less physiological perspective], through [authentic] empowerments[59] [the yogi] will bring his consort/*anima*-figure to [spiritual] maturity whose three indications are
Trust, steadfastness, and paucity of [divisive] notions.

➤ *Letting the intimacy mature*

Taking in her qualities he will [reciprocate by] offering his pristine awareness,
Reverberating with the intensity of [their] immediate experience, and,
For the time being, he will take this pristine awareness—heightened in its sensibility through Being's genuineness [operating in it], approximating in flavor [Being's nothingness replete with everything in highest perfection]—as the Mahāmudrā experience.[60]

46 [In the last analysis, however,] it is the Mahāmudrā in whom the "fluid" of the [supranatural] Lady/Goddess[61] is going to be engorged, who,
Once [the yogi] has made contact with her by knowing

how to time [this moment], will make him to become absorbed in the sky[62] in which no dichotomies obtain.

> *A detailed presentation of the solitary figure's social conduct*
> *His conduct in crowded places*

[By contrast with this "companionable" type of yogi a solitary and, by ordinary standards, eccentric yogi][63] will
Sometimes, when he stays in a market place, examine his [experience and his understanding of it] as to its stability [or instability] and
Having looked for the real [*don*, by means of what is only] similar [to the real] let the really real [*don-nyid*, take over] when and wherever it pleases.[64]

> *His conduct in fearsome places*

47 Sometimes, when he stays in a cremation ground, he will delight in the "lamps" and their "brightness";[65]
Fearlessly he goes to sleep in places haunted by spirits;
Making friends with the outcasts, he drags the cart carrying the corpses;
He does not accept as the norm what [others say] should not be done.

> *His conduct in festival gathering*

48 When he goes to gatherings where [men and women] sing and dance and amuse themselves with playing music,
He never gets tired of exalting his mind with [experiencing their dance as]
The dancing posture of Heruka and [their singing as] the songs of the six [consorts of the six supranatural regents in his entourage].

> *His apparel*

[As clothing] he puts a woolen blanket over his shoulders, covers his arms and legs with brass ornaments,
49 Ties his plaited hair [held together by] an [ivory] ring into a knot on his head and,

When he has adorned all his limbs with pieces of bones,
He wraps the upper and lower parts of his torso in an elephant's hide and a tiger's skin. [As accessories]
He holds in his hand a trident with a bell.[66]

➤ *The transported mystic's conduct*

50 Behaving like a mad elephant or playing the role of a dumb person, or
Going about life in an untroubled way,[67] a mystic,[68] with a mind that
Forever stays intoxicated, resembling an elephant having voluntarily gone into a pond,
May well engage in what is despicable [for others] and yet remain free—[thus] says Saraha.

➤ *V. Commitment*
Connecting what has been said before with what follows
E-ma—The mystical language of the Ḍāka/Ḍākinīs
Paying homage to one's innermost mentor whose greatness is illustrated by five similes
The goose/gander

51 He who shows the whole of the phenomenal reality in its multiplicity to have but the one flavor [of ecstatic experience]
Is the trustworthy innermost mentor[69] himself, and hence
You should reverently place on a clean [spot in the] crown of your head
This noble superior [whose discernment is] similar to the beak of a goose.[70]

➤ *The hero*

52 He who shows [one's] mind in which [the dual aspect of one's phenomenal reality[71]] has found its unity [to be Being having assumed the gestalt expressive of the experiencer's principle of humanity[72]] is the innermost mentor, and
The site [where it is going] to be shown is the disciple's heart.

Since through his understanding [of the mind's abidingness, this innermost mentor, as] a hero who overpowers in an instant all [one's] tribulations, is so very kind,

> *The physician*

53 Once you have seen what he has done for you, in order to repay his kindness
You always should go along with this king among physicians.

> *The helmsman*

There is no other such excellent boat that makes you cross the
Deep and vast ocean of samsara, [and]

54 Since with the help of this trustworthy helmsman ecstasy is won,
You should sincerely worship this your kinsman of such enormous might with all that is in your possession.

> *The universal ruler*

This sublime person—who turns [your] unknowing into the ecstatic knowledge [that only you yourself can know],
Through the bright rays of [his] pristine awareness that is like the sun,

55 Wise in the wonderful means of turning the whole of reality into pure ecstasy, similar to the philosopher's stone turning metal into gold—
Is always to be worshipped [like] a universal ruler.

> *The necessity of paying homage to him by way of remembering what he has done for you by being attentive to what he communicates to you through the nectar that flows from his mouth*

The altered state of your intellect, that is uncontrived and
In the possession of a pristine awareness, unobscured [by anything] without having had to give up anything, since

56 All dualistic views have been overcome [and swept away] by a river-like [visionary] experience,
Springs from the nectar [that flows from] the trustworthy innermost mentor's mouth.[73]

> *Through the beauty of his lotus-like mouth*

Turning the notions postulated by the mind and its operators
Into a yogi's friends [is effected by]
57 The lotus flower of the innermost mentor's mouth, [so that]
The transformation of all that is into helpful spiritual friends takes place from it.

> *Being attentive to his presence in a shape perceptible in its visionary experience*

Nobody is going to understand the mystery of [what it means] to become spiritually awake,
Encoded in ciphers and outside ordinary parlance,
58 Unless he sees with the eye of spiritual instruction and is suffused by its sensuous flavor, [which comes]
When by touching the dust on [the innermost mentor's] feet, pristine awareness becomes [his intimately known] ecstatic knowledge.[74]

> *Being attentive to his spirituality that is active as his compassionate concern for all that is alive*

Piercing the concrete things [of reality] in their multiplicity with the arrow of nothingness and
Experiencing this nothingness through the phenomenal
59 Is the seeing of the phenomenal in its lucency through knowing [what] appreciation in understanding [means].
This appreciation [in understanding] derives from [your] adamantine instructor.[75]

> *That is powerful in subduing your emotional vagaries*

[The fact that] all the emotions are changed into this

superb [ecstatic knowledge] through [the innermost mentor's] spiritually appropriate device, and

[The fact that this ecstatic knowledge] is unchangeable by any of the tribulations [that pertain to] divisive thought processes, [since it]

60 Derives from the vitalizing core intensity in [their] instructions,

Are [both] realized [by the aspirant] through the power of this noble superior [who is your innermost mentor].

> *The advice to heed the innermost mentor*

Therefore those who have [received] this revitalization [that comes through] their connectedness [with him and now being in] the lineage of the spirit,

Should always honor him in their wisdom concerning the time, the appropriate manner [of honoring him], and the service [done on this behalf].

> *VII. The Culmination*[76]
> *Connecting what has been said before with what follows*
> *E-ma—The mystical language of the Ḍāka/Ḍākinīs*
> *The culmination that is a deeply felt understanding*
> *The gist of the subject matter*

61 Once you have deeply felt and understood [the difference-without-separation][77] of operacy (*thabs*) and appreciation (*shes-rab*) in their ownmost dynamics [participating in Being displaying its principle] of the self-consistency,[78]

From [it as] the *lumen naturale*[79] [within yourself] you will gain the [experience of]

complementarity-in-spontaneity. It comes about by your becoming more and more familiar with this *lumen naturale*, similar to the waxing moon.

Its illumining [effect makes] you enjoy [the wholeness of your being] just as rice ripened in the light of sun and moon.

> *The primary reason for this deeply felt understanding*

62 The root of all achievements[80] is the *rdo-rje slob-dpon*,[81] who
From [the perspective of] our thoroughly cleansed [disposition to wholeness] is the cause-factor of why all realizations as its fruition occur in our bodily existence.

> *The culmination that has come to its end*[82]
> *The presentation of the subject matter*

In order to attune it to [the norms] of which He-who-has-passed-into-bliss[83] has spoken [in his profound] announcements,

The Lord of Ecstasy, the valiant mind [expressing Being's] pellucidity and consummation,[84] has uttered these maxims:

63 *chos-sku, longs-sku, sprul-sku,*
ngo-bo-nyid-kyi sku [and by implication *bde-ba chen-po'i sku*)[85] are to be known as standing in a cause-effect relationship.[86]

> *The detailed explanation of the five gestalts*
> *An explanation of what each is in substance*

[The pristine awareness in which] there is no duality, devoid of positive and negative imputations, is the *chos-sku*,
[Its open-dimensional field character is] the *ngo-bo-nyid-kyi sku*, [its feeling tone of ecstasy] is the *bde-ba chen-po'i sku*,[its spanning the individual's spiritual dimension] is the *longs-sku*,

64 And [its self-manifestation in concrete guiding images] according to the varied inclinations of all living beings is the *sprul-sku*.

> *The unitary function of these five gestalts*

The pristine awareness modes of [these five gestalts in their] indivisibility is the "authentic Self" [hidden] in [and being] the whole [of Being].[87]

> *The manner of its fulfilling as its most excellent double purpose*
> *A general explication*

Although [in these pristine awareness modes] nothing whatsoever of something to be created and someone creating is observed,

It is through the power of your having become accustomed to [the working of your dichotomizing mind that this duality with its apprehensions and] fears [has come about], but once these have been overcome [by these pristine awareness modes]

65 A double repercussion [is intimately felt and brought to life]: invaluable self-fulfillment and other-enrichment.

> *A summary of the above*

Although one speaks of them in terms of cause and effect, they are indivisible in substance.

> *How the well-being of the living comes about in view of the fact that the two perceptible gestalts of Being entertain no preconceptions*
> *A brief causal statement*

Through the power of your devotion to It and the compassion in It, Being's two [perceptibly experienceable] gestalts[88] come about.

> *The longs-sku acting without preconceptions*

Like an auspicious jar, a wish-fulfilling tree, and a precious jewel.

66 This gestalt that cannot be grasped concretely by anyone is most beautiful.

> *The sprul-sku acting without preconceptions*

Assuming different shapes on behalf of those to be guided.

All of them are its manifestations, inconceivable [by ordinary thought and inexpressible by word of mouth].

> *Linking cause and effect with respect to this most excellent self-fulfilment and other-enrichment*
> *The indivisibility of cause and effect with respect to the starting point, or Being itself*

By him who through felt images cultivates[89] this inconceivable pristine awareness, originated by itself,

67 All [its] repercussions are [in their] being cultivated through felt images [intimately experienced].

By taking these repercussions that are the unsurpassable vitalizing way of the Mahāyāna

As the way, he continues staying in these repercussions [that have existed] since the beginning.

> *The indivisibility of cause and effect with respect to other-enrichment*

[From among these] the invaluable other-enrichment [outcome] is a supreme repercussion [of this experience], in that

68 It has come about from the accumulation [of merits] that are of primary importance [because of their involving devotion and compassion] for the refinement [of your being].

> *The indivisibility of cause and effect with respect to self-fulfilment*

Ultimate release, however, comes from a further refinement [in which the accumulation of pristine awareness modes is of primary importance], and

Is obtained by you through the power of the uninterrupted streaming of that [genuine] mind[90] which is without anticipations [and fears].

> *Incidental effects of the culmination of the process detailed above*
> *A general statement*

In a precious individual in whom this divine substance[91] is born,

69 All poisons without exception subside in an instant.

> *Freedom from external calamities*

Lions, mad elephants, tigers, and bears,
Ferocious animals, poisonous snakes, fire, and precipices,
A death-sentence by a king, poison, lightning and thunder,
70 Are all harmless because they are of this very "stuff" [of which Being-in-its-beingness is made of].[92]

> *Freedom from internal calamities*

By conquering the powerful enemy of dichotomic thinking all these enemies are conquered.
By subduing the poison of the belief in a self-[entity], all poisons are subdued.

> *Advice*

Therefore value this jewel of [your] mind.

> *VIII. Overall advice*
> *Connecting what has been said before with what follows*
> *E-ma—The mystical language of the Ḍāka/Ḍākinīs*
> *In the ecstatic awareness of the mystery of Being's presence as a gestalt, as an announcement, and as spirituality there is no misunderstanding*

71 In a person who knows the [triune] mystery of [Being's] gestalt [character], announcement, and spirituality,
The dumbness [caused by his emotional and intellectual] poisons does not exist.

> *Advice on how to get rid of the subject-object dichotomy*
> *How mistakes are committed by persisting in this dichotomy*
> *Becoming fettered by this dichotomy*

A person who thinks of anything he does in terms of good and evil and
Exerts himself accordingly, I declare to be in league with poison;
72 [For] a person who comports himself in this manner fetters himself, and

Through this disease of his lasting devotedness to it he falls into samsara.

> *The fallacy in the logician's notion of immediacy of perception*

[For the understanding of Being's abidingness] the logician's ruminations are not necessary, through them [a person who falls for them] is going to be worse off than he was before,

Whatever he assigns an objective reality to, it obscures his release by being just such an assignment [and nothing more].

73 Even if he labels this objectified [content] as positive, through its [nature as an] illness, he falls into samsara, and

If he labels it as a mean action, its maturation [into evil consequences] will not stop.

> *Becoming free from the hold the subject-object dichotomy has on us by not making conscious efforts*
> *Experiencing the way without making conscious efforts*

A mind in which no labelling occurs stays like the [clear] sky; [but]

This sky that has no localizability is dissociated from [any objectifying] parlance.

74 Such a mind, dissociated from [any objectifying labels], is not in need of discursive reasoning [with its labelling]:

Restored to its ownmostness it stays as what it is [and has always been].

> *The reason for not making conscious efforts*
> *The mind pursues by itself its abidingness*

[As] the culmination it is intangible and stays in itself [as it has done] since the very beginning.

Therefore you do not have to [first] fetter [your mind] by expectations or fears and [then busy yourself with] what counters them.

> *It does so without needing any prompting*

75 This applies to the use of all conventional expressions, be they symbolic gestures or verbal propositions.
They are not the real; the "really" real is the domain of all wise persons.

> *Advice concerning one's sociocultural conduct*
> *Inauthentic conduct*[93]*; A brief statement*

The indivisibility of cause and effect is your vitalizing mind,[94]
You do not have to look for it all over [the world] in your attempt to experience it.

> *A detailed presentation*
> *Freedom is not won by depending on hearsay*

76 Serving a trustworthy person [as if he were the innermost mentor], listening [to his words] and thinking [about what he says] and absorbing [all of it];

> *Freedom is not won by merely going from one empowerment ceremony to another*

Feeling spiritually uplifted by the assertion that all virtues derive from the empowerments;

> *Freedom is not won by practising the developing stage*[95] *in meditative concentration*

Imbuing your intellect with in-depth appraisals and then tuning in to them and visualizing their images imaginatively; [and lastly]

> *Freedom is not won by pursuing a solitary and eccentric way of life*

Adopting an eccentric way of life[96] [in the belief that] this is the preliminary for [finding] the certainty of [what] is of ultimate value –

> *A summary of the above*

77 These are all ways of engaging in constructions set up by perverse notions.

> *Being's abidingness as the countermeasure against the above pitfalls*

The vitalizing mind is dissociated from [notions about] virtues and faults,
Its reality need not be established by activities of [acceptance or rejection]—
A mind that has discarded such activities is the very pinnacle of ecstasy.

> *Putting the mind in its real interiority (that has neither a within nor a without)*

78 Those who cling to the five worldly sciences[97] are in the grip of a demon;
Their very mind is pervaded by the poison of the belief in the concreteness [of the phenomenal].
This should be considered by those who dismiss the external world and turn their mind inward and
Engage in [what is] the vitalizing core [of their psychic life].

> *Concluding remarks*
> *Completing the ways leading to the spiritual levels and ultimately to Being itself*

79 He who understands this unsurpassed vitalizing core of his being
That derives from the sensuous experience of [Being's] wholeness immanent in him,
After the husk of logical rumination has been discarded
Stays on the fourteenth[98] [spiritual level that is pure ecstasy].

> *Making the basics of the wholesome available to all*

80 A yogi who wants [to live] this ultimate pristine awareness
May go about it in a gradual or instantaneous manner and,
Through having established himself in the citadel of this superb pristine awareness,
May [guide] the living beings to win the Mahāmudrā [experience].

Dohākośa nāma Caryā-gīti

A Treasure of *Dohā*: A Song on Human Action

(King *Dohā*)

> *A summary presentation of the starting point, the way, and the goal*[1]
> *Errancy emerging as the starting point*
> *The emergence of this errancy*

1 As calm water lashed by the wind
Turns into waves and rollers,
So the king thinks of Saraha
In many ways, although one man.

> *The mistaken idea about the difference between subject and object*

2 To a fool who squints
One lamp is as two;
Where seen and seer are not two—ah! the mind
Works on the thingness of them both.

> *Being's pristine awareness is all-encompassing*

3 Though the house-lamps have been lit,
The blind live on in the dark.
Though spontaneity is all-encompassing and close,
To the deluded it remains always far away.

> *The pristine awareness that understands the way*

4 Though there may be many rivers, they are one in the sea,
Though there may be many lies, one truth will conquer all.
When one sun appears, the dark—
However deep—will vanish.

> *Being neither increases nor decreases*
> *An analogy*

5 As a cloud that rises from the sea
Absorbing rain the earth embraces,
So, like the sky, the sea remains
Without increasing or decreasing.

> *The meaning of this analogy*

6 So from complementarity-in-spontaneity that is unique,
Replete with the [five] facets constituting the "Buddha"-dimension,[2]
Are all sentient beings born and in it come
To rest. But it is neither substance nor nonsubstance.

> *An analytical presentation of the above dismissing addiction—1*

7 They walk other paths and forsake true ecstasy,
Seeking the delights that stimulants produce.
The honey in their mouths and to them so near
Will vanish if at once they do not drink it.

> *Analytical presentation—2*

8 Beasts do not understand the world
To be a sorry place. Not so the wise
Who the heavenly nectar drink;
While beasts hunger for the sensual.

> *Analytical presentation—3*

9 To a fly that likes the smell of putrid
Meat, the fragrance of sandalwood is foul.
Beings who discard nirvana
Covet coarse samsara's realm.

> *Analytical presentation—4*

10 An ox's footprints filled with water
Will soon dry up; so with a mind that is firm
But full of qualities that are not perfect;
These imperfections will in time dry up.

> *Recognizing the subject matter—1*

11 Like salt seawater that turns
Sweet when drunk up by the clouds,
So a firm mind that works for others turns
The poison of sense-objects into nectar.

> *Recognizing the subject matter—2*

12 Though ineffable, never is one unsatisfied,
Though unimaginable, it is ecstasy itself.
Though from a cloud one fears the thunderclap,
The crops ripen when from it pours the rain.

> *Recognizing the subject matter—3*

13 It is in the beginning, the middle, and
The end; yet end and beginning are nowhere else.
All those with minds deluded by interpretative thoughts
Are in two minds, and so discuss openness/nothingness and compassion[3] as two things.

> *Recognizing the subject matter—4*

14 Bees know that in flowers
Honey can be found.
That samsara and nirvana are not two;
How will the deluded ever understand?

> *The pointing to the substance of the subject matter—1*

15 When the deluded in a mirror look
They see a face, not a reflection.
So the mind that has truth denied
Relies on that which is not true.

> *The pointing to the substance—2*

16 Though the fragrance of a flower cannot be touched,
'Tis all pervasive and at once perceptible.
So by unpatterned being-in-itself
Recognize the mystic circles and the vortices of energy.

> *The pointing to the substance—3*

17 When [in winter] still water by the wind is stirred,
It takes [as ice] the shape and texture of a rock.
When the deluded are disturbed by interpretative thoughts,
That which is as yet unpatterned turns very hard and solid.

> *The pointing to the substance—4*

18 Mind immaculate in its very being can never be
Polluted by samsara's or nirvana's impurities.
A precious jewel deep in mud
Will not shine, though it has luster.

> *The connectedness of cause and effect*
> *An analogy*

19 Knowledge shines not in the dark, but when the darkness
Is illumined, suffering disappears [at once].
Shoots grow from the seed
And leaves from the shoots.

> *Its meaning*

20 He who thinks of the mind in terms of one
Or many casts away the light and enters the world.
Into a [raging] fire he walks with open eyes—
Who could be more deserving of compassion?

> *The way / The wrong way—1*

21 For the delights of kissing the deluded crave
Declaring it to be the ultimate real—
Like a man who leaves his house and standing at the door
Asks [a woman] for reports of sensual delights.

> *The way / The wrong way—2*

22 The stirring of biotic forces in the house of nothingness
Has given artificial rise to pleasures in so many ways.
Such yogis from affliction faint for they have fallen
From celestial space, inveigled into vice.

> *The way / The wrong way—3*

23 As a brahmin, who with rice and butter
Makes a burnt offering in blazing fire,
Creating a vessel for nectar from celestial space,
Takes this through wishful thinking as the ultimate.

> *The way / The wrong way—4*

24 Some people who have kindled the inner heat and raised it to the fontanelle,
Stroke the uvula with the tongue in a sort of coition and confuse
That which fetters with what gives release,
In pride will call themselves yogis.

> *The way / The wrong way—5*

25 As higher awareness they teach what they [egocentrically] experience.
What fetters them they will call liberation.
A glass trinket colored green to them is as a [priceless] emerald;
Deluded, they know not a gem from what they think it should be.

> *The way / The wrong way—6*

26 They take copper to be gold. Bound by discursive thought
They think these thoughts to be ultimate reality;
They long for the pleasures experienced in dreams.
They call the perishable body-mind ever-lasting ecstasy.

> *The way / The wrong way — 7*

27 By the symbol EVAM [they think] self-clearness is achieved,
By the different situations that demand four seals;[4]
They call what they have fancied
complementarity-in-spontaneity.
But this is looking at reflections in a mirror.

> *The way / The wrong way — 8*

28 As under delusion's power a herd of deer will rush
For the water in a mirage that is not recognized,
So also the deluded quench not their thirst, are bound by chains
And find pleasure in them, saying that all is ultimately real.

> *The Mahāmudrā Way*
> *Its specificity*

29 Convention's truth is "memory" that [on closer inspection] turns out to be "nonmemory"[5]
And [thus a] mind which has become no-mind.
This is fulfillment, this the highest good.
Friends, of this highest good become aware.

> *Its details — 1*

30 In "nonmemory" mind is absorbed; and [in this process its]
Emotions become thoroughly pure.
Unpolluted by the good or bad of worldliness
This sovereign reality is like a lotus unaffected by the mud from which it grows.

> *Its details — 2*

31 Yet with certainty must all things be viewed as if they were a magic spell.
If without distinction you can accept or reject samsara
Or nirvana, steadfast is your mind, free from the shroud of darkness.
In you will abide [Being's] ownmostness, beyond thought and self-originated.

> *Its details—3*

32 This world of appearance has from its radiant beginning
Never come to be; unpatterned it has discarded patterning.
As such it is continuous and unique meditation;[6]
It is nonmentation, stainless contemplation, and nonmind.

> *Its details—4*

33 Mind, intellect, and the formed content of that mind are It;
The world and all that seems from it to differ are It;
All things that can be sensed and the perceiver are It;
Dullness, aversion, a mind spiritually awake are It.[7]

> *The experience of the way*

34 Like a lamp that shines in the darkness of spiritual unknowing,
It removes obscurations of a mind
As far as the fragmentations of intellect obtain.
Who can imagine the ownmostness of desirelessness?

> *The deeply felt understanding*

35 There is nothing to be negated or affirmed,
Nothing to be [egocentrically] grasped; for it can never be conceptually fathomed.
By the fragmentations of their intellect the deluded are fettered;
Indivisible [Being's] complementarity-in-spontaneity remains pure.

> *The freedom won through this understanding*

36 If you question ultimacy with the postulates of the many and the one, oneness is not given,
By a mere [flash of] insight sentient beings freed.
The recognition of [Being's] radiance [as the *lumen naturale* in you] and its continuous cultivation [that is your]
Unswerving mind is to be taken to be your authentic Self.

> *The flawless culmination*
> *Ecstasy and pristine awareness: The overarching gestalt experience*

37 Once in the realm that is full of joy
The seeing mind becomes enriched
And thereby for this and that most useful;
Even when it runs after objects it is not alienated from itself.

> *Its two gestalt expressions*[8]

38 The buds of joy and pleasure
And the leaves of glory grow.
If nothing flows out anywhere
The ecstasy unspeakable will fruit.

> *Self-fulfilment and other-enrichment*

39 What has been done and where and what in itself it will become
Is nothing: yet thereby it has been useful for this and that.
Whether passionate or not
The pattern is nothingness.

> *The summing-up*

40 If I am like a pig that covets worldly mire
You must tell me what fault lies in a stainless mind.
By what does not affect one
How can one now be fettered?

Notes to "People Dohā"

[1] These are the *Ṛgveda*, *Sāmaveda*, *Yajurveda*, and *Atharvaveda*.

[2] The text mentions only a one-pronged staff and a three-pronged staff. Karma 'Phrin-las, 21 (see above, chapter 1, note 1), elaborates this cryptic passage as meaning that the one-pronged staff symbolizes Śiva in his aspect as a solitary figure, that the two-pronged staff symbolizes him in his androgynous aspect, and that the three-pronged staff symbolizes him in his aspect of having a wife (Umā/Pārvatī) and a son (Gaṇeśa).

[3] *tha-dad-pa*. The original Apabhraṃśa text has *biṇuā*, which is said to be *vijñaka* in Sanskrit. The Tibetan translator seems to have understood this word in the sense of *bheda*, "difference," which is one of the categories in Indian logic that originated in Śivaite circles.

[4] Neither the original Apabhraṃśa text nor the Tibetan version is quite clear. The goose (*haṃsa*) is a symbol for Śiva and the late *Paramahaṃsa-upaniṣad* describes the path of an ascetic named Paramahaṃsa. As is well known, Śiva is the ascetic. In a longer version of the present text that is lost in its original form and also does not exist in an independent Tibetan translation but is found in Advayavajra's *Ṭīkā* (bsTan-'gyur, vol. *Mi*, fol. 240), this phrase *ngang-pas bstan-pa* is elaborated as:

> *rgyu-ba ngur-gyi ngang-pa'i skad*
> *bstan-pas gzhan 'dul chos ston-pa*
>
> [Others] roaming about proselyte
> By [uttering and] interpreting a heron's cry [as Śiva's word].

Instead of the customary *haṃsa* Advayavajra uses *kaṅka*, which has the double meaning of heron and a false Brahmin.

[5] These people seem to have been similar to the Antinomians who played a prominent role in Gnosticism. See *The Collected Works of C. G. Jung*, vol. 6, 17.

[6] This rendering follows the version given by Advayavajra in his *Pañjikā* (bsTan-'gyur, vol. *Mi*, fol. 202b) which reads:

> *yugs-sa-mo dang co-rag-mo 'di-'dra cha-lugs gzhan 'ongs-la*
> *dbang-rnams bskur-zhing bla-ma'i yon-rnams len-par byed-pa yin*

and which renders the original Apabhraṃśa text that reads:

> *raṇḍī muṇḍī aṇṇa bi besē*
> *dikkhijjai dakkhiṇa-uddese.*

However, the nowadays standard Tibetan translation preserved in the bsTan-'gyur reads:

> *khyo-med skra-med 'di-'dra gzhan-la ston*
> *dbang-rnams bskur-zhing bla-ma'i yon-rnams len.*

Karma 'Phrin-las explains the terms *khyo-med*, "without a husband," and *skra-med*, "without hair," as symbol terms for the lack of *thabs* (*upāya*), "efficacy," and *shes-rab* (*prajñā*), "insight," respectively. This interpretation he has taken over from Advaya Avadhūti, who explains *khyo-med* by *thabs-med-pa mo-rang-mo*, "one without means, a single woman," and *skra-med* by *go-ba med-pa*, "without understanding" (bsTan-'gyur, vol. *Tsi*, fol. 98b). Karma 'Phrin-las furthermore inverts the two lines and considers the last line as a critique of an indiscriminate conferring of initiations.

Advayavajra's *Ṭīkā* (fol. 240b) is highly relevant. It reads:

brda-med tshig-gis g.yo-sgyu byed
skra-med rgyan-bral rig-ma ston
thod-pas dur-khrod dbang-bskur byed
bla-ma'i nga-rgyal yon-rnams len

They deceive people with meaningless words and
Display a woman whose head has been shaved and from whom
 jewelry has been taken away as Wisdom-incarnate.
Conferring initiations in a cremation ground by means of a skull
In their arrogance of being spiritual teachers they charge a fee.

It is interesting to note that shaving a woman's head and taking away her jewelry was (and still is) a punishment for adultery in India. Although no direct link with Gnostic ideas is traceable, the similarity with the Gnostic idea of the *sophia prouneikos*, "Wisdom the Whore," is remarkable. For this idea in Gnosticism see Benjamin Walker, *Gnosticism* (Wellingborough, Northamptonshire: Crucible, 1989) 40, 152.

[7] *nam-mkha' yid-can*. This derisive term epitomizes the materiality-oriented belief system of the Jains, who considered the egological self (*bdag*) or one's egocentrically predisposed awareness (*yid*) to be as encompassing as the fundamental, material force called "sky/space" (*nam-mkha'*). For the Buddhists, who were mentality oriented, the Jains' conception of the way—a person's self-growth and ultimate self-transcendence as something materially static—was a contradiction in terms and a baneful farce. Thus, according to Saraha, the Jains deceive themselves by assuming that their hypostatized materiality-Self (*bdag-nyid*) is going into a state of emancipation.

[8] The Tibetan text is vague, but the Apabhraṃśa original is explicit. Obviously the Tibetan translator was unfamiliar with this custom among low-caste women in India. Reading between the lines one can readily see the glee with which Saraha sets out to shock and ridicule the moralistic Jain monks.

[9] This is a reference to the Digambaras's outfit: a broom of peacock's feathers or hair of the tail of a cow. For further details see Surendranath Dasgupta, *A History of Indian Philosophy* (Delhi: Motilal Banarsidass, 1975), vol. 1, 172.

[10] *bde-ba'i de-nyid*. As is amply borne out by the commentaries, for Saraha, ecstasy as the fusion of the physical and the spiritual is not only one's uncontrived (*gnyug-ma*) state of mind, but the very "stuff" (*ngo-bo*) of which the fabric of one's being is made. On the exact meaning of *gnyug-ma* see chapter 2.

[11] *ro-gcig*. This is one of the "four tuning-in phases" (*rnal-'byor bzhi*) developed in the framework of the Yogācāra (mentalistic) teaching, which is rejected

as an end in itself by this line. For further details on the tuning-in phases, see my *Meditation Differently*.

[12] This short line is a rejection of the Madhyamaka teaching, in particular its negativistic Prāsangika version. Saraha is quite explicit in his *Kāyakośa-amṛta-vajragīti*, fol. 78a:

> *bye-brag-pa dang mdo-sde snags-pa dang*
> *rnal-'byor-pa dang dbu-ma la-sogs de*
> *gcig-la gcig skyon 'gel-zhing rtsod-par byed*
> *snang-stong mkha'-nyam de-nyid mi-shes-pa*
> *lhan-cig-skyes-la rgyab-kyis phyogs-par 'gyur*
>
> The Vaibhāṣikas and Sautrāntikas,
> The Yogācāras, the Mādhyamikas and the rest
> Get into heated arguments by finding fault with one another.
> Not knowing Being-in-its-beingness [in which] the phenomenal and the noumenal are co-equal [in their being there] like the sky,
> They turn their back on [Being's] complementarity-in-spontaneity and become partial [to the one or other extreme].

[13] *'khor-lo*. Usually seven such vortices, Sanskrit *cakra*, are listed, and there exists an extensive literature about them both in India and the West. However, Buddhist and Hinduist literature differ in the number of these energy vortices.

[14] The fourth empowerment is an inner experience that expresses itself and is intimated by symbols and cannot be reduced to an objectivist's trivialities. For details see my *Meditation Differently*.

[15] *lhan-cig-skyes-pa* (*sahaja*). See chapter 2, pages 21–23, on the exact meaning of this term.

[16] What Saraha wants to emphasize is that the moment we start talking about something, be it the world "out-there" or an inner experience, it somehow becomes transformed into something else, something delimited by language and far removed from the immediacy of experience.

[17] This rendering reflects the wording in the original Apabhraṃśa text. All Tibetan commentators, to the extent that their writings have been preserved, seem to have read *snying* (heart) instead of *rnying* (old), and on the basis of this reading have interpreted it as "explaining the treatises in one's heart."

[18] This is the version commented upon by Advaya Avadhūti in his *Ṭīkā* (bsTan-'gyur, vol. *Tsi*, fol. 101b). In Advayavajra 's *Pañjikā* (fol. 205a) this line reads:

> *de-lta-bu-yi lta-ba ni mtshon-pa nus-pa yod-min-te*
> Such a visionary experience cannot be pointed out [as this or that]

and is linked to the three lines that follow it in the text.

[19] *gnyug-ma'i rang-bzhin*. For the exact meaning of this term, specific to Saraha and the authors in the sNying-thig tradition, see chapter 2.

[20] *ma-mtshon-pa*. Literally this term means "undemonstrable," but it is always understood in the sense given here. Advayavajra's *Ṭīkā* (fol. 253a) reads *ma-tshor-bas*, "since [Being's genuineness] is not directly sensed and felt [as some sort of thing]," and goes on to say that as a consequence the fool is deceived by his mistaken ideas and suffers.

[21] Karma 'Phrin-las, 39–40. understands the first "fool" as indicating a teacher who is caught in representational thought processes and lacks immediacy of experience, and the second "fool" as such a teacher's disciple of low intelligence who is doubly deceived by his own and his teacher's misconceptions.

[22] *bsam-gtan med-cing rab-tu byung-ba dag kyang med*. The manner in which this line is linked with the foregoing stanza or connects with the following line(s) has been of crucial importance to the various commentators. In *Pañjikā* (fol. 205b), Advayavajra leaves out the second line in the preceding stanza and links the first line with the first two lines of the subsequent stanza, intimating that by such behavior things will go from bad to worse. The attempt of the author to preserve the Indian emphasis on meditative concentration and renunciation is quite obvious. Apparently this interpretation is meant for "general consumption." On the other hand, in his *Ṭīkā* (fol. 253a) he interprets this line more in the spirit of Saraha—since Being's genuineness as an uncontrived presence in us is not some "thing," there is no point in concentrating on it as if it were. Since, furthermore, such concentration presupposes dichotomic thinking it merely reinforces attachments and aversions. It is also interesting to note that in the last line of this stanza (which for him is the last but one) he does not use the phrase *mDa'-bsnun nga ni* (I, Saraha), but lets Saraha speak of himself as *snying-po'i don mchog ldan-pa nga*, "I in whom Being's superb vitalizing dynamics have found its concrete expression." Mokṣākaragupta in his *Pañjikā* (bsTan-'gyur, vol. *Mi*, fol. 297b) agrees with the above interpretation by Advayavajra.

[23] *chung-ma dag*. In Advayavajra's *Ṭīkā* (fol. 253b) this plural form is presented as *chung-ma 'khor*, "(one's) wife and attendants." Advaya Avadhūti in his *Ṭīkā* (fol. 102b) conceives of the "home" as a person's biological foundation, his neural and metabolic mind (*dran-pa*), and of the "womenfolk" as three aspects or intensities of a higher-order mind (*shes-rab-ma*), summarily referred to as *dran-med*. On *dran-pa* and *dran-med* see chapter 2.

[24] On *rang-bzhin gnyug-ma* instead of the more common *gnyug-ma'i rang-bzhin* see chapter 2.

[25] See also above, chapter 2.

[26] The three terms *yid*, *sems*, and *bdag-nyid*, as well as the sequence in which they are introduced, are of singular importance. In Buddhist psychology *yid* (*manas*), corresponding to our notion of an egologically predisposed awareness and synonymous with *bdag* (*ātman*) indicating one's egological self, is related to *sems* (*citta*), usually rendered as "mind" but more precisely being a term for a feedforward/feedbackward process, in such a way that *yid* is a sector of *sems* as its wider background. For details see my *From Reductionism to Creativity*. If in terms of Jungian psychology we identify *yid* with "consciousness," *sems* would be the "unconscious." But both *yid* as "consciousness" and *sems* as the "unconscious" are enframements of a supraordinate reality that, in the wake of the Buddhist mentalistic conception of the universe, is referred to as *bdag-nyid*, here rendered as "authentic Self." Like Jung's "individuated Self," it is a dynamic whole (see *The Collected Works of C. G. Jung*, vol. 9/1, 275) and as such simultaneously the feeling of "ecstasy" (*bde-ba*) and "meaning" experienced in the gestalt of one's humanity (*chos-sku*). In this, its dynamics, it is autonomous vis-à-vis its environ-

ment (see Erich Jantsch, *The Self-organizing Universe*, 298), from which, as its social context, it is inseparable.

[27] The scorn that Saraha expresses is based on the fact that the literalist is unable to understand what "authentic Self" means because as a staunch reductionist he reduces it to and equates it with his petty egological self. The fact that it is the authentic Self that is the agent in the social activities listed in this stanza is clearly stated by Advayavajra in his *Ṭīkā* (fol. 255b), where the line

za-zhing 'thung-la gnyis-spyod-kyi dga'-bzhis

is made into two lines:

bdag-nyid za-zhing 'thung-la gnyis-sbyor te
dga'-ba'i yid-kyis sprod-par byed-pa ni

The authentic Self eats and drinks and has sex and
With a joyful mind engages [in such activities].

The second reason for Saraha to express his scorn is the fact that the literalist-objectivist is unable to understand that a human individual is a multilevel process structure in which each level has its own self-organizing dynamics. According to Karma 'Phrin-las, 45–46, the "lowest" ("outer," *phyi*) predominantly physical level in the literalist-objectivist-rationalist's approach to his being is his complacency with being a more or less successful co-ordination of behavior patterns and their ritual execution. For further details see my *The Creative Vision* (Novato, CA: Lotsawa, 1987), 120. The next "higher" ("inner," *nang*) level is an "imaginal" one on which the experiencer feels and images the vibrations and vibrational patterns of his live body. The third "higher" ("arcane," that is, "systemic," *gsang*) level is the organism's self-organizing dynamics in the direction of its becoming ever more self-reflexive. This level as process is summed up by the four code terms *dran-pa, dran-med, skye-med,* and *blo-'das.* For their meanings see chapter 2. The last and "highest" ("wholeness-beingness," *de-kho-na-nyid*) level is the very dynamics of Being itself in its being simultaneously a "ceaselessly ongoing radiation" (*gdangs 'gag-pa-med-pa*) and an "originless nothingness" (*gshis skye-ba med-pa*).

Lastly the four joys (*dga'-ba*) are phases of intensity that mark the lessening of dichotomic cognition (*rnam-rtog*) and the strengthening of a unitive pristine awareness (*ye-shes*). The intricate interplay between joy and awareness in the context of meditative concentration with strong sexual overtones has been detailed by Klong-chen rab-'byams-pa in his *mKha'-yang*, vol. 2, 285ff.

[28] A detailed analysis of all the points listed in this stanza, as offered by Karma 'Phrin-las, 47, would easily fill a whole chapter in a lengthy book. Here it must suffice to point to the hierarchically organized levels of which a human individual is composed. There is first of all the "physical" or biological level consisting of the biotic currents and what is best described as neural-metabolic mentation. The fact that in Buddhist thought "mind" (*sems*) is primarily a biological and physiological phenomenon presents considerable difficulties for a Westerner because of his dualistic notion of body and mind. The next higher level—remaining co-ordinated with the lower level—is the "psychic" level consisting of dichotomic thought patterns related to the individual's emotionally toned egologically predisposed awareness, his egological consciousness or egological self (*bdun-yid*), and their instinctual-spiritual assessment related to

the egological self as such (*drug-yid*). The third level is the "symbolic" one. As pointed out by Karma 'Phrin-las, there is over and above this descriptive presentation of an individual's complexity another more experiential account according to which the biotic currents (*rlung*) are the vehicle of consciousness and form the object phase (*gzung-rtog*) in an intentional arch, and mentation (*sems*) is consciousness as such and constitutes the act phase (*'dzin-rtog*). Together they form the current constituting one's karmic actions (*las-kyi rlung*). When this current ceases to be operative the current constituting one's pristine awareness modes (*ye-shes-kyi rlung*) takes over. The cessation or stoppage of which the text speaks occurs in the wake of the self-organizing dynamics of the "system"; it is not an artificially introduced phase, as Advayavajra in his *Pañjikā* (fol. 208a) points out. In his *Ṭīkā* (fol. 255ab) Advayavajra gives a different version of this stanza:

gang-du rlung dang sems ni mi-rgyu-zhing
thabs dang shes-rab 'jug-pa med gyur-pa
skyes-bu mi-shes-pa-dag gnas der ni
gnas-shing gnas-skabs sems ni dbugs-'byung-zhing

Where the biotic currents and neural-metabolic mentation no longer stirs and
[The system's] operacy and intelligence have ceased,
There, you ignorant people,
You should stay and from time to time have your mind take a breather.

29 *man-ngag*. This term signifies an "instruction" that comes from within an innermost experience and as such is quite different from an instruction a person may give to someone (*gdams-ngag*). We might paraphrase this sentence by saying that Being itself has instructed Saraha and that he has conveyed this instruction to his audience. What this instruction is, is the admonition in the subsequent stanza.

30 Advayavajra in his *Ṭīkā* (fol. 255b) seems to have understood this statement as meaning that Saraha himself has passed away into this zero-point and offers a text that includes the first line, though expanded, of the following stanza in the standard version:

snying-po' i don-gyi ye-shes de-kho-na
bdag-med-mas ni man-ngag bstan-nas song
gnyis-su mi bya gcig-tu rtog-na rnal-'byor spros-pa'i lam

The pristine awareness of [and in] the concrete presence of Being's vitalizing dynamics (*snying-po'i don*), [presencing in many guises, but experienced] in its beingness (*de-kho-na*)
Is without an egological self (*bdag-med-ma*)[, and yet is the mother (*ma*) of every self]; having given the instruction (*man-ngag*) [of its being nothing whatsoever], it has passed away. [Hence]
Do not create the duality (*gnyis*) [of an imagining agent and an imagined object], but if you were to conceptualize [what is your authentic Self] as a One (*gcig*), oh yogi, this would be the way of conceptual proliferations.

It should be noted that the term *bdag-med-ma* contains a pun. One of its meanings is that given in the translation; another is its "mythological" implication of being the experienced personification of "man's soul" as being feminine, *bdag-med-ma* = *nairātmyā*.

[31] According to Karma 'Phrin-las, 49, the duality refers to one's conceptual-representational thinking (*rnam-rtog*) and what is the gestaltism of (Being's pervasive) meaningfulness (*chos-sku*), in the sense that in its indivisibility (*sku*) is the object-phase in an intentional arch whose act-phase is *ye-shes*. The unity is the awareness of the complementarity of *rnam-rtog* and *chos-sku*.

[32] *rigs*. Karma 'Phrin-las begins his explanation by pointing out that *rigs* corresponds to *dhātu*, and then lists as synonyms *dbyings*, *khams*, and *rang-bzhin*. But then he goes on to draw a subtle distinction between *rigs*, which, in this context, he understands as *rang-bzhin*—"(Being's) ownmostness," "(Being's) Eigenstate"—and *khams* as denoting the thematization of *rigs*. It is true that Tibetan *dbyings* and *khams* render *dhātu*, but *dbyings* is used for what we would call "Being's 'radiation'-dominated expanse or field character" and *khams* for "Being's 'matter'-dominated expanse." From a dynamic perspective, *rigs* may be conceived of as twofold, threefold, or fivefold. In this aspect it comes close to our notions of "resonance domains" and "probability patterns" underlying and "shaping" our psychophysical being. In their radiation they display different colors visible as a person's aura. Mokṣākaragupta in his *Pañjikā* (fol. 298b) speaks of their five colors and also refers to the human system's "operacy" (*thabs*) and "intelligence" (*shes-rab*) modes as *rigs*, probabilistic modes resonating with the whole of Being. Advayavajra in his above-quoted *Ṭīkā* (fol. 256a) mentions three *rigs* and relates them to the three *khams* such that the "world of desires" (*'dod-khams*) is an actualization of the *rin-po-che'i rigs*, "the world of aesthetic forms" (*gzugs-khams*) an actualization of the *padma'i rigs*, and the "world of no-form" (*gzugs-med khams*) an actualization of the *rdo-rje'i rigs*.

[33] *khams*. These are the "world of desire," the "world of aesthetic forms," and the "world of no-form," mentioned in the preceding note. Their psychological correspondences are our sensuality, our heightened sensibilities, and what is otherwise known as the "detection threshold."

[34] Advayavajra in his *Ṭīkā* (fol. 256a) gives a considerably different version of the last four lines in this stanza and highlights the difference between ecstatic awareness and ordinary cognitions. His version reads:

> *mdun dang rgyab dang g.yas-g.yon phyogs-bcu-ru*
> *gang-du rtog dang myong-ba de-dag ni*
> *de ni 'khrul-pa'i lam-la mngon-par gnas*
> *rang-bzhin mtshon-cha chen-po rtogs-pa-na*
> *da ni su-la'ang dri-bar mi-bya'o*

> Wherever one [intellectually] conceives of and [emotionally] feels
> A front, a back, a right, and a left in the ten regions [of the compass] these [concretizations] pertain to and
> Reside on the way of errancy.
> In the deeply felt understanding [of ecstasy that] in itself is a gigantic sword
> One need not ask anyone any longer.

[35] *rang-gi ngo-bo*. Karma 'Phrin-las, 53, understands this term as referring to one's mind (*sems*) whose "stuff" (*ngo-bo*) is dichotomization. Advayavajra in his *Ṭīkā* (fol. 256b) reads this line as:

> *rang-gi ngo-bo ma-nyams dngos nyams-'gyur*
>
> The stuff we are made of [i.e., the energy/intensity-"stuff" that is Being itself] does not dissipate, its concretistic misplacements dissipate.

[36] *lhan-cig-skyes-pa'i lus*. This rather unusual term I understand as a contraction of *lhan-cig-skyes-pa'i ye-shes* and *ye-shes-kyi lus*. Spontaneity manifesting itself as a felt awareness of togetherness (complementarity-in-spontaneity) involves *ma-rig-pa* (*lhan-cig-skyes-pa'i ma-rig-pa*), one's cognitive capacity not being quite what it actually is or could be, and *ye-shes* (*lhan-cig-skyes-pa'i ye-shes*), a pristine awareness as a function of Being's ecstatic-supracognitive intensity (*rig-pa*). The meaning of the term *ye-shes-kyi lus* is clearly brought out in a sentence in the *dGongs-pa zang-thal*, vol. 4, 5:

> *Kyai, gsang-ba'i bdag-po sangs-rgyas chos-kyi sku ye-shes-kyi lus-su bzhugs-so. mtshan-ma'i lus med-do*
>
> Hey! Lord of the Mysteries! The gestaltism (*sku*) of Being's meaningfulness or Buddhahood presences as the embodiment (*lus*) of [Being's] pristine awareness; this embodiment is not a [physical] body having defining characteristics.

The *lhan-cig-skyes-pa'i lus* can thus be said to be our humanity, which we cannot but imagine as having an anthropomorphic form.

[37] *mtshams-su*. This in-between is, strictly speaking, the nonlocalizable transcendence of opposites.

[38] *rang-rig*. This term signifies an ecstatic-cognitive intensity (*rig*) that is self-reflexive (*rang*) in just being an intensity.

[39] *gnyug-ma'i yid*. On this key term in Saraha's writings see chapter 2.

[40] This is a favorite image with Saraha. It occurs again in stanza 88 and in his *Dohākośa-nāma mahāmudrā-upadeśa*, fol. 96b.

[41] That is to say, he confuses his petty egocentric mind with Being's wholeness; in other words, he attempts to reduce the whole to an artificial model, which he believes to have universal validity only because he has constructed it.

[42] "The root of your mental-spiritual disposition" (*sems-kyi rtsa-ba*) is a term for the dynamics of Being that extends over the three levels that constitute an individual in his hierarchical organization. Each level reflects Being's spontaneity as it manifests itself through the principle of complementarity "togetherness" (*lhan-cig-skyes-pa*). As Karma 'Phrin-las, 61, elaborates, an individual consists of the well-known triad of body, speech, and mind (not so much in an additive manner, but in a hierarchy that itself becomes ever more "dense"); but what is called "body" is, as we might say, the "concrete" end-phase of Being's "lighting-up" (*snang-ba*)—paradoxically, it is Being's nothingness (*stong/stong-nyid*). The same applies to "speech" as the end-phase of Being's "voicing" (*grags*)— that, too, is its nothingness. In the Western context the German psychologist Hans Lipps has recognized this long ago by stating that every word is surrounded by an "aura of the unexpressed." Lastly, "mind" is the end-phase of Being's "ecstatic intensity" (*rig-pa*)—that, too, is its nothingness. Another

interpretation by Advaya Avadhūti in his *Ṭīkā* (fol. 108a) links spontaneity to the experiences encoded in the terms *dran-med, skye-med,* and *blo-'das.* In his *Cittakośa-aja-vajra-gīti (Thugs-kyi mdzod skye-med rdo-rje'i glu,* lost in its original Apabhraṃśa, but preserved in its Tibetan translation in bsTan-'gyur, vol. *Tsi,* fols. 88a–89b; see 88a), Saraha exclaims:

lhan-cig-skyes-pa rnam-gsum nyams-su bde
zhen-pa med-phyir rtog-ge'i yul-las 'das

In the [sensuously felt] experience of the three aspects of Being's spontaneity there is ecstasy [to be found];
Because there is no addiction [to it as some thing] it surpasses the logician's realm [of understanding].

43 *man-ngag.* On this term see above, note 29.

44 The rendering of this line:

'khor-ba'i rang-bzhin sems-kyi ngo-bo-nyid yin-te,

is based on the interpretation by Karma 'Phrin-las, 62. The distinction between *rang-bzhin* and *ngo-bo/ngo-bo-nyid*—the particle *nyid* having only emphatic significance in this context—is reminiscent of the rDzogs-chen distinction: *ngo-bo* being a term for Being's facticity or its intensity-"stuff," that is its nothingness, and *rang-bzhin* being a term for Being's actuality or radiance as the former's symmetry transformation. See my *From Reductionism to Creativity,* 258; *Matrix of Mystery,* 52f., 76f., and *passim.*

45 *slob-dpon.* Note the distinction made between *bla-ma* (the innermost mentor as a guiding image operating from within one's self) and *slob-dpon,* who, if he really knows, conveys Being's message through his own being, which itself assumes the character of a symbolic gesture. Cryptically, Saraha refers to himself.

46 *rang-rgyud.* This term is synonymous with the authentic Self.

47 This is one of the most often quoted stanzas in Tibetan literature.

48 While Karma 'Phrin-las, 66–67, considers this stanza to present the gist of the imaginative process concerned with "inner calm" and the subsequent four stanzas as describing the progressive movement toward its climax, Advayavajra in his *Ṭīkā* (fol. 262a) considers the first four stanzas in the analytical assessment of the imaginative process by Karma 'Phrin-las as a description of how the mind is to be settled in its own vastness. With the exception of a few key terms, found also in the standard version of Saraha's Song, his version is very different and reads:

sems ni nam-mkha' 'dra-bar blta-bya ste
lus ni de-nyid yin-pas chags mi-bya
chos-rnams kun dang sems-nyid mnyam-pa ste
sems de bsam-gyis mi-khyab bsam-byas-nas
des ni bla-na-med-pa thob-par 'gyur

The mind [in its intensity-"stuff"] should be seen to be like the sky and
Since your body is [made] precisely of this [intensity-"stuff" of which your mind is made] do not be attached [to either].

All the entities of reality and the mind as a dynamic principle are
alike [in being Being's intensity-"stuff"].
Once you have thought of this mind as not being able to be
encompassed by representational thought
The unsurpassable [goal] will be attained.

He then adds another stanza:

nam-mkha'-la sprin byung-ba rlung-gis thim
sems-kyi de-nyid rtog-bya brtags-pas thim
snying-pos smras-pa nam-zhig nus-ldan-na
mi-rtag g.yo-ba myur-du spong-bar 'gyur

In the sky clouds arise but they are dispersed by the wind;
[So it is with] the mind's beingness, the notions that crop up are
dispersed by the scrutiny [of them by the innermost mentor,
who is none other than mind itself].
[Saraha, who is the concrete presence of] Being's vitalizing energy,
says: Once you are able [to do so]
[Everything] transitory and unstable will quickly be discarded.

49 The entire extant Tibetan version of this stanza, whose original Apabhraṃśa version is lost, is extremely elliptic and almost unintelligible without the help of the commentary on it by Karma 'Phrin-las, 68–69, and other related works dealing with the topic under consideration. In symbolic language the stanza describes the process of dying as experienced by a person in his becoming "dead to his everyday reality" whilst entering his *lumen naturale* (*'od -gsal*), which David Michael Levin in his *The Opening of Vision* (450) shows to be "an accurate phenomenological description of a deeply realized experience of being human."

The crucial term in this half of the stanza is "ambrosial water" (*bdud-rtsi*). Its lengthy indigenous hermeneutical explication, which I have translated in my *The Creative Vision*, 157 note 245, suggests that it was understood as an archetypal image. This ambrosial water has an immanent tension that—in view of Karma 'Phrin-las's opinion that this term is synonymous with *byang-chub-kyi sems*, which he goes so far as to qualify as being "moist" (*gsher-ba*)—acts as "the effectiveness principle of evolution," in the words of Erich Jantsch, *The Self-organizing Universe*, 308. The identity of water (*bdud-rtsi, chu*) and spirit (*byang-chub-kyi sems, ye-shes*) is not only well attested in Western alchemical writings (see *The Collected Works of C. G. Jung*, vol. 13, 76) but also in Buddhist literature (see the *sGra-thal 'gyur-ba*, 110: *ye-shes rlan*).

The symbolic character of the fundamental forces that constitute a living being is explained by Karma 'Phrin-las, 69, to the effect that "wind" (*rlung*) is our egocentric mind (*yid*) that unpredictably flits from one object to another; "fire" (*me*) is the raging of our emotions consuming our very being; "water" (*chu*) is our turbulent actions (*zag-bcas-kyi las*) that set up and embroil us in what we call samsara; "earth" (*sa*) is our psychophysical organism in interaction with its environment. "Ambrosial water" (*bdud-rtsi*), being both "water" and "spirit," is the conceptually undivided zero-point (*mi-rtog-pa'i ting-nge-'dzin, nirvikalpa-samādhi*) where, in modern terms, evolution is poised.

50 This statement refers to the old idea of the four cosmic fundamental

forces being gradually reabsorbed, one into the other, at the "end of the world" before they start proceeding one from the other to form another world. Experientially this process is experienced as the solidity of our being dissolving into fluidity, this fluidity dissolving into heat, this heat dissolving into a breeze (that under given circumstances may blow the other way and fan the fire), this breeze dissolving into the cognitive principle that in our enworldedness is our consciousness. At this moment a transformation, not to be confused with a reduction, takes place such that what was felt and judged to be quantitative now is experienced qualitatively as our *lumen naturale* that is sheer ecstasy. Another term for this ecstasy is *chos-sku*.

51 The version of this stanza given by Advayavajra in his *Ṭīkā* (fol. 262b) is quite different and reads as follows:

rlung dang me chu dbang-chen 'gags-pa-na
bdud-rtsi'i dangs-ma rlung-chen-la zhugs-pas
dhuti rlangs-pa sems-la 'jug 'gyur te
srid-pa'i sa-ru rdzogs-pa'i sangs-rgyas-nas
sbyor-ba bzang-po 'di-la snang-ba sems-la thim
nam-zhig sbyor-bzhi gnas-'gyur tshul-gyis ni
sems zhugs dus-su bde-ba che rgyas te
nam-mkha'i khams-su shong-min mnyon-ba'i tshul

When [what is felt and imaged as] wind, fire, water, and earth has ceased [to play a dominant role], then
By virtue of the subtly luminous "stuff" in the ambrosial water fusing with [your organism's] overall currents [as they move along the right and left channels of your body-schema]
The moisture in the central channel is being absorbed in the mind-"stuff" [of which the organism is made];
When in this possibilities-offering phase-transition the spiritual awakening process completes itself
In this glorious linking backward [to the source] the phenomenal subsides in the [noumenal aspect of your] mind-"stuff."
When through a qualitative transformation [effected by] a fourfold linking backward
The mind enters [and becomes its *lumen naturale*] ecstasy spreads.
It is experienced as not being containable in the dimension of [physical] space.

52 Advayavajra in his *Ṭīkā* (fol, 262b) adds:

dpa'-bo-rnams-kyis brtags-pa'i rigs
Spiritual heroes [that is, out-of-the-ordinary yogis] should consider this.

53 Karma 'Phrin-las stands alone in dividing what follows into two stanzas of two lines each.

54 Karma 'Phrin-las, fol. 74, understands "doing what is to be done" (*bya-ba byed*) and "not doing what is to be done" (*bya-ba mi-byed*) as referring to good and evil actions respectively. Avayavajra in his *Ṭīkā* (fol. 262a) understands the first phrase as indicating the phenomenal world in which the individual is involved by his dichotomic thinking, and the latter phrase as referring to Being's genu-

ineness. In contrast with Karma 'Phrin-las, who remains surprisingly conventional in his interpretation, Advayavajra has clearly understood Saraha's mysticism, which calls to mind Meister Eckhart's words: "God and Godhead are as different as doing and non-doing" (quoted in *The Collected Works of C. G. Jung*, vol. 6, 254). Advayavajra then goes on to link this idea to the first half of the following stanza. Advaya Avadhūti in his *Ṭīkā* (fol. 111a) agrees with Advayavajra and explicitly states that "doing what is to be done" refers to a person's samsaric mind, in mystical language spoken of as *dran-pa*, and "not doing what is to be done" to a person's nirvanic mind, in mystical language *dran-med*.

55 The same image is used by Saraha in his *Kāyakośa-amṛta-vajragīti*, fol. 84a.

56 Advayavajra in his *Pañjikā* (fol. 213b) explains this image by saying that if a camel is loaded it struggles with all its strength and tries to run away, but if the load drops off it stays calm and immobile.

57 The Tibetan translation of this stanza, lost in its original Apabhraṃśa, is far from uniform and varies with each commentator. The one given here is based on the rendering in the commentary by Karma 'Phrin-las, 75:

kye lags dbang-pos ltos-shig dang
ngas ni 'di-las ma-mthong-no

Advayavajra in his *Ṭīkā* (fol. 265b) offers the following reading and interpretation:

kye lags dpa'o ltos-shig dang
'di la nga ni mi-rtogs-so.

Hey-ho, [you] spiritual hero, have a look and
Do not understand [what you see] as an ego.

And Mokṣākaragupta in his *Pañjikā* (fol. 301b) reads:

kye lags dbang-po ltos-shig [dang]
'di-la ngas ni ma-rtogs-so

and explains the first line as meaning "look haughtily at the cloudless sky" and the second line as meaning "I have not split it with my mind."

58 Advayavajra in his *Pañjikā* (fols. 213b–214a) gives a slightly different version:

rlung spangs rang-nyid ma-sems-shig
shing-gi rnal-'byor-dag-gis kyang
sna-yi rtse-mor rab-tu bcing
e-ma'o skye-bo rmongs-rnams lhan-cig-skyes-pa'i mchog-tu son
srid-pa'i bag-chags 'ching-ba spongs

Do not think that discarding the biotic force [means that you become] your very self[, on the contrary it is death].
Even the "tree-trunk" yogis
Fetter [and hold it steady] at the tip of their nose.
Alas! you foolish people. You should go into Being's superb complementarity dynamics and
Discard the fetters that are the tendencies [operative in the transition phase that is the] probability [of your becoming] enworlded.

Needless to say, by using the derogatory term "tree-trunk" yogi (*shing-gi rnal-'byor*) Saraha expresses his contempt for such techniques.

59 The same sentiment is expressed by the German poet Novalis (Friedrich von Hardenberg):

> Es gibt nur *einen* Tempel in der Welt, und das ist der menschliche Körper.
>
> There is only *one* temple in the world, and that is the human body.

60 This stanza describes in evocative images the body as it is felt and imaged as process structure. For details see chapter 3.

61 Karma 'Phrin-las, 83, adds that these people also believe that these gods, each in his own way, have created the world, but this belief is an emotionally toned fiction that merely serves to keep the believers in bondage. According to him Brahma is the emotion (*nyon-mongs*) of dullness (*gti-mug*, *moha*), Viṣṇu is the emotion of irritation (*zhe-sdang*, *dveṣa*), and Śiva is the emotion of cupidity (*'dod-chags*, *rāga*). In order to link this line with the following one, he says that there are also people who do not accept any differentiation but they differ from the Buddhists by emphasizing the content of the experience rather than living the experiential process itself, for which *rdo-rje-'chang* is a guiding image, not a concretized reality "out there."

62 There is no corresponding Apabhraṃśa version to the first line in this stanza, which with minor variations is found in the commentaries by Karma 'Phrin-las, 84, Advayavajra (*Ṭīkā*, fol. 269), and Advaya Avadhūti (*Ṭīkā*, fol. 113a). Only Advayavajra (*Pañjikā*, fol. 216a) gives a line that to a certain extent tallies with the Apabhraṃśa text, which contains a reference to alchemical practice.

63 The last two lines in this stanza render a single line in the original Apabhraṃśa that reads:

> *kapparahia suhaṭhānu jaga ubajjaï tattha.*

The standard Tibetan rendering reads:

> *bde-ba'i gnas mchog rtog spangs-te*
> *'gro-ba nye-bar skye-ba nyid bzhin-no.*

A seemingly truncated version has been given by Advayavajra in his *Pañjikā* (fol. 216a). It reads:

> *bde-ba'i gnas mchog rang-bzhin spangs*
> *'gro-ba nye-bar skye-ba der.*

The difficulty offered by the term *rang-bzhin* in this context is solved by Advayavajra in his *Ṭīkā* (fol. 269b). His explication of Saraha's stanza (or half-stanza) is so important that it has to be presented in full:

> The abiding presence (*gnas*) of ecstasy (*bde-ba chen-po*) that by virtue of its ownmost dynamics (*rang-bzhin-gyis*) has become dissociated from divisive concepts is [one's] as yet undifferentiated psychic potential. Through its cultivation and its becoming its very superbness (*mchog*) all divisive concepts are discarded without exception. This is like persons growing up into the fullness of their being: just as a person's capacities become fully developed in the person's passage through childhood, adolescence, and adulthood, so also it is with this (*nyid*) as the quintessence and ultimacy of his being. When through its visionary experience,

its relishing, its deeply felt understanding, and its having reached its "end" [as a new beginning] in the fullness of a person's being, the [realized] meaningfulness of his existence (*chos-sku*), it expresses itself in and through his sociality (*longs-sku*) and his being a guiding-image to others (*sprul-sku*).

Ecstasy as a person's ownmostness comes, as Advaya Avadhūti in his *Ṭīkā* (fol. 113b) points out, from nowhere else than the person himself.

Mokṣākaragupta in his *Pañjikā* (fol. 304b) reads the first line of this stanza as:

> *bde-ba'i gnas mchog rtog-pa spangs-pa de ngas mthong*
> *'gro-ba nye-bar skye-bar byed-pa nyid bzhin-no*
>
> I have seen ecstasy's abidingness in its superbness as having discarded divisive concepts;
> This is precisely like letting a person grow up.

and explicates it as meaning the following:

> "Ecstasy's abidingness" means the "cause" [of the person's evolutionary process], Being's nothingness; "having discarded divisive concepts" means the "way" that is without divisive concepts; and "I have seen" means the immediacy of its experience. "Letting a person grow up" means that it is like a child growing in its mother's womb—it is the birth of unfailing ecstasy.

64 *dran-pa*. There is no corresponding term in the original Apabhraṃśa version. It is significant that the unknown Tibetan translator used this term instead of the more common *rnam-shes* (*vijñāna*) in such listings. This shows that he thought about the material he was translating and that he was well versed in the line of thought that was cognizant of what we now call the biological foundation of psychic life.

65 Karma 'Phrin-las, 86ff., divides this section into five major divisions, each of them having many subdivisions and subdivisions of subdivisions. The major divisions have been marked by Roman numerals.

66 Although the standard version as well as Advaya Avadhūti (*Ṭīkā*, fol. 114b) read *don-mang*, "having many meanings," corresponding to the Apabhraṃśa text that has *bahu attha*, the latter makes it quite clear that *don-med*, "meaningless," is intended. Advayavajra in his *Ṭīkā* (fol. 267b) reads the verse line as having *don med*.

67 The following fourteen lines have not been preserved in their original Apabhramṣa.

68 *tshad-ma*, *pramāṇa*.

69 Advayavajra in his *Ṭīkā* (fol. 271a) reads *rnam-par 'byed-pa* "introduce differentiations" instead of *rnyed-pa* "obtain," "get," "come up with," found in the other commentaries.

70 This extremely condensed stanza has found different interpretations, the gist of which is that the stupid are caught in their reductionism and shun Being as if it were an untouchable thing. What cannot be touched by the intellect (that is, intellectually reduced to the commonplace and trivial) is, literally and figuratively, "untouchable" (so Advaya Avadhūti in his *Ṭīkā*, fol. 115a) because any contact with him (it?) would "soil" and make one untouchable. By contrast, the wise, who take Being and its message as authoritative, eagerly enter the house of the untouchable, and, like the untouchable himself, cannot be "soiled."

[71] The implication is, as Karma 'Phrin-las, 88–89, points out, that even a beggar might come to realize what he really is: a king in the spiritual sense. He would then have no need for a begging-bowl nor would he have to bother with the affairs of state, since he has risen above any such involvement.

[72] These two lines are only found in Advaya Avadhūti's *Ṭīkā* (fol. 115b) and in Karma 'Phrin-las, 89, on whose interpretation the above rendering is given. The deeper meaning is that in your beingness as *chos-sku* you are invariant, in your sociality as *longs-sku* you are not biased in one way or another, and in your worldly presence as *sprul-sku* you are a guiding image for others.

[73] As Advaya Avadhūti in his *Ṭīkā* (fol. 115b) explicates, there is a kind of reciprocity between nirvana, as Being's nothingness/openness (*stong-pa*), and samsara, as Being's "lighting-up" (*snang-ba*). Being's nothingness is adorned by Being's lighting-up and Being's lighting-up is adorned by Being's nothingness. In more modern terms, Being's nothingness is in its lighting-up, though not in the sense of Being's lighting-up being some container, and Being's lighting-up is Being's nothingness, though not in the sense of a mathematical equation.

[74] The same image is used by Saraha with reference to the experience of the spread of an unbounded pristine awareness (*ye-shes*), in his *Kayākośa-amṛta-vajragīti*, fol. 84b.

[75] This rendering reflects the interpretation given by Karma 'Phrin-las, 91, of the Tibetan translation of the Apabhraṃśa original that reads:

> *so paramesaru kāsu kahijjaï*

and in Tibetan:

> *dbang-phyug dam-pa de ni su-la bstan nus-sam.*

According to Karma 'Phrin-las, the term *dbang-phyug*, corresponding to the Apabhraṃśa *paramesaru* and the Sanskrit *parameśvara*, is a metaphorical expression for the "pristine awareness (aspect) in Being's complementarity dynamics" (*lhan-cig-skyes-pa'i ye-shes*). Advayavajra in his *Ṭīkā* (fol. 272a) turns the phrase *dbang-phyug dam-pa* into a full verse line as *dbang-phyug bde-ba rang-bzhin med-pa ste* and links this verse line with the preceding one, so that the resulting three lines would mean:

> As is the case with a young woman's innermost yearning for the
> pleasures of sex
> So it is with Śiva, who may be said to be the pleasures of sex:
> Can [this force or "person"] be shown to anyone?

The unspoken implication is that the experience of Being's genuineness may be said—as far as language can be used to express the unexpressible—to be "ecstasy" (*bde-ba/bde-ba chen-po*), but ecstasy cannot be reduced to sex alone. For the Buddhists the gods of any denomination are instances of what Alfred North Whitehead has called "misplaced concreteness." It is against this misplaced concreteness that the Buddhists leveled their often scathing critique.

[76] As Advayavajra in his *Ṭīkā* (fol. 272b) points out, it is to these notions of substance and non-substance that it owes its origin.

[77] *bla-med lus*. This is the reading of the standard version; it fails, however, to bring out the fact that it is a rhetorical question. In the original Apabhraṃśa the line reads:

tāba ki dehānuttara pābasi

and is rendered in Tibetan as a simple statement:

de-tshe bla-med lus ni thob-par 'gyur.

Advayavajra in his *Ṭīkā* (fol. 272a) reads this line as

de-tshe bla-ma'i lus-su 'grub-pa nyid

Then you are established as the embodiment of the innermost mentor.

[78] Advayavajra in his *Ṭīkā* (fol. 272a) takes this line as a concluding sentence and, in elaborating the above idea in three verse lines instead of two, reads:

de-ltar bstan-pa-nyid-la nges rtogs-pas
ma-'khrul-pa-yi ngo-bor rdzogs sangs-rgyas
rang-gi(s) rang-la legs-par shes-par bya

Through the certain and deeply felt understanding of what has been shown
You become fully spiritually awake in the energy/intensity-"stuff" [of Being);
Properly know this to have come about in you by itself.

[79] This is the claim of the Hīnayāna Śrāvakas.

[80] This is the claim of the Hīnayāna Pratyeka-buddhas.

[81] This is the claim of the Mahāyāna Yogācāra philosophers.

[82] Advayavajra in his *Ṭīkā* (fol. 272b) takes the following sentence to be the conclusion of this stanza.

[83] Advayavajra in his *Ṭīkā* (fol. 273a) simply says: "It is not a stupid person's meditative concentration that can be thought and spoken about."

[84] As Karma 'Phrin-las, 95–96, points out, the following contains a critique of the rational approach of various philosophical systems, summed up under the generic term *hetuyāna* or *lakṣanayāna* (*mtshan-nyid-kyi theg-pa*), with their division of the world into irreconcilable opposites, cause and effect, subject and object, the instinctual-emotional, and the intellectual-spiritual. By contrast, in those disciplines, referred to as *phalayāna* (*'bras-bu'i theg-pa*), that start from the whole and are process-oriented, there is no sharp separation between opposite aspects of reality; rather, the opposites include each and assist each other.

[85] Mokṣākaragupta in his *Pañjikā*, (fol. 307a) concisely states that the biotic forces (*rlung*) are the root of samsara. The traditional image is that the biotic forces are the swift horse and the mind the lame rider.

[86] In modern terms, Being, the whole, of which the innermost mentor is a symbol, remains invariant under all and any transformations. But then, also, each of us is the whole and yet only part of it; and so it is with the images of the whole.

[87] *rnal-'byor-ma, yoginī.* Mokṣākaragupta in his *Pañjikā* (fol. 307a) explains *rnal-'byor-ma* as *sgyu-ma'i rnal-'byor-ma,* which in an attempt to capture the mythological spirit I translate as "the Lady of Enchantment." The implication of this beautiful passage is that when we die and return to the immutable source from which we have sprung, the world that for so long has captivated us, fades—and with it the images under whose spell we have lived. The world is not an illusion, but an enchanting play.

[88] Advayavajra in his *Ṭīkā* (fol. 274b) adds the following line:

gar 'gro sems-dang kye-ho dpa'-bo-rnams
Hey-ho, you spiritual heroes, think about where you are going!

[89] The term *buddha* has always been understood as describing the "state of being spiritually awake" and so refers to an experience that is nowhere else than in the experiencer as an "embodied" being. In other words, our "body" is our "spirituality," though not in the sense of a mathematical equation. See also figure 1, page 45.

[90] The rendering of *lom-sems* as "unruly" is tentative and based on the explication of this passage by Karma 'Phrin-las, 99. The word *lom/lom-pa* is not listed in any dictionary. It is used by Saraha once again in his *Kāyakośa-amṛta-vajragīti*, fol. 84a:

de-nyid shes-na snang-ba longs-spyod yin
lcags-kyus btab-pas glang-chen thim-pa bzhin
bya-bral bzhag-pas glang-chen lom-pa bzhin
dran-pa dran-med ngo-shes gnod-pa med

If one knows Being-in-its-beingness the phenomenal is [a source of] pleasure and enjoyment;
It is like an elephant having become docile when touched by the hook in the mahout's hand, or
It is like an elephant romping when it is left without work.
In the recognition of [what] *dran-pa* and *dran-med* [mean] none can do any harm.

On *dran-pa* and *dran-med* see chapter 2 and on the image of the elephant see stanzas 125–28.

[91] The above rendering of the Tibetan text, which has no corresponding version in Saraha's original Apabhraṃśa, is based on the commentaries, which themselves differ among each other. The general idea is that the elephant is a metaphor for one's mind as a biological phenomenon. Its unruliness is likened to the fluctuations of the biotic forces as long as the harmonization and balancing out of their contrary aspects has not been effected.

[92] This rendering is based on the wording of this line as preserved in the commentary by Karma 'Phrin-las, 99, and in Advaya Avadhūti's *Ṭīkā* (fol. 121b):

'di-ltar rtogs-na gang-du'ang 'dri-sa med

Advayavajra in his *Ṭīkā* (fol. 275a) and Mokṣākaragupta in his *Pañjikā* (fol. 307b) read:

de ni 'di-ltar rtogs-so chos ci dgos
Understand it in this way; what more do you need?

[93] The same image is used by Saraha in his *Kāyakośa-amṛta-vajragīti*, fol. 84a and in his *Dohākośa-nāma mahāmudrā-upadeśa*, fol. 96a.

[94] Generally speaking there are two realities or universes: the external world in which the rationalist and realist believes as if it were a matter-of-fact world, forgetting or ignoring the "fact" that facts are what he has made and is making of them; and the inner world of the psyche with its images or "ideas." In whichever "reality" the experiencer (or observer) finds himself, it is assigned an exclusively "real" status. Advaya Avadhūti in his *Ṭīkā* (fol. 122b), varying the

theme already found in the *Kāśyapaparivartasūtra* (paragraph 67), speaks of a painter who paints a beautiful woman and is so fascinated by his painting that he believes this painted woman to be real. The illustration of this situation by a black rope seen as a poisonous snake is therefore not an instance of an illusion, the rationalist's clumsy attempt to reduce everything to the narrow level of his perception, but an account of how it feels to be in the one or the other situation.

95 Advayavajra in his *Ṭīkā* (fol. 277b) elaborates these illustrations as follows:

> Just as fish are obsessed with tasting the foam [floating on the water], so a yogi is obsessed with tasting Being's beingness; just as a moth is obsessed with what can be touched [and felt], so a yogi is obsessed with pleasurable sensations, first in his body and then in his mind; just as an elephant is obsessed with the fragrance of sandalwood, so a yogi is obsessed, less with [physical] scent, but with the fragrance of Being's nothingness; just as bees are obsessed with the colors of flowers, so a yogi is [obsessed with] the limpid knowledge of the Mahāmudrā, [the experience of himself as being the expression and the expressed] of Being's meaningfulness [comprising] the phenomenal and its possibilizing dynamics; and just as deer chase after the sound of music, so a yogi runs after the song [sung by] the indivisibility of ecstasy and nothingness.

96 Advayavajra in his *Ṭīkā* (fol. 277b) offers a slightly different version of these two lines, such that they read:

gang-zhig sems-la rnam-par 'phro-bar snang
de-srid mngon-po-la ni rang-bzhin te

which he interprets as meaning:

Whatever appears in the mind as its projections
Is an encounter with the trustworthy guardian-lord; there is no other dynamics than the one He is.

97 In his *Dohākośa-nāma mahāmudrā-upadeśa*, fol. 96b, Saraha turns this question into an admonition: "Do not conceive of the [ocean's] water and its waves as different [entities]."

98 *dgongs-pa*. On the meaning of this term see my *From Reductionism to Creativity*, 89, 93, 94.

99 Advayavajra in his *Ṭīkā* (fol. 278) and Mokṣākaragupta in his *Pañjikā* (fol. 308b) base their interpretation on quite a different version of this stanza:

gang-zhig ston-te gang-gis thos-pa-yi
dgos-pa gang-yin dam-pa skyong-ba-na
gdug-pa'i skugs-sa rdul-bzhin rlag-par byed
snying-ga nyid-du nub-par 'gyur-ba yin

If you meticulously guard what is essential [for your growth]
As it is being shown [to you by the truthworthy innermost mentor] and as you listen [to Him],
You will destroy the stake of poison as if it were just dust [which]
Will then subside in your heart.

He explains "poison" to mean one's divisive notions (*rtog-pa*). Instead of *ston-te* Mokṣākaragupta reads *bstan-te*, "what has been shown," and instead of *dam-pa skyong-ba* he reads *dam-par skyol*, "carrying it wisely with you." Lastly he explains "poison" to mean the emotions (*nyon-mongs*) and "stake" to mean one's basic mind (*rtsa-ba'i sems*). In fol. 309a he clarifies the use of "one's basic mind" by differentiating it from what he terms *ngo-bo sems*, "mind as the energy-intensity-'stuff'," that is, Being. Advayavajra concludes his interpretation by stating that "subsiding in your heart" points to a deeply felt understanding, as illustrated by the subsequent stanza.

[100] Advayavajra in his *Ṭīkā* (fol. 278b) offers a slightly different version and interpretation:

> *ji-ltar chu-la chu bzhag-na*
> *de nyid chu-ru ro-mnyam gyur*
> *ji-ltar mar-la mar gzhag mtshungs*
> *sems dang snang-ba de-bzhin smra*
> *skyon dang yon-tan rnam(s) dang ldan-pa'i sems*
> *mngon-po sus kyang mtshon-par mi-'gyur-ro*

> Just as when one pours water into water
> It acquires the same taste as the water [into which it has been poured]—
> Similar to butter put on butter
> I declare [the similarity of] the mind and what is a presence [to and in the mind].
> The mind that has both defects and qualities
> Cannot be pointed out [and understood as some thing] by anyone, be he the guardian-lord [or a Buddha and so on].

Mokṣākaragupta in his *Pañjikā* (fol. 309a) reads *mnyam-ldan*, "equally present," instead of *rnam(s) dang ldan-pa*, "having" or "being endowed with," and offers a valuable interpretation. "Water" is a metaphor for Being's nothingness (*stong-pa*), "water poured" is a metaphor for Being's compassionate dynamics (*snying-rje*), and "same taste" is a metaphor for their indivisibility and non-duality (*gnyis-med*). "Defects" he explains as a term for one's basic mind in its indestructibility (*rtsa-ba'i sems mi-shigs-pa*) and "qualities" as a term for mind as the energy/intensity-"stuff" that is Being in its indestructibility (*ngo-bo sems mi-shigs-pa*). He then goes on to say that the "stuff" (*ngo-bo*) the qualities are made of is the "stuff" the mind is made of and that this "stuff" is luminous, Being's *lumen naturale*. In other words, we as "mind"-beings are the "mind" of the universe and we as luminous beings carry this light with us, "preserving it and handing it down in its endurance," in the words of Martin Heidegger (*Early Greek Thinking*, New York: Harper & Row, 1975, 129),

[101] The rendering of this stanza, only moderately similar to the Apabhraṃśa version, is based on the interpretation by Karma 'Phrin-las, 105–106, who explains the first line as meaning that the fools do not go beyond good and evil thoughts. Advayavajra in his *Ṭīkā* (fol. 278b) gives a different reading of the text and a highly original interpretation:

> *rmongs-pa dag-la gnyen-po gang-yang med*
> *khyod ni stong-pa-nyid-la zhen tam-ci*
> *nags-la mched-pa'i me-lce ji-bzhin-du*
> *gong-du bab-pa 'di-ltar snang-ba kun*
> *ji-ltar snang dang graags-pa'i dngos-po-rnams*
> *rtsa-ba stong-pa-nyid dang lhan-cig byos*

In the as-yet-undifferentiated psychic potential (*tha-mal-gyi shes-pa*)
that is a foolishness of which none could be greater (*rmongs-pa chen-po*), there is nothing that is of aid or hindrance to it.
Therefore, my dear mind, what is this obsession of yours with a nothingness that is no-thing-whatsoever?
Like the flames of a forest fire that descend on this no-thing-whatsoever just mentioned—so is the whole of your phenomenal reality.
Just as the things you see and hear
Have their root [in what is the experience of you being the expression and the expressed of Being's meaningfulness, *chos-sku*] so deal with them in their togetherness with the nothingness of Being itself.

An as-yet-undifferentiated psychic potential (*tha-mal-gyi shes-pa*) is the most natural state of the whole in being "intelligence" (*shes-pa*) through and through, and as such, as the Buddhist texts over and again emphasize, is present in the fool and/or the child. Here one is immediately reminded of what Heinrich von Kleist says about gracefulness: "Gracefulness appears purest in a human body which has either no consciousness, or infinite consciousness, that is, in the puppet or in the god" (see Erich Jantsch, *The Self-organizing Universe*, 311).

102 Being's nothingness, which, precisely because it is not some thing or other, is felt to be so pleasing, is constantly on the verge of being reduced to some specific feeling about it. These specific feelings are the pleasurableness (*bde-ba*) that through its becoming concretized fetters the experiencer in the world of his desires; the lucency (*gsal-ba*) that through its concretization into luminous figures—gods and goddesses, in the language of imagination and mythology—fetters the experiencer in the world of aesthetic forms; and the suspension of dichtomizing thought (*mi-rtog-pa*) that through its concretization fetters the experiencer in the world of formlessness. This is the explanation given by Advaya Avadhūti in his *Ṭīkā* (fol. 122b). Advayavajra in his *Ṭīkā* (fol. 278a) gives a different reading of the first two lines:

gal-te yid-du 'ong-ba mnyam-pa'i sems
snying-la gces-spras byams-pa'i sems-nyid-la

If [you were to turn your] mind, at one with [what is so] pleasing
[Being's pleasurableness, lucency, conceptual undividedness, and no-thing-whatsoever-ness],
Into a mind of love holding dear in your heart [the disturbing presence of some divisive thought]. . . .

103 Mokṣākaragupta in his *Pañjikā* (fol. 309a) explains this stanza to the effect that a pig and an ox may be alike in being animals, but neither is ever the other. He then applies this to characterize the Buddhists. They all, he says, emphasize Being's nothingness, but the various philosophical disciplines merely talk about nothingness, while those for whom experience is of primary importance, live it. Advayavajra in his *Ṭīkā* (fol. 279a) reverses the first two lines and gives a larger version of this stanza:

grogs-po phag dang glang-po smyon-pa ltos
de-ltar yin-pa de ni ma-yin-no

rtog-bral brtan dang chags-pa'i gza'-gtad bral
rnal-'byor rtog-klong(s) dmag-bzlog sdig-par bral

Friends, look at a pig, an elephant, and a madman;
Being like this, they are not so:
Without discrimination, firm, and without anything to be attached to;
The yogi has done with divisive notions, routed the army, and is
without evil.

He explains the two last lines as meaning that just as a pig is not discriminating in what it eats, so a yogi eats anything without making any discrimination as to whether the food is clean or unclean; just as an elephant is undaunted in mind and stands firm (in battle), so a yogi cannot be deceived by Mara, heretics, outsiders, and outer and inner distractions and stands firm; and just as a madman has nothing to be attached to, so a yogi is not attached to anyone and roams about as he pleases. But a yogi is different from that with which he has been compared so far. He has upset the lair of divisive notions; he has routed the army of (spiritual) foes; and he is without the evil of destroying life.

[104] This poison appeared when the gods and demigods were churning the ocean for the potion of immortality. It was so virulent that none of the gods or demigods could drink it except Śiva, whose throat was turned blue by it—hence his name *nīlakaṇṭha*, "he with the blue throat." Mokṣākaragupta in his *Pañjikā* (fol. 309b) says that the term *kālakūṭa* is a name for "experience" (*nyams-su myong-ba*), and Karma 'Phrin-las, 111, makes the significant statement that the very utterance of this word would destroy what is the deeply felt understanding (*rtogs*) of Being-in-its-beingness.

[105] Advayavajra in his *Ṭīkā* (fol. 280a) adds the following lines:

de ni bsam-med rtogs-pa ma-yin-no
kye-ma rnal-'byor bsgom-pa rang-la dris
snying-po rang-bzhin dag-pa rtogs-pa-la
rang-bzhin gnas-pa'i sems-kyis blta-bar rigs

This is not something for representational thought and [hence]
cannot be understood [conceptually].
Hey-ho! You yogi, the active imagination [of
Being-in-its-beingness] is a self-questioning.
The deeply felt understanding of Being's energy that in its
ownmostness is utterly pure
Must be looked at by a mind abiding in Being's ownmostness.

[106] *bsgom dang mi-bsgom*. The term "active imagination" was coined by C. G. Jung and contrasts with mere fantasy or passive daydreaming. Both imagination and dreaming make use of images simply because no psychic activity can do without images. But each uses them in a different way. An excellent account of this difference has been given by Robert A. Johnson, *Inner Work* (San Francisco: Harper SF, 1989), 21–26 and *passim*. In the Buddhist context *bsgom* corresponds to Jung's "active imagination," while *mi-bsgom*, in spite of the negative particle *mi*, does not mean a negation of *bsgom*, but only that it is not "actively" employed. As is obvious from Saraha's insistence on their inseparability in actual life, we need both and at the same time.

This stanza and the following one are not found in the version of Saraha's

Dohā that was the basis for Advayavajra's *Ṭīkā* and Mokṣākaragupta's *Pañjikā*. Advayavajra (fol. 280b) has instead:

de-nas phyi-nang mnyam-par shes-pa dang
shes-byed de 'gog-par ni bla-ma'i lung
mgo snying lte gsang rkang lag spangs-pa ste
ngas mthong bsam-pa'i yul ni mchod-par byed
gzhan-dag bsam-pa'i yul ni 'gags-par 'gyur

Then, with the recognition of the external and internal being alike [in their being Being's nothingness]
The cognizing act [phase that made the object phase possible], too, has to cease [to be operative]—such is the innermost mentor's message.
When I have dismissed [the images of there being] a head, a heart, a navel, genitals, feet, and hands,
What I see [as] the object of my imaging is to be venerated;
Everything else [as] the object of my imaging passes away.

Mokṣākaragupta (fol. 310a) says even more poignantly:

de ni bsam-med sus kyang rtogs ma-yin
kye-ma mgo snying lte gsang spangs-pa ste
gzugs-med gzugs-bzang dam-pa ste
sna-tshogs gzugs-can yid-las skyes
bsam-pas yul ni mtshon-par byed
gzhan-dag bsam-pa rlung 'gag-'gyur

This is not something for representational thought and nobody is going to understand it [conceptually].
Hey-ho! When you have dismissed the images of a head, a heart, a navel, and the genitals,
This which has no form is the real and most beautiful form.
That which has various forms is born from your egologically predisposed awareness
But this [formless] object is perceived and understood by a thinking [that is not conceptual].
Everything else [pertains to conceptual] thinking [that here together with the] biotic force [that keeps this sort of thinking alive] ceases [to be operative].

107 In other words, the longer I look at something the more it will lose its objective reference, and what has been termed "pure sensation" will come about.

108 The text uses the term *sems* twice, each time indicating a different function reflecting the mentalistic Yogācāra position with its idea of an all-pervasive mentalistic foundation, the *kun-gzhi*, in many aspects similar to the notion of the unconscious in modern depth psychology and its idea that what we call consciousness is more like ripples passing over this substratum. As Karma 'Phrin-las, 115, points out, this "showing" is not meant in an ostensible manner. Instead of the somewhat elliptical second line of this stanza in the standard version that Karma 'Phrin-las uses, Advayavajra in his *Ṭīkā* (fol. 280b) reads:

rlung dang yid ni mi-g.yo brtan-par 'gyur
The biotic force and the egological mind are no longer stirring and stay firmly [rooted].

[109] The same image is used by Saraha in his *Kāyakośa-amṛta-vajragīti*, fol. 84a.

[110] *mnyam-pa/mnyam-nyid*. Identity of self and other or of samsara and nirvana is not the same as a mathematical equation. The Buddhists were fully aware of the problem of identity and difference as discussed by Martin Heidegger in his *Identity and Difference* (New York: Harper & Row, 1974). His statement on 27, "Identity itself speaks out in a pronouncement which rules as follows: thinking and Being belong together in the Same and by virtue of this Same," may, in Saraha's terms, be paraphrased as "I (myself) and Thou (the other) belong together in the Same (*mnyam*) and by virtue of the Same."

[111] The original Apabhraṃśa version of these two lines,

ekku deba bahu āgamẽ dēsaï
appaṇu icchẽ phuḍa paḍihāsaï,

seems to have presented considerable difficulties to the (various) Tibetan translators and interpreters. Thus, Mokṣākaragupta in his *Pañjikā* (fol. 310b) comments on a stanza that reads:

lha gcig-la ni lung-rnams mang-po mthong
rang-'dod-pa-yis so-sor snang

In the one divinity one sees many directives [that]
According to one's liking appear individualized [so as to suit one's taste].

Advaya Avadhūti in his *Ṭīkā* (fol. 127b) reads these lines as:

lha cig-la ni lus-rnams mang-por mthong
rang-'dod-pa-yi mang-po gsal-bar snang

Assuming that in view of the poor spelling in unedited Tibetan texts *lus*, "body," stands for either *lung*, "directive," or *lugs*, "method," this stanza might then be translated as:

In the one divinity one sees many directives/methods [that]
In this multiplicity due to one's liking present themselves clearly.

Karma 'Phrin-las, 119, reads *lhan-cig* instead of *lha gcig* and explains it as Being's possibilizing dynamics (*chos-nyid*), ultimate reality (*don-dam-pa'i bden-pa*), and Being-in-its-beingness that remains conceptually inaccessible (*spros-pa dang bral-ba'i de-kho-na-nyid*). He seems to have followed Advayavajra's *Pañjikā* (fols. 223b–224a), in which Saraha's stanza begins with *lha gcig*, which in his commentary he replaces with *lhan gcig*.

Advayavajra, in his *Ṭīkā* (fol. 281ab), presents a considerably different version:

rtags gcig-la ni lugs-rnams mang-po mthong
'ongs-pa ma-mthong phyis kyang de mthong med
rang-'dod-pa-yis rang-rig gsal-bar smra
rang-bzhin 'jig-cing gzhan dang 'gal-ba yin

In [Being's reality as its own and] single argument [for it] one sees many methods [one may adopt];
[From where] they have come [as objective realities], one does not

see; and even at some later time one will not see them [as objective realities].
[Then there are the Yogācāra philosophers who] by way of their wishful thinking say that this is one's self-knowledge in its clarity.
[This claim, like the preceding one,] collapses because of its own weakness and is at odds with all other arguments.

The use of the term *rtags* (*linga*) is intriguing, because it belongs to the vocabulary of the logicians (Nyāya-Vaiśeṣikas), and Advayavajra's elaboration shows that in all likelihood he was conversant with Uddyotakara's (sixth century) *linga-paramarśa*. For details see Surendranath Dasgupta, *A History of Indian Philosophy*, vol. 1, 351.

[112] The standard Apabhraṃśa version,

appanu nāho aṇṇa biruddho
gharẽ gharẽ so siddhānta pasiddho

which may be translated literally as:

The Ātman [Self/self] is the lord, the other is the opponent.
In each and every house he is famed as an article of faith

has found different translations in the Tibetan tradition. The standard version reads:

mgon-po bdag-nyid gcig-pu gzhan-rnams 'gal
khyim dang khyim-na grub-mtha' de grub-bo

but Advayavajra in his *Ṭīkā* (fol. 281a) reads:

mgon-po bdag-nyid gcig-pu bzhin dang ldan
khyim dang khyim-na grub-mtha' de grub-bo

The problem is with the first line, which Advayavajra explains as meaning that the guardian-lord, the authentic Self alone, "has the face of Being's ownmost dynamics" (*rang-bzhin-gyi bzhin-ldan*). There may be a pun involved with the phrase *rang-bzhin 'jig* (for metrical reasons short for *rang-bzhin-gyis 'jig*) to the effect that the "face" (*bzhin*), the philosophical systems, each in its own (*rang*) way, cannot bear scrutiny. Looking at the guardian-lord is to look into the "face" of Being itself. Even with respect to the second line in this stanza the commentators differ in their interpretation. According to Karma 'Phrin-las, 120, the first time the term "house" (*khyim*) is used it refers to those who have completely wrong notions about the guardian-lord, and the second time the term is used it refers to those who have only a partial understanding of him. According to Advayavajra, the first house refers to the guardian-lord as giving out instructions and the second house to him as experiencing these instructions. From a dynamic perspective, inherent in his way of thinking, not only is Being becoming ever more self-reflexive, so also is the human individual in his co-evolution with his universe. All commentators agree that by the term *guardian-lord* the authentic Self Saraha is meant, and so it refers to himself. Advayavajra further states that the "belief system" through which the authentic Self becomes self-reflexively aware is one that has nothing to do with the ordinary squabbles of affirmation and negation.

113 None of the Tibetan renderings of this line can be said to offer a literal translation of the Apabhraṃśa original:

ekku khāi abara aṇṇa bi polaï.

Advaya Avadhūti in his *Ṭīkā* (fol. 128b) comments on a rendering of *polaï* as *'tshig*, "burnt/consumed by fire." Karma-phrin-las, 120, even has *tshig* instead of *'tshig* and understands this line to mean "by eating this one (belief system) all others are understood to be mere words." Mokṣākaragupta in his *Pañjikā* (fol. 311a) prefers the reading *tshim*, "saturated with," and explains this line to the effect that "one" refers to "consciousness" (as one of the five groupings, *skandha*, into which traditional Buddhism analyzed human existence, but which in later Buddhism was given primary status), "eating" refers to the transmutation of it into the flavor of ecstasy, and the rest of the line as meaning that in the wake of this transmutation all the remaining groupings become saturated with this flavor. However, he is aware of the alternative reading *'tshig* and illustrates the use of this word by saying that when one tree is burning the flames may spread to the other trees in the forest and consume all of them. Advayavajra in his *Ṭīkā* (fol. 281a) reads *tshim-par 'gyur* and then continues to give a slightly enlarged version of this stanza:

nang-gzhag phyi-rol song-nas khyim-bdag tshol
btsal kyang ma-mthong phyis kyang de med de
'dug-par 'gyur kyang de-yis ma-shes-so

Although [the authentic Self as] the master of the house is within [himself in the house] he goes outside to look for him.
Though he may look for him he will not see him, and even at some later time there will be no trace of him [anywhere outside].
Even if he were to sit right there he would not recognize him because of [the mistaken notions heaped upon him by the logicians].

114 The original Apabhraṃśa,

ṇittaraṅga paramesarū ṇikkalaṅka bohijjaï

has enjoyed several different Tibetan translations. One, found in Advaya Avadhūti's *Ṭīkā* (fol. 128a), has served as the version that was commentated upon by Karma 'Phrin-las, 121, and has been translated here. It reads:

rba-rlabs med-pa'i dbang-phyug mchog
rnyog-pa med-pa'i bsam-gtan gyur.

Another version is found in Advayavajra's *Pañjikā* (fol. 224b) and reads:

dba'-rlabs med-pa'i dbang-phyug-mchog
rnyog-pa med-pa bsgom-par bya

The supreme powerful lord [who is like the ocean] without waves
Is [also] to be imaged as being without mud.

Still another version is given by Advayavajra in his *Ṭīkā* (fol. 281b):

rba-rlabs med-pa'i dbang-phyug chen-po mchog
rnyog-pa med-pa'i bsam-gtan ci ma-gzhag

Why should one not place one's meditative concentration [not marred by] the mud [of conceptualization]

Into the supreme powerful lord [who like the ocean] is without
waves?

Mokṣākaragupta in his *Pañjikā* (fol. 311a) does not offer a complete stanza, but after having given its first four syllables merely says: "The rest is easy to understand."

115 Advayavajra in his *Ṭīkā* (fol. 282a) reads this line as:

'gro dang 'ong-ba ro-gcig mi-'dor-ro
[Since whatever] goes or comes is of the same flavor [as Being's
nothingness] it is not to be discarded,

and in (his) *Pañjikā* (fol. 224b) he reads:

'gro dang 'ong-ba mi-'dor-ro
[Whatever] goes and comes is not to be discarded,

and takes this line as an introduction to the following stanza, intimating that the "dancing-girl" is coming and going on her own and is the experiencer's anima (in modern Western Jungian terminology) or *rnal-'byor-ma /yoginī* (in Buddhist terminology).

116 This word, *gang-yang*, is only found in the version(s) on which Advaya Avadhūti (fol. 128b) and Karma 'Phrin-las, 121, wrote their commentaries. As Karma 'Phrin-las points out, this word is meant to introduce the stanza as an illustration of the subject matter of the preceding one.

117 That is, Being-in-its-beingness or, in the traditional diction, nothingness.

118 This rendering is based on the explanation provided by Advayavajra in his *Ṭīkā* (fol. 283a) and by Mokṣākaragupta in his *Pañjikā* (fol. 311b). In Advayavajra's work this line begins with the words *rang-rig gzugs*, while in all other commentaries it begins with the words *rang-gi gzug*, corresponding to the original Apabhraṃśa *appaṇa rūa*.

119 Advayavajra in his *Ṭīkā* (fol. 283a) comments on a version in which these two lines are inverted and then are followed by a lengthy dissertation on the non-concretistic and non-concretizable character of the unity of the composure and post-composure experiences:

de-tshe thams-cad -mkhyen-pa thob-pa ste
dbyer-med ngang-la gzhag-pa thob med kyang
brda'-ru mtshon-nas gzhag dang thob-par smra
smras-pa'i tshig-tu zhog-la de don bsgoms
bsgom-par bya-ba rdul-tsam med-pa ste
med-pa'i ngang-la gzhag-tu med-pa'i ngang
de-la gnas-na rnal-'byor snying-po'i lam
snying-po med-de brjod-pa ma-yin-gyi
dngos dang sems-su shes-shing shes-pa med
med-pa'i rdo-rje de-la 'jug-par bya

Then and there omniscience [the "Buddha"-experience] is gained.
Although in its indivisible dimension there is neither composure
nor post-composure
One metaphorically speaks [of it] in terms of composure and
post-composure—

Let these words be words and [instead] concentrate on what is meant.
But there is not so much as an atom that one could concentrate on.
If you stay in this dimension that is not something that as composure can be put into the dimension of "non-existence"
This is the way of the vitalizing energy in [your] tuning-in to [the dynamics of the whole].
This vitalizing energy is non-existent [as something] and cannot be expressed by word of mouth.
One knows it as the things [of one's world] and as one's mind, but this knowing is not [some representational] knowing.
Get into it [as being] the diamantine force of "non-existence" [that is beyond existence and non-existence].

120 *khyim-bdag*. According to Karma 'Phrin-las this term refers to the subject-object dichotomy such that *khyim* indicates the objective pole and *bdag* the subjective pole in this intentional structure.

121 The rendering of this stanza is based on the Tibetan translation on which Karma 'Phrin-las and Advaya Avadhūti (124 and fols. 128b–129a) wrote their commentaries. The original Apabhraṃśa version,

gharabaï khajjaî gharaṇiĕhi jahi deśahi abiāra,

was rendered into Tibetan as:

khyim-bdag zos-nas khyim-bdag-mo longs-spyod
yul ni gang gang mthong de spyad-par ba

and

khyim-bdag khyim-bdag-mo-yis zos
yul de gang mthong dpyad mi-bya

The country in which one sees the master of the house being devoured by the mistress of the house
Is not to be investigated.

The clue to the solution of the problem posed by these two different translations lies in the attitude of the experiencer to his encounter with the unconscious—a psychic realm that may be either a fearful dimension or the source of the experiencer's creativity. Karma 'Phrin-las, as we have noted, conceives of the master of the house as the subject-object dichotomy that marks our consciousness (and, as the texts imply, is devoured by the unconscious). Advayavajra, who in *Pañjikā* (fol. 225a) comments on the second translation, cautions the experiencer against delving into the unconscious. Advaya Avadhūti in his *Ṭīkā*, however, is not afraid of the unconscious and explains this stanza as meaning that the master of the house, referred to by the code term *dran-pa* (on which see chapter 2) is overcome by the mistress of the house, referred to by the code term *dran-med*, who now can enjoy the three (outer) worlds that are simultaneously (inner) levels and manifestations of *dran-pa*, without fear.

As against these versions there is a third version, which is commented upon by Advayavajra in his *Ṭīkā* (fol. 283b) and by Mokṣākaragupta in his *Pañjikā* (fol. 311b).

The version, fully given in Advayavajra's work, reads:

khyim-bdag dang ni khyim-bdag-mo longs-spyod
yul ni gang mthong-ba de bshad-par bya

The master and the mistress of the house have a good time and
What they see they call it "This."

As Advayavajra explains, this "This" is the "stuff " of which the gestalt is made, in and through which Being's meaningfulness is seen (*chos -sku'i ngo-bo*). In letting the master and the mistress of the house be "together," Advayavajra has captured the spirit of Saraha's claim that the composure and postcomposure experiences are a single experience that is divided into two facets for descriptive purposes only.

122 Although what follows in this section is couched in the traditional terminology, the presentation itself is of enormous complexity. Not only did the Tibetan translators of Saraha's Song have difficulties with the original Apabhraṃśa in which it was composed, but also with its interpretation. From a comparison of the original Apabhraṃśa with the various Tibetan versions it becomes evident that the Apabhraṃśa version has been preserved in a rather fragmentary way. By way of introduction it may suffice to point out that *chos-sku,* intentionally left untranslated and not even given in its Sanskrit equivalent (*dharmakāya*) because of the many misconceptions that have accrued to it in the wake of a still-prevalent reductionism, is an "archetypal image," as defined by Naomi R. Goldenberg, *Changing of the Gods* (Rutland: Charles E. Tuttle, 1962), 64, of tremendous energy that as energy has no gender. Phenomenologically speaking, *sku* is the expression and the expressed ("object" phase) of a perceptual act (the "act" phase in an intentional arch). Because of the experiencer's presence as an embodied being in any perceptual (cognitive) situation he/she cannot but "visualize" this expression of what is his or her own dynamics in an anthropomorphic shape that is immediately meaningful (*chos*). Saraha images this energy as "feminine"—the *yoginī*, the Mother—not so much in the sense of a doctrinally prescribed content of this image, but as the intensity with which this image affects us and which as such mediates between the human level of our experience and the divine realm of our beingness, between the part and the whole that is needed to give meaning to the part(s) that constitute it. Particularly, it is through the image of the feminine that a man can relate to a woman in the physical world and to the realm that is much larger. See also Caitlín Matthews, *The Elements of The Goddess* (Longmead, Shaftesbury, Dorset: Element Books Limited, 1989), 13.

123 Actually Saraha does not speak of five gestalt experiences as intimated by Karma 'Phrin-las, who in his effort to bring out Saraha's emphasis on ecstasy falls into the trap of quantification by representational thought.

124 These two lines are not found in Advayavajra's *Pañjikā*. Karma 'Phrin-las, 124ff., explains the "I" in this stanza as the *chos-sku,* the "play" as the two concretely (materiality-toned) gestalt experiences (*longs-sku* and *sprul-sku*), and the "children" as ordinary persons caught in their belief systems, who become "tired and exhausted" by attempting to reduce what is a deeply moving experience to some triviality. Advayavajra in his *Ṭīkā* (fol. 283a) explains the "I" as "spirituality" (*sems-nyid*) and likens her "play" to the rays of the sun that illumine

what is our phenomenal world, and depicts the "children" as those who have never experienced ecstasy and who "become tired and exhausted" by their being led deeper and deeper into samsara due to their lack of understanding. Mokṣākaragupta in his *Pañjikā* (fol. 312a) explains the "I" as complementarity-in-spontaneity (*lhan-cig skyes-pa*) and the "play" as so many manifestations of it, the "children who have become tired and exhausted" as those who do not understand. It is not without interest to note that "spirituality," a somewhat inadequate rendering of the German word *Geistigkeit*, is feminine in tone, and thus contrasts sharply with the traditional Western notion of the Logos as masculine. As Stephan A. Hoeller, *The Gnostic Jung and the Seven Sermons to the Dead*, 140, points out, Jung defines *Geistigkeit* "as a power that receives and comprehends, and in this sense because of its receptivity is described as feminine," and continues on 142 by saying: ". . . the feminine principle in the sermon is none other than Logos: it is receptive and more importantly comprehending. There can be little doubt, if any: the Sermons present us with . . . a feminine Logos."

Advayavajra in his *Ṭīkā* (fol. 283a) adds two further lines:

me byung-ba ni spra-ba ste
me ni spra-ba-nyid-la 'bar

A fire's origin is tinder,
But the fire itself is the tinder ablaze.

Mokṣākaragupta, in his *Pañjikā* (fol. 312a), gives only the last line of the above.

125 The original Apabhraṃśa version,

māi re para tahi [mooned-i] ki ubajaï bisaria joini-cāra
Oh Mother, where else does such an unusual way [for a] yoginī
come about?

is preserved in three different Tibetan translations. Karma 'Phrin-las, 125, and Advaya Avadhūti in his *Ṭīkā* (fol. 129a) have:

a-ma gzhan-nas bu de skye mi-'gyur
de'i phyir rnal-'byor-spyod-pa dpe dang bral-ba ste.

Here for metrical reasons *rnal-'byor* (*yoga*) is a short form for *rnal-'byor-ma* (*yoginī*), as attested to by the Apabhraṃśa original.

Advayavajra in his *Ṭīkā* (fol. 283a) has:

kye-ma'o gzhan yod ma-yin gzhan ma-yin
rnal-'byor-spyod-pa skye dang bral-ba ste

Hey-ho! [She] is not something other that exists, but [she also] is
not something other [than herself].
The way of the Lady does not come into existence [as something
and by consequence does not pass out of existence].

Mokṣākaragupta's interpretation (*Pañjikā*, fol. 312a), is similar to Advayavajra's, but somehow clarifies the Tibetan difference between *yod*, "to exist," and *yin*, "to be [so and so]":

e-ma gzhan ni yod ma-yin
gzhan yin-nam 'on-te rang yin
rnal-'byor-ma ni dpe dang bral-ba ste

Hey-ho! [She] is not something other that exists,
Is [She] then [herself] something other? No, [She] is herself.
The Lady is without compare.

[126] This rendering is based on the version of Saraha's Song as commentated upon by Karma 'Phrin-las, 126–27., Mokṣākaragupta, *Pañjikā* (fol. 312a), and Advaya Avadhūti, *Ṭīkā* (fol. 129b). This stanza deals primarily with cutting the emotional ties that fasten us to the phenomena of our enworldedness summed up under the two headings of samsara and nirvana. Attachment (*chags*) involves two intensities of joy: ordinary joy (*dga'-ba*) and heightened joy (*mchog-tu dga'-ba*); the attachment-free phase (*chags-bral*) refers to the minimum stimulus energy to excite the experiencer and still have him attached to what he senses; hence its inherent joy, termed *dga'-bral*, is not a joyless phase in the strict sense of the word. After all, nirvana, an approximation-"wholeness," has its joy, even if it cannot be compared with the degrees of intensity with which we respond to things of the world. What actually matters is to gain the joy that is commensurate with the whole that is, if we may still speak about it, joy through and through (*lhan-cig-skyes-pa'i dga'-ba*), ecstasy (*bde-ba chen-po*).

Advayavajra in his *Pañjikā* (fol. 225b) gives a version that corresponds exactly to the Apabhraṃśa original:

ghara-baï so khajjaï sahaje rajjaï rāa-birāa
ṇia pāsa baïṭhṭhi citte bhaṭhṭhi joiṇī mahu paḍihāa

and reads:

bdag-po za-shing lhan-skyes mdzes-par bya
chags dang chags-bral byas-nas gnyug-mar zhugs
gnyug-ma'i drung-gnas sems nyams-pa'i
rnal-'byor-ma ni nga-yis mthong

By eating the master [of the house] the
complementarity-in-spontaneity dynamics [of Being in you] is
to be enhanced in beauty.
Having turned attachment and the attachment-free phase [into a
state of equal flavor] let it enter Being's genuineness.
Next to this genuineness I have seen the lady in whose
Mind the [dichotomic thinking] has deteriorated.

[127] Advayavajra in his *Pañjikā* (fol. 225b) and his *Ṭīkā* (fol. 284a) reads the third line in this stanza as:

phyi-rol-par sems sdug-bsngal 'dzin
The thought of them as external realities is courting frustration.

[128] The *longs-sku* prefigures the psychosocial context in which the experiencer is seeing himself installed. In a certain sense this context is the projected dimension of Being's spirituality as a kind of detour the experiencer must make in order to reach Being's beingness that is not directly accessible to him, while like a beacon light drawing him to his authenticity.

[129] As Mokṣākaragupta in his *Pañjikā* (fol. 313a) points out, these three levels are what is ordinarily called the triad of body, speech, and mind. Through the presence of Being's flawlessness in them, not in the sense of their being containers, but as their organizing and transformative principle, they can and are

made to evolve into their "original" luminosity. With minor changes in the order of words this stanza is found only in Karma 'Phrin-las, 130, and in Advaya Avadhūti's *Ṭīkā* (fol. 129b).

[130] This stanza is found only in Karma 'Phrin-las, 130–31, and in Advaya Avadhūti's *Ṭīkā* (fol. 130a). Other commentators do not quote the full stanza, but seem to have been aware of its content. What is so remarkable about this stanza is Saraha's extension of a binary *thabs/shes-rab* relationship to a ternary relationship including "ecstasy" (*bde-ba*) as the principle that underlies creativity at all levels and whose first manifestation, if we may say so, is Being's complementarity-in-spontaneity principle. Although we may speak of a ternary relationship, it has to be borne in mind that on this strictly experiential level there prevails as yet an undivided reality that in its dynamics is on the verge of giving actuality to what so far were only probabilities. One is the experiencer's operacy or efficacy (*thabs*) that binds him to the phenomenal world (*snang-ba lhan-cig-skyes-pa*), the second is the experiencer's appreciative awareness (*shes-rab*), seemingly "nothing" (*stong-pa*) that binds him to his inner world (*stong-pa lhan-cig-skyes-pa*), and the third is the experiencer's ecstasy (*bde-ba*) that binds him to Being's "unoriginatedness" – the whole does not originate nor does it end (*skye-med lhan-cig-skyes-pa*).On this ternary relationship see also above, note 42.

[131] The idea of a *ngo-bo-nyid-kyi sku*, usually listed at the end of the enumeration of the traditional three *sku* (*chos-sku*, *longs-sku*, and *sprul-sku*) and somehow said to sum them up, has been a stumbling block for all who have tried to reduce it to some objective reality. It should be noted, right at the beginning, that Saraha recognizes five *sku*, and in his discussion of them assigns the *ngo-bo-nyid-kyi sku* a central position such that the following "sequence" results: *chos-sku*, *longs-sku*, *ngo-bo-nyid-kyi sku*, *bde-ba-chen-po'i sku*, and *sprul-sku*. Strictly speaking, there is no sequence. What we have is a mandala, a centered four. The term *ngo-bo-nyid* has been explained in a small work by Padmasambhava, the *Rin-po-che spyi-gnad skyon-sel thig-le kun-gsal-gyi rgyud* (in *rNying-rgyud*, vol. 6, 230–37), 236:

> *dngos-med-pa mi-dmigs-pa kun-'byung-gzhi*
> It has nothing to do with substance, is non-referential, and the
> "ground" of the universe.

Though spoken of as a "ground," it is a ground that is itself not grounded anywhere, and "having nothing to do with substance" in terms of which we tend to deal with the universe, it makes itself come to the fore holistically (*kun-'byung*). As such it is a matrix of intensity, intense matter whose dynamics is described in the *rDzogs-pa-chen-po thig-le gsang-ba de-kho-na-nyid nges-pa'i rgyud* (in *rNying-rgyud*, vol. 5, 515–25), 516 as

> *ngo-bo-nyid-kyi snang-ba-la*
> *ngo-bo-nyid-kyi sku shar-bas*
> *nam-mkha' dang ni nyi-ma bzhin*
>
> In the lighting-up [coming-to-presence] of Being's prime matter
> There has arisen its gestalt –
> Like the sky and the sun.

This stanza occurs also in the *Thig-le kun-gsal chen-po'i rgyud* (in *rNying-rgyud*, vol. 5, 124–289), 127, where in addition the significant statement is made that, though we may speak of a *ngo-bo-nyid-kyi snang-ba* and a *ngo-bo-nyid-kyi sku*, they do not form a duality. The statement on page 132 of the above-mentioned work that "since [Being] has become the 'stuff' (*ngo-bo*) of which all our reality, samsara and nirvana, is made, it is [spoken of] as *ngo-bo-nyid-kyi sku*; since this is an auto-presencing, it is spoken of as *ngo-bo-nyid-kyi snang-ba*" is quoted verbatim by Klong-chen rab-'byams-pa in his *Zab-yang*, vol. 2, 216.

132 This stanza contains a subtle play on words. The Tibetan term *yi-ge* renders Sanskrit *akṣara* (in Apabhraṃśa *akkhara*), which means either a "linguistic symbol" or "imperishable," "indestructible"—a term applied to the syllable *OṂ*, associated by the Śaivas with Śiva in his form of *nādatanu*, "he whose body is sound." In this context the connecting link would be Śiva's sensuously perceived body (*tanu*) and Being's sensuously felt gestalt (*sku*). The above rendering is based on the interpretation given by Karma 'Phrin-las, 131. Mokṣākaragupta in his *Pañjikā* (fol. 313a) explains this stanza as meaning:

> Among all the living beings
> There is none who does not have defining characteristics;
> If his notion of defining characteristics has ceased [to dominate his thinking],
> He will understand all propositions.

He adds another line to the above and interprets the two lines,

> *de-srid yi-ge rab-tu shes*
> *yi-ge-med-pa yi-ge yin,*

to the effect that the word *yi-ge* in the first line means *akṣara* "unchanging bliss," that *yi-ge-med-pa* in the second line means "the nonexistence of dichotomic thinking" and that *yi-ge yin* means "bliss with no dichotomic notions entering."

133 *cig-shos*. Intended is what is otherwise known as the ultimately real, Being's abidingness (*gnas-lugs*)—Karma 'Phrin-las, 132; Mokṣākaragupta in his *Pañjikā* (fol. 313b) explains *cig-shos* as "the gestalt Being's nothingness has assumed" (*stong-gzugs*).

134 The number fourteen is arrived at from adding up the six levels of the world of desires, the four levels of the world of aesthetic forms, and the four levels of the world of no-form. The fourteenth level is the so-called "detection threshold."

135 *sgrub-yig bzhi*. Because of the different translations of the Apabhraṃśa word *paḍhiaü* "to have read" as either *ston* "to teach" (as in Advayavajra's *Pañjikā*, fol. 226b and in his *Ṭīkā*, fol. 285b) or as *bton* "to recite, read aloud" (as in Mokṣākaragupta's *Pañjikā*, fol. 314a and Advaya Avadhūti's *Ṭīkā*, fol. 131a), this line presents considerable difficulties. In the Brahmanical context, as pointed out by Karma 'Phrin-las, 134, the four opening words have first been spoken by Brahma himself and later in the human teacher-disciple context by the teacher. In the original Sanskrit these four opening words are *siddhir astu* and have been incorporated in this form in the Apabhraṃśa text. Their Tibetan translation as *grub-par gyur-cig*, "may the work succeed," bringing out the imperative mood, is recorded in the version of this line as presented in Advayavajra's *Pañjikā* (fol. 226b). In the Buddhist context the four opening words/syllables are *evaṃ mayā*, "thus by me (it has been heard)." They stand at the beginning of the discourses given by the historical Buddha as recorded by

his disciples. The *e* is interpreted according to the rules of Sanskrit as the locative of *a*, the primal sound as well as the first letter in the alphabet.

136 *khu-ba*. This word denotes the "cream" in butter and is used synonymously with *snying-po*, "the quintessence, the best in something." The word also indicates the life-giving force of what is popularly known as the elixir of immortality or, in the interpretation of it by Karma 'Phrin-las and Advaya Avadhūti, the "unoriginated" (*skye-med*), symbolized by the vowel *a*.

137 There is again a subtle play on words involved: *yi-ge*, which means both a "letter" and the "imperishable" (both of which were conceived of as resounding), and *ming* (*nāman*), which means both a "word" and a "name." What Saraha wants to say is, once one has gone to the source and drinks from it, one no longer bothers about by which names the source may be called.

138 The following two stanzas of two lines each have not been preserved in their Apabhraṃśa form and are found only in the version of Saraha's Song that has been commented upon by Karma 'Phrin-las and Advaya Avadhūti. Still another version is found in Mokṣākaragupta's *Pañjikā* (fol. 314b) and Advayavajra's *Ṭīkā* (fol. 286a).

139 Karma 'Phrin-las, 137, explains the "divine" (*lha*) as the *lumen naturale* and the "that does not go wrong" (*zag-med*) as the triune body-speech-mind organization experienced from the viewpoint of Being's nothingness. The version of this stanza as commented upon by Mokṣākaragupta reads:

> *nags khrod gsum na yi-ge gcig*
> *yi-ge gsum-gyi dbus-na lha.*

He expains the *nags khrod gsum*, which literally may mean "three dense forests," as metaphors for the triad of body, speech, and mind, and the *yi-ge gcig* as the resounding letter *a* that is irrepressible. The *yi-ge gsum* in the next line he understands as referring to the transformations of the vibration (*rlung*) in the primary *yi-ge* into the (mystic) syllables *oṃ*, *āḥ*, *hūṃ*. These syllables, as vibrant (sound) patterns, "structure" what becomes one's body, speech, and mind in the form of standing wave patterns, and shape its experience of the "divine" (*lha*) as the "tangible and auditive" presence of Being as formulated nothingness (*stong-gzugs*). In Advayavajra's *Ṭīkā* (fol. 286a) this stanza reads:

> *nags khrod gsum-na yi-ge nag-po gcig*
> *yi-ge gsum-gyi dbus-nas blta-bar bya.*

It will be noted that he does not speak of something "divine" but rather suggests that the experiencer "look for or at" this resounding letter. He explains the phrase *nags khrod gsum* as: *nags*, "forest," stands for the flesh of one's body, *khrod*, "pile," for the bones in one's body, together forming, as we might say, the matter-system for a process structure that is imaginal, in the sense that none of its "three" components (*gsum*)—chreods (*rtsa*), motility (*rlung*), and information (*thig-le*)—are strictly mental-material. The *yi-ge* in this line he explains as the inseparability of ecstasy and Being's nothingness (*bde-stong dbyer-med*), the *nag-po*, "black," as indicative of its invariance (*mi-'gyur-ba*), and the *gcig*, "one," as the singular experience of being spiritually awake (*sangs-rgyas nyag-gcig*). The *yi-ge gsum*, "three resounding letters," indicate the three worlds of desire, aesthetic forms, and no-form as well as the triad of body, speech, and mind.

140 The so-called "third empowerment," the irruption of a pristine aware-

ness mode through the individual's appreciative acumen pushed to its limits (*shes-rab ye-shes*), is the moment of the realization of Being's unoriginatedness (*skye-ba med-pa/ skye-med*), to be "followed up" by the experience of "pure transcendence" ("beyond the scope of the intellect," *blo-las 'das-pa*).

141 The "fourth" joy is wholeness itself—"complementarity-in-spontaneity" as the inseparability of the phenomenal from the noumenal, as we might say. This idea of a "fourth" is a direct continuation of the Upanishadic idea of the *turīya* ("fourth") that is "ecstasy/bliss" or "joy" (*ānanda*), and is of supreme importance in a person's life.

142 A metaphor for the sun. Its association with misery and suffering reflects the scorching heat that only one who has lived in the tropics or subtropics knows.

143 A metaphor for the moon, whose gentle light in the coolness of the night favorably contrasts with the glare and heat of the sun.

144 *'khor-lo*, popularly known by the Sanskrit term *cakra*.

145 *dkyil-'khor*, also popularly known by the Sanskrit term *maṇḍala*.

146 *rang-grol* describes an auto- (*rang-*) emancipatory process (*grol*) for which there is no adequate term in any Western language. *Rang-grol* is a process term involving what Alfred North Whitehead called a "vector feeling-tone" and as such is quite different from a transitive verb (*sgrol-ba*) or an intransitive verb (*'grol-ba*).

147 Advayavajra in his *Ṭīkā* (fol. 228a) sounds a word of caution. A person who has been cured of a disease may say that he has won freedom from (this) disease, but such a statement remains within the framework of objectifying thought and is not the last word in the matter. Freedom/emancipation is a feeling-tone that approximates the ecstasy that is Being-in-its-wholeness.

148 Mokṣākaragupta in his *Pañjikā* (fol. 315b) adds a further line:

> *de-la rtogs-pas ma-'dri zhig*
> If you have understood it don't ask [any further questions].

Advayavajra in his *Pañjikā* (fol. 288b) leaves out this line and lets Saraha's stanza close with the line Mokṣākaragupta added. Advayavajra in his *Ṭīkā* (fol. 289a) combines the "questioning" and the "no-more-questioning" in a single stanza.

149 This rendering is based on the interpretation by Karma 'Phrin-las, 144. According to Advayavajra in his *Pañjikā* (fol. 228b), the lake is a metaphor for ecstasy. Mokṣākaragupta in his *Pañjikā* (fol. 316a) explains this stanza in terms of the imaginal body schema of the experiencer according to which the sky is the "head," the mountain the "body," the drinking of the water the "sensation of (its) vitality," and the shore the "developing lines along which the force of (Being's) genuineness moves."

150 This rendering is based on the Apabhraṃśa version that reads:

> *bisaa-gaenda-karẽ gahia jaṇi māria paḍihai,*

and on Advayavajra's version in his *Pañjikā* (fol. 228b), which, faithfully rendering this line, reads:

> *yul-gyi glang-po'i snas blangs-nas*
> *ji-ltar gsod-pa ltar snang yang.*

However, there seem to have existed different Apabhraṃśa versions that were accordingly translated differently into Tibetan. Thus Advayavajra in his *Ṭīkā* (fol. 289b) replaces *snas* by *lag-pas* and *glang-po* by *dbang-po*, and Advaya Avadhūti in his *Ṭīkā* (fol. 134) inserts *rang-dbang* before *snang*, which both he and Advayavajra render by *snang-bar 'gyur*. These differences may have been the reason that the stanza in Karma 'Phrin-las, 145, reads:

> *yul-gyi glang-po dbang-pos lag-pas blangs-nas-su*
> *glang-po gsod-par rang-dbang snang-bar 'gyur*

which he explains as meaning that

> Once the elephant, living in the jungle of the sensuous objects, has been seized by its trunk by the mahout [holding] in his hand the elephant-hook, which he puts on the elephant's forehead, the mahout seems to be free, should he so desire, to kill the elephant.

Advaya Avadhūti, who also has *rang-dbang*, interprets this stanza as meaning:

> Once the elephant, the sensuous object, has been seized by its trunk
> It seems to [retain its] independence even it it looks as if it had
> been killed.

The point to note is that *lag-pa* (Apabhraṃśa *kara*) means both "hand" and "trunk" and that *dbang-po* means "the sensory apparatus" and also "master."

Mokṣākaragupta in his *Pañjikā* (fol. 316a), does not say anything about the elephant being killed, but seems to have read *khrid-nas ji-ltar skyod-par snang yang* as meaning "being conducted [by the king], seems to move about of its own" (*rang gang-dga'-bar*). All commentators agree that Saraha's use of the image of the elephant likely to run wild again, once its control by the mahout weakens, is to show that a control psychology is of no avail to overcome the frustrations of dichotomic thought.

151 The following three stanzas are not preserved in their Apabhraṃśa version and also are not found in Advayavajra's *Pañjikā*. However, all other commentators quote and elucidate them. Together these three stanzas show that Saraha conceived of the egological mind (*yid*) as a hierarchically organized process structure with each level in this hierarchy having an external and internal aspect, such that what is the internal aspect of one level is the external aspect of the other level.

152 These related statements refer to the early Buddhist realism that analyzed a cognitive situation as consisting of a mind as a substance and the object or the reference of its cognition as another substance. There are, however, as the Buddhists noted, also nonreferential cognitive situations that were, in the wake of the prevailing reductionism in early Buddhist thought, defined as being such that the absence of an external (concretely objectifiable) reference was equal to its nonexistence or nothingness that, in turn, was realistically made into a nothingness-thing.

153 These are the images that the psyche produces and through which the experiencer may directly come into contact with the inner forces in himself that are clothed in these images and as symbols will deeply affect him. In other words, they carry with them a kind of ecstasy, but this ecstasy is not yet pure ecstasy (*bde-ba chen-po*) because the dichotomical thinking (and feeling) that

characterizes the egological mind has not yet been completely transcended and wholeness has not yet been realized.

[154] This idea reminds us of what the ancient Greeks called the Kairos, and of which C. G. Jung wrote: "We are living in what the Greeks called the *καιρός*—the right moment—for a 'metamorphosis of the gods', of the fundamental principles and symbols. This peculiarity of our time, which is certainly not of our conscious choosing, is the expression of the unconscious man within us who is changing" (*The Collected Works of C. G. Jung*, vol. 10, 304). The "unconscious man" has no sexist connotations; rather, like the Buddhists' "authentic self" (*bdag-nyid*) or the "innermost mentor" (*bla-ma, guru*; on its meaning see chapter 2), it intimates the individual's process of unfoldment.

[155] This may be the strongest statement ever made to the effect that we cannot wait for someone to do the job for us. There is no God to redeem mankind—mankind redeems itself.

[156] *byang-chub, bodhi*. Its Tibetan hermeneutical rendering is based on the perception of it as an ontological, not epistemological, concept. For the Buddhists, who emphasize experience and its understanding rather than its explanation, the universe was "intelligent" and "spiritually awake." But these adjectives are not so much descriptions as vector feeling-tones, inseparable from the process itself. The process involves the refinement (*byang*) of one's psyche and through it the realization of wholeness (*chub*).

[157] The transition from *yid* to *sems* is to be noted: *yid* always refers to the individual's more or less "closed" egologically predisposed awareness. Though firmly settled into the "normal" patterns of experiencing its world in terms of an "I" and an "it," it is yet "open" to a wider dimension, of which it gets a glimpse through the feedback link between the "I" and the "Thou." This feedback link carries with it a feeling-for-the-other and thus is the first step in the individual's opening-up. This opening-up points beyond itself and paves the way to an awareness of wholeness that throughout the process has been its guiding force. This opening-up and openness is intimated by the term *sems*.

[158] *sangs-rgyas*, literally meaning "the dissipation [of darkness] and the spreading [of light]," describes the process of an individual's becoming "spiritually awake" (*buddha*). The Western, commonly accepted, notion of what is designated as Buddha or Buddhahood as something static completely misses the process character of Buddhist thought.

[159] This "stuff" is "intense matter," not just "matter" (*ngo-bo*), but rather "intensity" (*nyid*).

[160] With the above two stanzas Saraha links his conclusion with the opening statement about what the quintessence of Buddhism is or should be—the unity, not an abstract synthesis, of the "fullness of Being's nothingness" (*stong*[*-pa*]*-nyid, śūnyatā*) and its "compassionate concern" (*snying-rje, karuṇā*) in full resonance with itself and everything else.

[161] In other words, the belief in a self is tantamount to turning selfishness into an absolute principle.

Notes to "Queen Dohā"

[1] This is the title given to the first canto in Saraha's eight-canto essay by his commentator Karma 'Phrin-las. The term "abidingness" (*gnas-lugs*) is a process word whose meaning is similar to Henri Bergson's idea of duration (*durée*), of which he says in his *Matter and Memory*, 186: "[Duration is] a continuity which is really lived, but artificially decomposed for greater convenience of ordinary knowledge" and "The duration *wherein we see ourselves acting*, and in which it is useful that we should see ourselves, is a duration whose elements are dissociated and juxtaposed. The duration *wherein we act* is a duration wherein our states melt into each other." But, then, the meaning of "abidingness" is also similar to Martin Heidegger's idea of *Dasein*, of which he says, "The being that we ourselves are, the Dasein, cannot at all be *interrogated* as such by the question *What* is this? We gain access to this being only if we ask: *Who* is it? The Dasein is not constituted by whatness but—if we may coin the expression—by *whoness*. The answer does not give a thing, but an I, you, we" (*The Basic Problems of Phenomenology*, Bloomington: Indiana University Press, 1988, 120).

The term *gnas-lugs* in the compound *dngos-po'i gnas-lugs* "the abidingness of the 'concrete' " is found in Saraha's *Kāyakośa-amṛta-vajragīti* (fol. 82a) and in the *Bi-ma snying-thig*, vol. 2, 364. As *dngos-po gshis-kyi gnas-lugs* this term has been frequently used by Padmasambhava (eighth century) and his contemporary Vimalamitra, who in his *rDo-rje rtse-mo 'dus-pa'i rgyud* (456; in *rNying-rgyud*, vol. 5, 441–69), declares that *gnas-lugs* comprises six "aspects": *chos-kyi sku'i gnas-lugs* (Being's abidingness in its gestaltism expressive of its meaningfulness), *rang-byung ye-shes chen-po'i gnas-lugs* (Being's abidingness as a self-originated super-pristine awareness), *sku'i gnas-lugs* (Being's abidingness in our experience of it as a gestalt), *gsung-gi gnas-lugs* (Being's abidingness in our experience of it as an announcement of its presence), *thugs-kyi gnas-lugs* (Being's abidingness in our experience of it as its and our spirituality), and *dbyings-kyi gnas-lugs* (Being's abidingness as a "field"). As a term descriptive of the experience of our existentiality, *gnas-lugs* is frequently found with authors dealing with the question of being—foremost amongst them sGam-po-pa (1079–1153), the initiator of the bKa'-brgyud lineage. Karma 'Phrin-las conceives of *gnas-lugs* as a process described in terms of a starting point (*gzhi*), a way (*lam*), and a goal (destination point, *'bras-bu*) as well as a "whole" in which everything has the flavor of uniqueness, and it is in the light of this "fourfold" that he writes his commentary on Saraha's first canto.

[2] *byang-chub sems-dpa' bde-ba'i mgon-po*. The above rendering reflects the Tibetan translator's understanding of the Sanskrit technical term *bodhisattva*. For details see my "Bodhisattva—The Ethical Phase in Evolution" (in *The Bodhisattva Doctrine in Buddhism*, ed. Leslie S. Kawamura, Waterloo, Ont.: Wilfrid Laurier University Press, 1978, 112–21). "Lord of Ecstasy" is one of the guiding

images that have an enormous impact on the life and, by implication, spiritual development of the holder of such images. As such it is "archetypal" in the ultimate Jungian sense of regulating and stimulating creative imagination (see *The Collected Works of C. G. Jung*, vol. 8, 204–205). In a sense, our word "ecstasy" is a feeble expression to convey the intensity of the experience that is *ek-stasis* in the true sense of the word, a standing (and continuing) outside "one's egologically conditioned self" both in its cognitive ("supracognitive" *rig-pa*) and feeling ("feeling-qua-feeling," not feeling as judgment) qualities. Lest the term "Lord" be theistically misconceived and misrepresented, it must be emphatically stated that *mgon-po* (*nātha*) does not denote a celestial tyrant or dictator, but a protector caring for the helpless. Through this tender guiding image a personal relationship between the experiencer and the forces working in and through him is established. While Saraha speaks of Him as the ecstasy (*bde-ba chen-po*) that as one's valiant mind is the whole of one's psychic potential, Klong-chen rab-'byams-pa speaks of Him as "one's invariant *lumen naturale*" (*'od mi-'gyur-ba*). See, for instance, his *Zab-yang* I, 230.

[3] *rang-bzhin*. On the meaning of this term see chapter 2.

[4] *gnyis-med rang-bzhin*. According to sGam-po-pa, *Collected Works*, vol. *Sa*, fol. 9a, "non-duality" is synonymous with *tha-mal-gyi shes-pa* "the (as yet) undifferentiated psychic potential."

[5] *de-bzhin-nyid-kyi ye-shes*. As the commentator points out, this awareness has a self-reflexive intentionality. In other words, it is an ontological, not epistemological, concept.

[6] It is important to note that Tibetan texts (whether they be translations from Sanskrit, Prakrit, or indigenous works) distinguish between *sems* and *sems-nyid*, a distinction the Sanskrit language is unable to make. While *sems* more or less corresponds to our "mind" or, more precisely, "one's psychic background," *sems-nyid* refers to what for want of a better term I have paraphrased as "Mind as a dynamic principle," in the sense that it makes a "mind" possible, but is not the same as this "mind."

[7] *snying-po*. In the narrower sense, this term refers to the vitalizing dynamics of Being. For details see my "Being's Vitalizing Core Intensity" (in *Journal of Naritasan Institute for Buddhist Studies* 10, 75–112).

[8] *chos 'di thams-cad*. While from the viewpoint of our prevailing "materialistic-realistic" ideology it is permissible to speak of "entities of reality," we should bear in mind that in life we do not deal so much with "things" as with "meanings," and while Buddhism started from a realistic-reductionist premise, in the wake of its growing mentalistic perspective the old term *chos* came to be used in the sense of "meanings in material concreteness." Naturally the old idea of materiality persisted, specifically among Brahmanical philosophers of the Nyāya-Vaiśeṣika persuasion.

[9] *rang-bzhin gnas-su grol-ba*. It has already been pointed out that *grol* is not so much an adjective like our "free," but a verb for which there is no equivalent in any Western language. The term *rang-bzhin gnas*, which occurs again in stanza 31, emphasizes the abidingness (*gnas-lugs*) of Being's ownmost dynamics as a presence (*gnas*).

[10] "Existence" is a free translation of what in the strict sense of the word

means "a particular existent." The stanza is a critique of what C. G. Jung once called the "thingness of thought" that makes us think of things in such a way that we even turn a no-thing into a thing. These extremes, the naive concretism of the realist philosophers (Nyāya-Vaiśeṣika and Hīnayāna Buddhism) and the sophisticated negativism of the Buddhist Madhyamaka system, are, according to the commentator Karma 'Phrin-las, the points where an individual gets stuck on his journey from his as yet unrealized wholeness to his wholeness fully realized, simply because he fails to "see" that the going is the way. The point to note is that the Mahāmudrā way is a spiral movement in which the starting point in its dormant wholeness is formally identical with the goal, which is different in being a vibrant wholeness.

[11] This blunt statement by Saraha is reminiscent of *Īśā-upaniṣad* 9:

> Into a blinding darkness go those who delight in unorigination,
> Into an even greater darkness go those who delight in origination.

[12] "Being's meaning-rich gestalt" (*chos-kyi sku*) is an image through which the experiencer "sees" and "feels" himself as a whole that he cannot but refer to as presenting a "gestalt" (*sku*) that is irreducible to its parts and also cannot be constructed from adding its parts together. Psychologically speaking, this gestalt is the symbolic formulation of the experiencer's authentic Self and has nothing to do with the egological structure hypostatized as self.

[13] Although works like Vasubandhu's *Abhidharmakośa* declare that the three terms *sems*, *yid*, and *rnam-shes* are synonymous, there is a marked difference in the functions they describe. For details see my *From Reductionism to Creativity*. In the present context *yid* seems, for metrical reasons, to stand for *gnyug-ma'i yid*, frequently used by Saraha in his larger *Dohākośa*, nicknamed the "People *Dohā*." The term *gnyug-ma'i yid*, on which see chapter 2, is, according to Karma 'Phrin-las, synonymous with *sems-nyid*, "mind as a dynamic principle." The emphasis is on the immediacy of experience in which all dualities that govern our ordinary mind are suspended. Following the explanation by Karma 'Phrin-las, the above phrase could be paraphrased as "Ask your (subjective) mind in the moment of its experiencing itself in its wholeness about this wholeness."

[14] On this term see chapter 2.

[15] This triad sums up the the individual's progress from the starting point to his/her destination from a spiritual perspective. For this reason I have avoided the mechanistic rendering of *sangs-rgyas* (the Tibetan hermeneutical translation-interpretation of the Sanskrit word *buddha*) by "Buddha(s)," preferably written with a capital letter in order to make sure that there is such a *thing*-Buddha.

[16] *spang-gnyen*, *prahāṇa-pratipakṣa*. This terminology and the notion behind it reflect the old dualistic view of a static cosmos for which opposite notions ("good" and "evil") are sharply separated. From a dynamic perspective, which Saraha espouses, opposite notions are not only complementary to each other but, in addition, point to the common source from which they evolved.

[17] The implication of this key term is that the *ek-stasis* of the immediacy of experience is not some emptiness, but a fullness "fuller than full." sGam-po-pa, *Collected Works*, vol. *Cha*, fol. 11a and elsewhere, has given this idea its classical form:

sems-nyid lhan-cig-skyes-pa chos-kyi sku
snang-ba lhan-cig-skyes-pa chos-sku'i 'od

Mind as a dynamic principle is in its spontaneity [and complementarity to its lighting-up in the phenomenal] Being's meaning-rich gestalt;
The phenomenal is in its spontaneity [and complementarity to the mind] the light of Being's meaning-rich gestalt.

We may compare with sGam-po-pa's famous dictum the words of Mark Johnson, *The Body in the Mind* (Chicago: The University of Chicago Press, 1987), 151:

> We are thus brought to a momentous conclusion about the importance of human imagination, namely, there can be no meaningful experience without imagination, either in its productive or reproductive functions. As productive, imagination gives us the very structure of objectivity. As reproductive, it supplies all of the connections by means of which we achieve coherent, unified, and meaningful experience and understanding.

18 Being's character as a "field" or "expanse" (*dbyings*) where meanings (*chos*) are born provides the coherence of experience of which Mark Johnson (see previous note) has spoken. The relationship between the "(meaning-rich) gestalt'"and the "(meaning-rich) field" can be viewed theoretically as the "gestalt" being the excitation of the "field," in no way independent of it.

19 While the first canto is devoted to "vision" (*lta-ba*) as a deep and deepening understanding of the unity of experience and world, inner life and outer reality, the second canto aims at laying bare and "cutting off" the inveterate tendencies that narrow the "opening of vision" (a phrase coined by David Michael Levin) and, by implication, impoverish us and make us suffer. The indivisible unity of the vision—*dbyer-med* in rNying-ma terminology, emphasizing indivisibility, and *lhan-cig-skyes-pa* in bKa'-brgyud terminology, emphasizing coemergence or togetherness—presents a dynamic tension field such that "vision-proper" stands at one end of the psychic spectrum and what we have called "pitfalls" at the other end, so that "vision-proper" may be said to be "innovative" and the "pitfalls" may be conceived of as attempts (only too often successful) to curtail the scope and to undermine the intensity of the vision. There are three major forces or pitfalls. The first is our addiction (*zhen-pa*) to the status quo presenting a triadic hierarchy of levels: the "physical" marked by our addiction to the sensuous and sensual offered by our senses; the "rational" marked by our addiction to a reductionist view that attempts to explain everything in terms of a naive cause-effect mechanism; and the "spiritual" marked by our addiction to egologically defined images of our fantasy, euphemistically called "meditation." The second major pitfall preventing us from growing into the fullness of being is our ignorance (*mi-shes-pa*) of the vast potential in us and of the interplay of the lower and higher levels of our being, the working of the higher level symbolized by the guiding image of the innermost mentor and the lower level by our stubbornness and unwillingness to learn. The third major pitfall is the most terrifying one: knowingly and willingly rejecting the Being that we are.

20 *rang-bzhin bral-ba'i de-nyid*. The term *rang-bzhin bral* occurs once again in stanza 26. Saraha's thrust is against the reduction of wholeness into some total-

ity from which the one or the other item can be singled out for "meditation" (*sgom*).

[21] Here Saraha uses *yid* in the traditional epistemological sense. Special attention is to be paid to the contrast between *yid* and *sems*—*yid* being our tendency to get involved in lifeless dichotomies at the expense of our vitalizing spirituality (*byang-chub sems*).

[22] *bdud-rtsi*. On the hermeneutical interpretation of this term see my *The Creative Vision*, 157, note 245.

[23] *rig-pa*, short for *rang-rig*, emphasizes the immediate and hence intimate character of knowledge that alone carries with it the sense of certitude and finality.

[24] This is an allusion to popular accounts of the tortures with which denizens of hell must live.

[25] Ever since the time of Plato, "imagination" has been suspected of being a false mode of knowledge quite arbitrarily identified with reason and its epistemological orientation. This view reflects a deep-rooted fear of the creative function of the imagination that manifests itself in symbolic presentations of itself and metaphorical projections, all of which are indispensable for the meaningful structuring of "vision" (*lta-ba*). Imagination as the exploration and cultivation of presences deeply felt and "seen" within ourselves is primarily concerned with the imaginal as contrasted with the conceptual. On the recently rediscovered importance of imagination see Mark Johnson, *The Body in the Mind*, 138–72.

[26] The imaginative process is rooted in what for brevity's sake I have rendered as "our spiritual core," whose dynamics have two aspects. The first aspect is its inner calm (*zhi-gnas*), discussed at length in many Sutras and demanding effort, especially on the part of the beginner, to "get hold of it" (*zin-pa*), and its second aspect is its wider visionary scope (*lhag-mthong*), also discussed at length in many Sutras but demanding no effort, since its "understanding" (*rtogs*) or, more appropriately, "innerstanding," derives directly from its "inner calm." These two "operations"—getting hold of it and understanding it (through itself)—occur on each of the four levels in the hierarchical organization of the psyche, referred to as "external" (*phyi*), "internal" (*nang*), "arcane" (*gsang*), and "just this and nothing else" (*de-kho-na-nyid*). Of these four levels the first three constitute our psychic reality, while the fourth level—if "level" can still be used—is of a higher dimensionality, irreducible to the lower levels that it encompasses and through which it is made apparent or effectual in our life. The so-called external level has two aspects, one referred to as "real in a conventionally accepted sense" (*kun-rdzob*), and the other as "real in an ultimate sense" (*don-dam*). Of these two aspects the first comprises two phases: "aspiration" (*smon*), involving effort in "getting hold of it" (*zin-pa*), and "involvement" (*'jug*), involving "understanding" and imperceptibly fusing with the "real in an ultimate sense."

[27] *dam-pa*. A superior person is an individual through whom, in mythological language, that person's innermost mentor (*bla-ma*) is made apparent in the human world. The text uses the plural, but Karma 'Phrin-las understands it as referring to a single person.

[28] "Sun" is a symbol for the phenomenal, Being's lighting-up (*snang-ba*), and "moon" is a symbol for the noumenal, Being's openness (*stong-pa*). The "center" is a symbol for their ontologically indivisible unity (*zung-'jug, lhan-cig-skyes-pa*). See also stanza no. 21 of the "People *Dohā*."

[29] *sna-rtse*. Literally this term means "tip of the nose." In its technical use, restricted to the "arcane" level in the hierarchical organization of the psyche, its meaning is as above.

[30] There is a double polarity involved. The one is the polarity between the masculine and the feminine, which in the social dimension of humankind is represented by men and women. Although in the present context of the imaginative process psychological forces are intended, they lend themselves easily to the Whiteheadian "misplaced concreteness" in terms of actual men and women. The other polarity is the one between quantity and quality. Quantity is intimated by "intensification" (*tshad*, "measure") in the sense that, to give an example, the "accumulation of merits" (*bsod-nams-kyi tshogs*) is pushed to its limits (*tshad dang ldan-pa*) when the vector momentum (*sna-rtse*) in this accumulation leads this mass into what is termed the "accumulation of awareness" (*ye-shes-kyi tshogs*) that dissolves in an ecstatic intensity that is and can be known only by the experiencer himself (*rang-rig*). Quantification, preceding, as it were, its qualitative assessment, is deemed to be a masculine activity. Quality as a value and function of aliveness (*mtshan*) is associated with the feminine, who puts, figuratively speaking, the final touch on what has been prepared by the masculine. It is not without deeper significance that the term used for this "feminine confirmatory activity" is *phyag-rgya*, short for *phyag-rgya-ma*. This dual male-female, masculine-feminine activity extends over all the four levels of psychic life.

[31] See also stanza no. 22 of the "People *Dohā*."

[32] "Fourfold" not only points to the four levels in the hierarchical organization of the psyche, but, in the context here, to the four confirmations or "seals" (*phyag-rgya bzhi*) and the four "symbol terms" (*brda bzhi*). The four "seals" are:

chos-rgya, summing up the unity of the phenomenal and noumenal (*snang-ba dang stong-pa zung-du 'jug-pa*) and pertaining to the "external";

yes-rgya, summing up the unity of the noumenal and the ecstatic (*stong-pa dang bde-chen zung-du 'jug-pa*) and pertaining to the "arcane";

las-rgya, summing up the unity of the ecstatic and the individual's experienced immediacy of cognition (*bde-chen dang rang-rig zung-du 'jug-pa*) and pertaining to the "internal"; and

phyag-chen, summing up the unity of the individually experienced ecstasy of cognition and the "beyond-the-intellect" (*rang-rig dang blo-'das*) and pertaining to the "just this and nothing else."

The four "symbol terms" are *dran-pa*, *dran-med*, *skye-med*, and *blo-las 'das*, whose meanings and functions have been discussed in detail in chapter 2.

[33] In support of the above, Karma 'Phrin-las, 257, quotes the four stanzas, beginning with the words "Let the elephant of your mind" and ending with "come back [of its own]." See stanzas 125–28 of the "People *Dohā*."

[34] *sems-kyi snying-po*. See also above note 7.

[35] *rdo-rje'i sems*. The qualification by "adamantine" points to what we might

call the "fine-structure" of the mind (*sems, citta*), which, in Buddhist thought, is not so much a state of consciousness, altered or unaltered, but a complex process structure. For details see my *From Reductionism to Creativity*.

[36] That is, to be spiritually awake (*sangs-rgyas*), always conceived of as a dynamic experience.

[37] In support of the above, Karma 'Phrin-las, 259, quotes the lengthy stanza no. 23 in the "People *Dohā*."

[38] *yon-tan*. This term does not so much refer to static properties of Being as to the dynamics in Being that are thoroughly positive.

[39] "Encounter" can be stated simply as our coming-face-to-face with what we really are, which implies that we do not allow ourselves to be trapped in a preconceived end-state that is but a projection of the seeker's preferences. In a sense, encounter is both the strengthening and safeguarding of the fullness of what has been and is being cultivated in self-reflexive imagination (*sgom-pa*), as discussed in the previous canto, and a linking with the fullness of engagement (*spyod-pa*), alluded to by Saraha at the end of this canto and discussed at length in the next canto. sGam-po-pa, *Collected Works*, vol. *Ra*, fol. 11b, discusses five phases in the process of encountering what we really are—an inward movement leading to the disinterested (as Kant would say) but therefore truly ecstatic and all-encompassing experience of bliss supreme. According to sGam-po-pa the five phases with their resultant inner "feelings" are:

1) Encountering the phenomenal as the (projective working of the) mind (*snang-ba sems-su ngo-sprad*), whereby the experience of having lost all interest in the external world as if it were an objective reality, comes about;
2) Encountering the (projective working of the) mind as being an openness/nothingness (*sems stong-par ngo-sprad*), whereby the experience of mind (commonly assumed to be an inner reality) as having no founding or root, comes about;
3) Encountering this openness/nothingness as the *lumen naturale* (*stong-pa 'od-gsal-du ngo-sprad*), by which the experience of Mind-as-a-dynamic-principle (*sems-nyid*) as a steady brilliance (*'od-gsal ma-yengs-pa*), comes about;
4) Encountering the *lumen naturale* as a unifying principle (*'od-gsal zung-'jug-tu ngo-sprad*), whereby the experience of the phenomenal becoming one's friend, comes about; and
5) Encountering this unifying principle as ecstasy (*zung-'jug bde-ba chen-por ngo-sprad*), whereby the experience of (feeling) like brandishing a spear in the unbounded sky comes about.

[40] *brda*. Phenomenologically speaking, this term describes Being as "speaking" or "languaging," and as such corresponds to what Ernst Cassirer has called "expressive meaning" which "cannot be explained by any causal derivation because it must be presupposed by any causal explanation" (*The Philosophy of Symbolic Forms*, New Haven: Yale University Press, 1953–1957, vol. 3, 176). Expressive meaning is a primary phenomenon, an Urphänomenon, a term Cassirer has borrowed from Goethe's *Naturwissenschaftliche Schriften*. Related to this "expressive meaning" is Cassirer's idea of "symbolic pregnance," of which he gives this definition: "By symbolic pregnance we mean the way [*die Art*] in

which a perception as a 'sensory' experience ['*sinnliches*' *Erlebnis*] contains at the same time a certain nonintuitive 'meaning' ['*Sinn*'] which it immediately and concretely represents" (*The Philosophy of Symbolic Forms*, vol. 3, 302).

41 Grammatically the text uses the "dual," but the "singular" is clearly intended. The innermost mentor is Being in its wholeness.

42 That is to say, the "material" entities are the sensory objects with which we deal in the light of what we might "get out of them" for personal gratification; the "immaterial" entities are the same sensory objects but enjoyed in a contemplative mood and with heightened sensibilities.

43 According to Rang-byung rdo-rje, *Zab-mo nang-gi don*, fol. 97a, these forces are:

1) a "root"-force that stands dissociated from conceptual-propositional proliferations (*rtsa-ba spros-bral-gyi thig-le*), which he defines as *yid-med* "without subjectivity";
2) an errancy low-level cognitive force (*'khrul-pa ma-rig-pa'i thig-le*), defined as *yid*, "the individual's subjective mind"; and
3) a force that countermands the latter force (*de'i gnyen-po thig-le*), defined as *dran-pa*, which, in all probability, is meant here as contemplative "inspection."

Whether Rang-byung rdo-rje's interpretation of the three forces of Being was derived from a different version of Saraha's line

thig-le gsum dang yid dran-pa dang dran-med dang,

or whether under his influence other commentaries that are seemingly lost changed Saraha's line into

thig-le gsum dang yid dran-pa dang yid-med cing,

must be left undecided.

The problem is made more complex by the fact that these three forces are related to the "mystical language of the Ḍāka/Ḍākinīs." Karma 'Phrin-las solves this problem by conceiving of Rang-byung rdo-rje's *yid* as implying *dran-pa*, of *dran-pa* as implying *dran-med*, and of *yid-med* as implying both *skye-med* and *blo-'das*.

44 See above, note 38.

45 This statement by Saraha is strikingly similar to Ernst Cassirer's statement concerning the phenomena of spatiality and temporality as exemplifications of the Urphänomenon of meaning in *The Philosophy of Symbolic Forms*, vol. 3, 124:

> What is given here points to a not-here, and what is given now points backwards to a not-now; without this the phenomenon of an intuitive [*anschaulich*, that is, perceived by the senses] world could not be understood or even described.

46 In Buddhist thought and literature a clear distinction is made between *dka'-thub*, literally meaning "that which is difficult to do or achieve" and usually associated with ascetism (*tapas*) and its attendant tolerance of and, often, infliction of suffering (as an imaginary self-improvement by a denial and denigration of the body as if self and body could be neatly separated and compartmentalized), and *brtul-zhugs*, said by Rong-zom Chos-kyi bzang-po in his commentary on Padmasambhava's *Man-ngag lta-ba'i phreng-pa* (see *gSung thor-bu*, 112) to represent *varta* (misspelled as *vartha* by the copyist) and defined as *ngang-tshul*

bsgyur-ba "change of disposition/character/temperament." Karma 'Phrin-las, 270–71, paraphrases Saraha's *brtul-zhugs spyod-pa'i rnal-'byor-pa* to mean: "an eccentric yogi who lives up to his having brought under control (*brtul*) all that does not really matter in life and having set out (*zhugs*) on his journey in the direction of emancipation."

[47] This technical term denotes a sociocultural setting for experiences as well as these experiences themselves that, according to the participating individual's levels of understanding, range from mere group sex to the ecstasy and rapture felt in the union and unity of the "masculine" (*thabs*, introducing divisions where there are none) and the "feminine" (*shes-rab*, restoring the lost unity in a new harmony), which cannot but have a tremendous impact on the experiencer's life-world. Karma 'Phrin-las explains the term *tshogs-kyi 'khor-lo* (*gaṇacakra*) in the following way. The first term in this compound means "crowd" and is here understood as the "unity of *thabs* and *shes-rab*"; the second term literally means "wheel," but is here understood to be a "bioenergetic vortex" that on every level of the multidimensional structure of the living individual checkmates whatever is not in harmony with the organism. See also my *The Creative Vision*, 120.

[48] *brda*. Thereby the masculine or "actional" (*thabs*) is intimated and related to the yogi.

[49] *dam-tshig*. Thereby the feminine or "appreciative" (*shes-rab*) is intimated and related to the yoginī.

[50] The coming-face-to-face with what we really are, outlined in the previous canto, may be said to climax in the searcher's "embodied self-knowledge"—"embodied" in view of the fact that a person's "self-knowledge" never occurs independently of our physical existence through which we find ourselves already in a social context with others, constantly structured and interpreted by our actions, which means that one's "self-knowledge" cannot but be lived in the concrete. In the Western world, two basic models of the sociocultural context are discernible and have been described by Riane Eisler, *The Chalice and the Blade* (San Francisco: Harper SF, 1987), xvii, as "the dominator" model in which one half of humanity is ranked over the other, and "the partnership" model in which the male and female diversity of our species "is not equated with either inferiority or superiority." This distinction is applicable to the East as well, with one remarkable modification—in India the feminine was never completely repressed or excluded, as it was in the West. The gods, whether they be Śiva or Viṣṇu or Brahma, are never without their consorts. The principle of complementarity that underlies such thinking intimates the importance of partnership, without which an individual cannot realize his much needed wholeness and merely stays on in stultifying one-sidedness. Therefore the first step in recovering and reliving wholeness is "to find a partner" (*grogs btsal*), who for a man is a woman, be this a real woman or an anima-figure, although in actual life the "flesh" and the "spirit" are inextricably interwoven, and then "to win the partner's cooperation" by gifts in the sense of "sharing."

It should be noted at the outset that this canto can be read as having two meanings, a literal one and a symbolic one, whose basic unity it is extremely difficult to convey in English or in any other Western language because of their having developed in the direction of placing emphasis on the literal and conceptual at the expense of the imaginal and symbolic. The piquancy of Saraha's presentation lies in the fact that he associates the literalist temperament with the non-Buddhist yogis and the imaginal one with the Buddhist yogis.

51 With this term Karma 'Phrin-las in his commentary indicates a psychic image to highlight the difference between the Śivaite approach that remains within the realm of the searcher's physical reality, and the Buddhist approach that is preeminently psychological without contradicting the sensuous and even sensual character of this image. Closely related to *rig-ma* is *phyag-rgya-ma*. The former term emphasizes the intensity of the ecstatic experience, the latter the impact this experience has on the life of the experiencer.

52 This reference to "low-caste people" (*dman-pa*) is highly revealing. In the Indian context, low-caste people usually lived on the outskirts of settlements and were socially avoided by the upper-caste people. Psychologically speaking, "going into the settlement of low-caste people" means a descent from the crisp, clear heights of consciousness into the murky and often fearful world of the unconscious. In this context the reference to "without fear" gains added significance.

53 As usual, the text is ambivalent. The term *rdzas* is paraphrased by Karma 'Phrin-las as meaning "the objects of sensual pleasures" (*'dod-yon*) and/or "degrees of intensity in the joy one feels" (*dga'-ba*). In modern terms, the Śaivite yogi presses his physical charms on her, the Buddhist yogi shares the joys of togetherness with her.

54 *rigs*. This technical term is extremely rich in meaning depending on the context in which it is used. This context not only involves family relationships and social ranking, but also the various levels in an individual's hierarchical psychophysical organization, usually referred to as the "external," the "internal," and the "arcane" level, as well as the individual's attunement to the dynamics of an all-embracing universe reaching into and patterning the individual as presenting a fivefold (a centered four) of resonance domains or force fields. For further details see chapters 3 and 4. The female partners to whom Saraha refers as playing an important role in this sociospiritual nexus are, by ordinary standards, those who are to be avoided because they are either blood-relations or low-caste and/or outcaste women. But to leave the topic at this point is to overlook the imaginal implications that are inextricably intertwined with the literal. The imaginal, that is, the abundance of images and symbols, demands that it be not identified with or reduced to one particular explanation but prompt the experiencer to drink deep of life and meaning, as explicitly stated in *Hevajratantra* I.v.16–18.

55 *kha-dog*. A living individual is experienced as a complex pattern of interrelated and interacting force fields that vibrate in different frequencies, which in ordinary perception we see as colors, but as a person's aura once our sensibilities have been heightened and our ordinary seeing has become visionary seeing. A highly readable account of the auric phenomenon has been given by David Tansley in his *The Raiment of Light: A Study of the Human Aura* (London: Arkana, 1983).

[56] *gso-ras-kyis 'tsho-ma*. The translation is tentative since the word is not found in any dictionary and also not explained by Karma 'Phrin-las.

[57] *rgyud sbyangs-pa*. "Personality disposition" is a makeshift translation of the term *rgyud* which refers to a human being in his/her psychophysical enframement as a reduction of Being. This reduction allows itself to be "upgraded" into the original wholeness that is Being by cultivating and refining (*sbyong/sbyangs*) the potential.

[58] This term comprises the anatomical-physiological aspects of the female genitals as well as their spiritual aspects that ultimately derive from the *lumen naturale* as intimated by the reference to light. In other words, the "flesh" (the vulva of a woman and the penis of a man) is, in modern terms, the densest level of light energy.

[59] Empowerment(s) (*dbang*) and maturity (*smin*) form an indissoluble unity. Empowerment means the energizing of the potential that is already latently present in an individual, and maturity means the having-come-to-full-bloom of this potential.

[60] *gnyug-ma'i ye-shes phyag-rgya*. While in the preceding stanza Saraha had made reference to so-called Karmamudrā (*las-kyi phyag-rgya*), a concrete woman who can be "manipulated" and who also "manipulates," in this stanza he speaks of the so-called Jñānamudrā (*ye-shes-(kyi) phyag-rgya*), a woman who is simultaneously appreciated and inspiring, a "meaning" (maybe in material concreteness, but not solely material, *chos*). Through her something of Being's openness/nothingness (*stong-nyid*) and Being's genuineness (*gnyug-ma*) is tangibly experienced. In the area of lived experiences the Buddhists have been singularly adept in describing the subtle nuances of Being's nothingness or dynamic fullness.

[61] *btsun-mo'i śukra*. The term *btsun-mo* refers to the cosmic feminine principle in anthropomorphic guise and implies the co-presence of the cosmic male principle. The Sanskrit term *śukra* originally meant "brightness" and was already in Vedic times used as an adjective with *payas*, "fluid," which, under the impact of the then prevailing male-dominated and male-oriented social order, became exclusively associated with the notion of "semen," the generative principle and force that, in Indian-Buddhist thinking, pervades the whole universe, whose dynamics was always considered to be male-female. It may be of interest that the idea of the male and female contributing equally to generation gained credibility in the Western world not before the late seventeenth century. For details of this development see Londa Schiebinger, *The Mind Has No Sex? Women in the Origins of Modern Science* (Cambridge: Harvard University Press, 1989), 178ff. It should be noted, however, that in spite of these seemingly gross physicosexual overtones the psychic (psychological) implications were never lost sight of. Thus, Mokṣākaragupta, commenting in his *Pañjikā* (fol. 298b) on stanza no. 20 of Saraha's "People *Dohā*," remarks that "eating" means "the experience of pleasure" (*bde-ba*), "drinking" means "the experience of rapture" (*śukra*), and "copulating" means the "warmth" (*drod-pa*) that comes in the wake of intraorganismic anabolic and catabolic processes. In view of Saraha's reservation about the Karmamudrā as a Brahmanical oversexed yogi's sole concern and his own high esteem for the Lady/Goddess, we may ask ourselves if under the symbol of a brilliant fluid (*śukra payas*) not another symbolic meaning lies concealed—

payas also means "milk" and the compound *payodhara* means both a "cloud" and a woman's "breast"; both rain and milk are nourishments, the one for the earth and the other for a child. As to the latter, Erich Neumann (*The Child*, 37) declares:

> It is neither a wild exaggeration nor a materialistic concretization to say that the "milk" of the Great Mother encompasses the supreme symbol, the "milk of Sophia" which feeds the philosopher; such a statement merely expresses and draws the implications of a symbolic reality, valid for all levels of life, namely, that all individual beings and things are nurtured by the Great Mother of Life, without whose *flowing* [italics added] abundance all existence must languish.

62 The sky is a symbol for the dynamic openness/nothingness of Being.

63 See above note 46 for the term *brtul-zhugs spyod-pa*. According to Karma 'Phrin-las, 281, what now follows in Saraha's canto refers to this type of yogi.

64 There is a subtle play of words involved. The term *don* has many meanings according to the context in which it is used. In the context of business it means any item for sale and its price and, in ancient India as in the modern world, people look for bargains by comparing the quality and the price of the item for sale. In the context of experience it means that which is valuable, and so the experiencer, too, looks for reliability and is not satisfied with the pseudovaluable, but goes for the "really real" (*don-nyid*).

65 Karma 'Phrin-las, 282, merely states that the lamps mean the "five kinds of flesh (*sha*)" and their brightness the "five kinds of nectar (*bdud-rtsi*)." "Flesh" and "nectar" are symbols, too; both are, as Jung says, "the sensuously perceptible expression of an inner experience" (*C. G. Jung Letters*, vol. 1, 59). Without going into details, the "five kinds of flesh" reflect the fivefold character of the human body as an energy field that is experienced as being simultaneously "physical-material" and "psychic-nonmaterial." The "five kinds of nectar" reflect the "spiritual" in the fivefold "material." As to the "connection" between the lamps and the flesh, so familiar to the Buddhists, it may not be out of place to point out that the idea of the "radiance of the flesh" in the Western world was first put forward by Maurice Merleau-Ponty, who stated, "all flesh, and even that of the world, radiates beyond itself" (*The Primacy of Perception*, 186). The contrast between two different perspectives on life, as already intimated in the preceding stanza, is here still more poignantly expressed by Saraha's comparison of the yogi's aliveness with the inertness of the corpses amongst which he stays.

66 The symbolic significance of the dress items and the accessories has been elaborated in *Hevajratantra* I.vi.2-4a; 17 and II.vi.12 and 14. For further details see also my *The Creative Vision*, 87–95.

67 According to Karma 'Phrin-las this phrase refers to the behavior of a small child, frequently used to describe higher mystic experiences.

68 The text itself has no corresponding noun, which is supplied by Karma 'Phrin-las, who states that this last stanza deals with what is technically known as *gsang-chen spyod-pa*. There is thus a triarchic aspect to an individual's sociocultural being-in-the-world. The first type of individual, the "companionable" one, tries to find spiritual fulfilment through "inspiration" from without; the second type, the "solitary" and by ordinary standards "eccentric" one, tries to find it by exploring his inner world and living the images it provides; the third type,

the "mystic," who does not fit into either category, finds it by being in the world but not of it. The ideal, however, is not to proceed from one level to a next "higher" one, but to harmonize them all and to live them at the same time.

[69] *bla-ma dam-pa*. The "innermost mentor" is a guidance image of the highest order in the life of a person. Its multiple aspects have been described by Saraha in five images, each of which has its own "symbolic pregnance."

[70] In Indian myth and folklore the goose (*haṃsa*) is known for its intelligence. It separates milk from water and only drinks the milk.

[71] Without Karma 'Phrin-las's commentary this line would be quite unintelligible. The dual aspect of phenomenal reality is referred to by the technical term *snang-srid*, which means Being's "lighting-up" or "coming-to-presence" (*snang*), and its "interpretation" (*srid*), the possible meanings the phenomenon may have for the experiencer. The "phenomenon" and its "interpretation" do not constitute a sequence, but "co-emerge in experience as indivisible" (*lhan-cig-skyes-pa*).

[72] *chos-sku*. This highly technical term is descriptive of an experiential process. It does not refer to a "thing" or some merely postulated "objective" reality, be this, in philosophical language, termed objective or subjective idealism. Being's meaningfulness, which has been an incontestible fact for the Buddhists, crystallizes in the experiencer into a meaningfulness that is his/her humanity.

[73] This and the following paragraph refer to the innermost mentor's announcement of himself (*gsung*) and his speaking, in the voice of silence, *to* the experiencer *through* the experiencer.

[74] This paragraph refers to the innermost mentor's presence, sensuously felt by the experiencer as a gestalt (*sku*).

[75] *rdo-rje slob-dpon*. This technical term indicates the link between the disciple and his teacher. The adamantine instructor is the quintessential embodiment of the innermost mentor's spirituality (*thugs*) and compassionate concern (*thugs-rje*), indicated by this and the following paragraph.

[76] The use of the term "culmination" for *'bras-bu* rather than the older and more customary "goal" reflects an attempt to avoid the rather static connotation of the latter term. In the Buddhist sense, culmination is both the perennial search for authentic self-realization "within" and the activation of this realization in the "without." It never means a passive dissolution in a sterile absolute.

[77] *rtogs*. Karma 'Phrin-las, 294, elaborates this verb as meaning *sor-rtogs* = *so-sor rtogs-(pa'i ye-shes)*, which is one of the five *ye-shes* and here closely linked to *mnyam-pa-nyid* (*mnyam-pa-nyid-kyi ye-shes*). See also figure 1 in chapter 3.

[78] *thabs dang shes-rab rang-bzhin mnyam-pa-nyid rtogs-nas*. The above rendering attempts to convey something of what only immediate experience and continued contemplation can convey. The construction of the sentence presents a sequence of "codes" in the order in which the items they denote occur and are connected in immediate experience. Thus, the experienced unity of *thabs* and *shes-rab* is their experienced ownmost dynamics, which, in turn, are experienced as Being's self-consistency. Although in ordinary parlance *mnyam/mnyam-pa* means "alike" or "same," in its technical use it means "the principle (*nyid*) of self-consistency (*mnyam-pa*)" that states that whatever comes into existence or

operation must be consistent with itself and with everything else. It does not indicate a mathematical equation.

[79] The *lumen naturale* (*'od-gsal*) is the irruption or symmetrical transformation of Being's "virtual" light (*'od*) into the brilliance (*gsal*) of Dasein (*rang-bzhin*).

[80] *dngos-grub*. Traditionally two kinds of achievements have been distinguished: ordinary or worldly (*thun-mong*) and supraworldly (*'jig-rten-las 'das*). What is understood by these terms varies in each case, however. According to Klong-chen rab-'byams-pa, *Bla-ma yang-tig*, part 2, 219–20, ordinary achievements have a markedly social character, modalities of concerned action; supraworldly achievements are "spiritual" in the sense of being expressions of a fully integrated personality.

[81] See also above, note 75. Over and above him is the innermost mentor (*bla-ma*) who is the indivisible wholeness of Being, enframed, as it were, in the continuity of our own being (*rang-gi rgyud*), thus guaranteeing our movement in the direction of openness and wholeness. The difference between the *bla-ma* and the *rdo-rje slob-dpon* is an ontological one that can only be understood in an experience grounded in the very openness of Being. (It is not too much to say that the association—if not identification—of the *rdo-rje slob-dpon* with a particular person is a prime example of what Alfred North Whitehead has called "misplaced concreteness.") This difference has been indicated by Karma 'Phrin-las by introducing the following line in the above stanza with the words *de-bas kyang che* "over and above" and then speaking of this higher or highest level as Mahāmudrā/innermost mentor.

[82] *mthar-thug-gi 'bras-bu*. "End" is here understood as a "new beginning"—the world of the spirit is built "anew."

[83] *bde-bar gshegs-pa*. This term emphasizes the feeling-tone in what is the experience of wholeness "projected" as a guiding image, otherwise termed innermost mentor. Synonymous with *bde-bar gshegs-pa* is *de-bzhin gshegs-pa* "He-who-has-passed-into-the-beingness-of-Being," emphasizing the rational (reductionistic) aspect of the experience of wholeness.

[84] The same phrase occurs in the invocation. See note 2 above. There is a subtle play of words and ideas. In the invocation "Lord of Ecstasy" refers to the innermost mentor; here this term refers to Saraha himself as the "advocate of ecstasy."

[85] I have intentionally left these technical terms untranslated and without Sanskrit equivalents, because of the many misconceptions that have accrued to them due to the fact that in the prevailing climate of reductionism their character as symbol has been deliberately ignored. An honest assessment of each of these terms would easily fill many volumes. Saraha is unique in speaking of five *sku* instead of the traditional three or four. First of all it has to be noted that *sku* is a generic term for experienced forms in which the qualities and functions of the wholeness that is Being become expressed and to whose open possibilities the experiencer remains sensitively aware. In other words, each *sku* is the expression and the expressed of a pristine awareness (*ye-shes*) that is primary and constitutive of what is a human being. These forms are "gestalt experiences" that as guiding images act as "normative forecasts" (to use a term coined by Erich Jantsch). Because of their openness they preclude any foreclosure and

hence are not categories of representational (discursive-analytical) thinking. Yet, because of the presence of our "body" (*lus*) in all our experiences, it itself is formative in the sense that it shapes the experience in its "image" as a distinct gestalt (*sku*). The *chos-sku* is of primary importance in being the gestalt experience of our spirituality (*Geistigkeit*) as the matrix of all experiences. As a "matrix" the *chos-sku* is distinctly feminine, and Saraha even speaks of "it" as "mother" and addresses "it" as "sweetheart" (*grogs-mo*). See stanza 107 of the "People *Dohā*." This spiritual principle allows itself to be assessed in terms of presenting the "stuff" that the universe and this principle itself is made of—energy-"stuff," as we might say, termed in this perspective *ngo-bo-nyid-kyi sku*. It also allows itself to be assessed in terms of its feeling-tone, in which case it is known as *bde-ba chen-po'i sku*. There is an inner connectedness of these three facets in what is a unitary experience: as a dynamic principle our spirituality (*chos-sku*) is inseparable from the operational field that is the whole of Being or the energy-"stuff" (*ngo-bo-nyid-kyi sku*) as its gestalt experience, as well as from its feeling-tone gestalt experience or ecstasy (*bde-ba chen-po'i sku*) that provides and ensures the much-needed fluidity and flexibility in the individual's development by giving it a kind of direction.

The *longs-sku* (short for *longs-spyod rdzogs-pa'i sku*) refers to the gestalt experience of the individual's "sociality" as elucidated in the Western context by Calvin O. Schrag, *Experience and Being*, 186:

> There is a sociality of situation which precedes objectifying distinctions and which antedates the methodological scaffolding of the social sciences. This sociality of situation is my situation as lived through with the other. It is the situation of awareness and action in which meanings contributed by the other both limit and enrich my own existence as a project of meaning.

Lastly, the *sprul-sku* is the experience of the other as a guiding image in its concreteness that retains its gestalt character.

[86] The first three "gestalts" (*chos-sku*, *ngo-bo-nyid-kyi sku*, and *bde-ba chen-po'i sku*) are the "cause," the two remaining "gestalts" (*longs-sku* and *sprul-sku*) are the "effect."

[87] *kun-gyi bdag*. "Authentic Self" is a term borrowed from Heidegger and succinctly stated by David Michael Levin, *The Body's Recollection of Being* (London: Routledge & Kegan Paul, 1985), 6, to be "that implicit dimension of our existence which is always and already enjoying a primordial attunement to Being-as-a-whole." Note Levin's terms "dimension" and "enjoying," which aptly fit into the Buddhist conception of *longs-sku* as stated above.

[88] These are the *longs-sku* and *sprul-sku*.

[89] *bsgom*. The traditional rendering of this term by "meditation" fails to convey the self-reflexive character of the process—self-reflexive in the sense that it does not end up with something labeled as either "objective" or "subjective."

[90] The text has only *sems*, but Karma 'Phrin-las, 304, paraphrases it by *gnyug-ma'i sems* to emphasize that this "mind" has nothing egological about it.

[91] *lha-rdzas*. That is, Being's nothingness has become a tangible reality.

[92] That is to say, all these tangible realities are Being's nothingness.

[93] *bcos-ma'i spyod-pa*. The term "inauthentic" as a rendering of *bcos-ma*, literally meaning "artificial," "contrived," "insincere," has been chosen in order to

emphasize the conformist's conduct. A conformist merely behaves and cannot be held responsible for his actions.

[94] *snying-po'i sems*. This is a key term in works dealing with inner experiences. Related to *snying-ga*, "heart," *snying-po* denotes, figuratively speaking, the "heart-felt" energy of Being-as-a-whole.

[95] *bskyed-rim*. This is basically an exercise in effecting a transformative vision through which the world, including ourselves, is symbolically re-created. For details see my *The Creative Vision*.

[96] *brtul-zhugs spyod-pa*. See also above note 46.

[97] They are: the science of healing, the science of language, the science of good reasoning, the science of dialectics, and the science of mechanics.

[98] Traditionally, ten spiritual levels were recognized. They were augmented by the two preparatory ways of a "build-up phase" and a "probability-of-a-breakthrough phase" (for details see my *From Reductionism to Creativity*, 151–65), each conceived of as a specific level, and a third level, the "Buddha"-experience. Ecstasy is a supraordinate level and hence counted as a fourteenth level.

Notes to "King Dohā"

[1] The rendering of the Sanskrit term *caryā* (*spyod-pa*) by "human action" in the title is prompted by the following consideration. The noun *caryā* is related to the verb *carati*, "to go about (one's way)," which in the Buddhist context has the connotation of "setting an example" by acting in such a way that concern for the other is uppermost. This concern is technically known as *karuṇā* (*snying-rje*), usually rendered as "compassion." The word *karuṇā* derives from the same root, *kṛ*, as the word *karma*(*n*), which describes a person's blundering through life. By contrast, *karuṇā* is always "concerned" action—"operacy" (*upāya* , *thabs*), inspired, so to speak, by an appreciative awareness (*prajñā*, *shes-rab*) that is truly "open" (*śūnya/śūnyatā*, *stong-* [*pa*]/*stong-nyid*). This is reflected in the dual complementarity of *śūnyatā-karuṇā* and *prajñā-upāya*. This Buddhist insight of their forming a complementarity-in-interaction—where interaction is lacking, a person has lost or does not come up to his/her humanity—is probably the strongest indictment against the still-fashionable behaviorism, reductionism pushed to its limits.

[2] *rgyal-ba'i phun-sum-tshogs*. As a concession to popular taste I have retained the term "Buddha" for the Tibetan term *rgyal-ba*, which, like its Sanskrit equivalent *jina*, literally means "victor" in a spiritual sense—"he who has won the victory over the deadening forces of the world." The term *phun-sum-tshogs* refers to hierarchically organized dimensions, each of them forming a mandala with (1) a center who is the "teacher," (2) a periphery that is the "audience," (3) a meaning that is the "teaching," (4) a space that is specific to the mandala under consideration, and (5) a time that, too, is specific to the particular mandala.

[3] See also note 2 above.

[4] These are the mudrās discussed in chapter 2.

[5] On the precise meaning of *dran-pa* and *dran-med* see chapter 2.

[6] Saraha here uses the conventional term *bsam-gtan* (*dhyāna*) but infuses it with a new meaning.

[7] There is a deeper meaning to this stanza. Saraha uses *bdag-nyid*, "the authentic or individuated Self," for what is here rendered "It" in an attempt to link it up with the *bsam-gtan* in the preceding stanza, intimating the mind's self-reflexivity. Saraha here speaks from wholeness deeply felt and understood, and at the danger of being misunderstood by those engrossed in pathological egomania, we might paraphrase Saraha's exultant utterance by saying "all this is Me, the authentic Self."

[8] These are the traditional *longs-sku* (*sambhogakāya*) and *sprul-sku* (*nirmāṇakāya*).

Bibliography & Index

Selected Bibliography

A. WORKS IN WESTERN LANGUAGES

BACHELARD, Gaston. *The Psychoanalysis of Fire*. Boston: Beacon Press, 1964.

BAGCHI, P. C. *Dohakosa*. Calcutta Sanskrit Series, no. 25c. Calcutta, 1938.

BATESON, Gregory. *Mind and Nature: A Necessary Unity*. New York: E. P. Dutton, 1979.

BERGSON, Henri. *Matter and Memory*. New York: Zone Books, 1988.

BOHM, David. *Wholeness and the Implicate Order*. London and Boston: Routledge & Kegan Paul, 1980.

CARR, B.J., and M.J. REES. "The Anthropic Principle and the Structure of the Physical World," *Nature* 278, 605 (April, 1979).

CASSIRER, Ernst. *The Philosophy of Symbolic Forms*, 3 vols. New Haven & London: Yale University Press, 1953–1957.

CHANDRA, Lokesh, ed. *mKhas-pa'i dga'-ston*. New Delhi: International Academy of Indian Culture, 1959.

CONZE, Edward, I.B. HORNER, David SNELLGROVE, and Arthur WALEY, eds. *Buddhist Texts through the Ages*. Oxford: Bruno Cassirer, 1954 (reprint, New York: Harper & Row, 1964).

DASGUPTA, Surendra Nath. *A History of Indian Philosophy*. Delhi: Motilal Banarsidass, 1975.

de BONO, Edward. *I Am Right—You Are Wrong*. New York: Viking Penguin Inc., 1990.

ECO, Umberto. *Art and Beauty in the Middle Ages*. New Haven and London: Yale University Press, 1986.

EISLER, Riane. *The Chalice and the Blade*. San Francisco: Harper & Row, 1987.

GADON, Elinor W. *The Once and Future Goddess*. San Francisco: Harper & Row, 1989.

GETTY, Alice. *The Gods of Northern Buddhism*. Rutland: Charles E. Tuttle, 1962.

GOLDENBERG, Naomi R. *Changing of the Gods*. Rutland: Charles E. Tuttle, 1962.

GORDON, Antoinette K. *The Iconography of Tibetan Lamaism*. New York: Columbia University Press 1939; rev.ed., Rutland, Vt.: Charles E. Tuttle Co., 1959.

GUENTHER, Herbert V. *The Life and Teaching of Nāropa*. Oxford: Oxford University Press, 1963.

______. *The Royal Song of Saraha*. Seattle: University of Washington Press, 1969; Berkeley and London: Shambhala Publications, pbk. 1973.

______. "Bodhisattva—The Ethical Phase in Evolution," in Leslie S. Kawamura, ed. *The Bodhisattva Doctrine in Buddhism*. Waterloo, Ont.: Wilfrid Laurier University Press, 1978.

______. *Matrix of Mystery*. Boulder and London: Shambhala, 1984.

______."Being's Vitalizing Core Intensity," *Journal of Naritasan Institute for Buddhist Studies* 10, 1987.

______. *The Creative Vision*. Novato, CA: Lotsawa, 1987.

______. *From Reductionism to Creativity: rDzogs-chen and the New Sciences of Mind*. Boston and Shaftesbury: Shambhala, 1989.

______. *Meditation Differently*. Delhi: Motilal Banarsidass, 1992.

HEIDEGGER, Martin. *Identity and Difference*. New York: Harper & Row, 1974.

______. *Early Greek Thinking: The Dawn of Western Philosophy*. New York: Harper & Row, 1975.

______. *The Basic Problems of Phenomenology*. Bloomington and Indianapolis: Indiana University Press, 1988.

HOELLER, Stephan A. *The Gnostic Jung and the Seven Sermons to the Dead*. Wheaton, IL: The Theosophical Publishing House, 1985.

JANTSCH, Erich. *Design for Evolution*. New York: George Braziller, 1975.

______. *The Self-organizing Universe*. Oxford: Pergamon Press, 1980.

______ and Conrad H. WADDINGTON, eds. *Evolution and Consciousness*. Reading, MA: Addison-Wesley, 1976.

JOHARI, Harish. *Chakras: Energy Centers of Transformation*. Rochester, VT: Destiny Books, 1987.

JOHNSON, Mark. *The Body in the Mind: The Bodily Basis of Meaning, Imagination, and Reason*. Chicago and London: The University of Chicago Press, 1987.

JOHNSON, Robert A. *Inner Work*. San Francisco: Harper SF, 1989.

JUNG, Carl Gustav. *C. G. Jung Letters, Volume 1: 1906–1950*. Selected and edited by Gerhard Adler in collaboration with Aniela Jaffé. Translated by R. F. C. Hull. London: Routledge & Kegan Paul, 1973.

———. *The Collected Works of Carl Gustav Jung*, 20 vols. Translated by R. F. C. Hull. Bollingen Series 20. New York: Pantheon Books, 1957–1970.

———. *Memories, Dreams, Reflections*. Recorded and edited by Aniela Jaffé, translated by Richard and Clara Winston. New York: Vintage Books, 1961.

KAUFMANN, Walter. *Critique of Religion and Philosophy*. London: Faber and Faber, 1958.

LAUGHLIN, Charles D. Jr., John MCMANUS, and Eugene G. D'AQUILI. *Brain, Symbol and Experience*. Boston: Shambhala, 1990.

LEVIN, David Michael. *The Body's Recollection of Being*. London: Routledge & Kegan Paul, 1985.

———. *The Opening of Vision*. New York and London: Routledge, 1988.

MACLEAN, Paul D. "A Triune Concept of the Brain and Behavior," in T. Boag and D. Campbell, eds., *The Hincks Memorial Lectures*. Toronto: University of Toronto Press, 1973.

MATTHEWS, Caitlín. *The Elements of The Goddess*. Longmead, Shaftesbury, Dorset: Element Books Limited, 1989.

MERLEAU-PONTY, Maurice. *Phenomenology of Perception*. London: Routledge & Kegan Paul, 1962.

———. *The Primacy of Perception*. Evanston: Northwestern University Press, 1964.

MINDELL, Arnold. *Dreambody: The Body's Role in Revealing the Self*. Santa Monica: Sigo Press, 1982.

MOTOYAMA, Hiroshi. *Theories of the Chakras: Bridge to Higher Consciousness*. Wheaton: The Theosophical Publishing House, 1981.

NEUMANN, Erich. *The Child*. Boston: Shambhala, 1990.

ROERICH, George N. *The Blue Annals*. Calcutta: Royal Asiatic Society of Bengal, 1949, 1953.

RYLE, Gilbert. *Dilemmas*. Cambridge: Cambridge University Press, 1954.

SCHIEBINGER, Londa. *The Mind Has No Sex? Women in the Origins of Modern Science*. Cambridge: Harvard University Press, 1989.

SHAHIDULLAH, M. *Les Chants Mystiques de Kāṇha et de Saraha. Les Dohā-koṣa (en apabhraṃśa, avec les versions tibétaines) et Les Caryā (en vieux-bengali) avec introduction, vocabulaires et notes.* Paris: Adrien-Maisonneuve, 1928.

SCHRAG, Calvin O. *Experience and Being.* Evanston: Northwestern University Press, 1969.

SHELDRAKE, Rupert. *The Presence of the Past.* Times Book, 1988.

SINGER, June. *Androgyny: The Opposites Within.* Boston: Sigo Press, 1989.

SMITH, Fritz Frederick. *Inner Bridges: A Guide to Energy Movement and Body Structure.* Atlanta: Humanics New Age, 1986.

SPENSER-BROWN, G. *Laws of Form.* London: Allen & Unwin, 1969.

TANSLEY, David. *The Raiment of Light: A Study of the Human Aura.* London: Arkana, 1983.

TEILHARD de CHARDIN, Pierre. *The Phenomenon of Man.* New York: Harper & Row, 1959.

VIRA, Raghu, and Lokesh CHANDRA. *A New Tibeto-Mongol Pantheon,* vol. 21, Śata-piṭaka Series of Indo-Asian Literatures, New Delhi: International Academy of Indian Culture, 1961.

VON FRANZ, Marie-Louise. *On Dreams and Death.* Boston: Shambhala, 1986.

WALKER, Benjamin. *Gnosticism.* Wellingborough, Northamptonshire: Crucible, 1989.

WHITEHEAD, Alfred North. *Process and Reality.* New York: Harper Torchbooks, 1960.

WHITMONT, Edward C. *The Symbolic Quest.* New York: Putnam, 1969.

ZANER, Richard M. *The Problem of Embodiment.* The Hague: Martinus Nijhoff, 1964.

B. TEXTS AND EDITIONS

TIBETAN

Abhayaśrī. *Grub-thob brgyad-cu-rtsa-bzhi'i rtogs-pa'i snying-po rdo-rje'i glu (Grub-thob brgyad-cu-rtsa-bzhi'i dohā).* See Gyaltsen, N. & N. Lungtok, eds.

Advaya Avadhūti. *Dohā mdzod-kyi snying-po don-gyi glu'i 'grel-pa (Dohākośa-hṛdaya-artha-gīti-ṭīkā)*. bsTan-'gyur, Peking ed.: vol. *Tsi*, fols. 97a–138a.

Advayavajra. *Do-hā mdzod-kyi dka'-'grel (Dohākośa-pañjikā)*. bsTan-'gyur, Peking ed.: vol. *Mi*, fols. 199a–231a.

______. *Mi-zad-pa'i gter-mdzod yongs-su gang-ba'i glu zhes-bya-ba gnyug-ma'i de-nyid rab-tu ston-pa'i rgya-cher bshad-pa (Dohānidhi-kośa paripūrṇa-gīti nāma nijatattva-prakāśa-ṭīkā)*. bsTan-'gyur, Peking ed.: vol. *Mi*, fols. 231a–295b.

rGod-kyi ldem-'phru-can. *(rDzogs-pa chen-po) dGongs-pa zang-thal*. 5 vols. (Reproduced from prints of the A-'dzom Chos-sgar blocks). Leh: Pema Choden, 1973.

sGam-po-pa (Dvags-po lha-rje bSod-nams rin-chen). *Collected Works*. Ri-bo-shanti, n. d.

GYALTSEN, N. and N. Lungtok, eds. *'Phags-yul grub-chen brgyad-cu'i rnam-thar*. 1970.

'Jam-mgon Kong-sprul Blo-gros mtha'-yas. *gDams-ngag-mdzod*. 11 vols. (Reproduced from a xylographic print from the dPal-spungs blocks). Delhi: N. Lungtok and N. Gyaltsan, 1971.

Karma-'Phrin-las. *Dohā skor-gsum-gyi ṭīkā 'bring-po sems-kyi rnam-thar ston-pa'i me-long*. (Reproduced from rare manuscripts preserved at O-rgyan-chos-gling in Bum-thang). Thimphu, Bhutan: Druk Sherig Press, 1984.

Khrag-thung Rol-pa'i rdo-rje. *Dag-snang ye-shes dra-ba-las gNas-lugs rang-byung-gi rgyud rdo-rje'i snying-po*, n. p., n. d.

Klong-chen rab-'byams-pa. *Bla-ma yang-tig*. Reprint of the Derge edition, New Delhi, 1970.

______. *mKha'-'gro yang-tig*. Reprint of the Derge edition, New Delhi, 1971.

______. *mKha'-snying* (= *mKha'-'gro snying-tig*). Reprint of the Derge edition, New Delhi, 1983.

______. *sNying-thig ya-bzhi* (= *Bi-ma snying-thig*). Reprint of the Derge edition, New Delhi, 1983.

______. *Tshig-don* (= *Tshig-don rin-po-che'i mdzod*). Reprint of the Derge edition, New Delhi, 1983.

______. *Zab-mo yang-tig*. Reprint of the Derge edition, New Delhi, 1971.

______. *Chos-dbyings* (= *Chos-dbyings rin-po-che'i mdzod*). Reprint of the Derge edition, New Delhi, 1983.

______. *Theg-mchog* (= *Theg-pa'i mchog rin-po-che'i mdzod*). Reprint of the Derge edition, New Delhi, 1983.

Mokṣākaragupta. *Do-hā mdzod-kyi dka'-'grel* (*Dohākośa-pañjikā*). bsTan-'gyur, Peking ed.: vol. *Mi*, fols. 295b–317b.

Padma las-'brel-rtsal. *Rin-po-che dbang-gi phreng-ba* (in Klong-chen rab-'byams-pa, *mKha'-'gro yang-tig*, vol. 1, 121–225).

Padmasambhava. *Man-ngag lta-ba'i phreng-ba*. See Rong-zom Chos-kyi bzang-po.

______. *sPros-bral don-gsal chen-po'i rgyud* (in *rNying-ma rgyud-'bum*, vol. 6, 374–607).

______. *Rin-po-che spyi-gnad skyon-sel thig-le kun-gsal-gyi rgyud* (in *rNying-rgyud*, vol. 6, 230–37).

Rang-byung rdo-rje. *Zab-mo nang-gi don*. n. p., n. d.

Rong-zom Chos-kyi bzang-po. *gSang-'grel* (= *rGyud-rgyal gsang-ba snying-po'i 'grel-pa*). n. p., n. d.

______. *Selected Writings* (*gSung thor-bu*). Leh, 1974.

Saraha. *Dohākośa-gīti* (*Do-hā mdzod-kyi glu*, "People *Dohā*"). bsTan-'gyur, Peking ed.: vol. *Mi*, fols. 74b–81b. Western editions: see P. C. Bagchi and M. Shahidullah.

______. *Dohākośa-upadeśagīti* (*Mi-zad-pa'i gter-mdzod man-ngag-gi glu* "Queen *Dohā*"). bsTan-'gyur, Peking ed.: vol. *Tsi*, fols. 34a–39b.

______. *Dohākośa nāma caryāgīti* (*Do-hā mdzod ces-bya-ba spyod-pa'i glu* "King *Dohā*"). bsTan-'gyur, Peking ed.: vol. *Tsi*, fols. 31b–34a.

______. *Kāyakośa-amṛta-vajragīti* (*sKu'i mdzod 'chi-med rdo-rje'i glu*). bsTan-'gyur Peking ed.: vol. *Tsi*. fols. 78a–85a.

______. *Vākkośa-rucira-svara-vajragīti* (*gSung-gi mdzod 'jam-dbyangs rdo-rje'i glu*). bsTan-'gyur, Peking ed.: vol. *Tsi*, fols. 85a–88a.

______. *Cittakośa-aja-vajragīti* (*Thugs-kyi mdzod skye-med rdo-rje'i glu*). bsTan-'gyur, Peking ed.: vol. *Tsi*, fols. 88a–89b.

______. *Dohākośa-nāma mahāmudrā-upadeśa* (*Do-hā mdzod ces-bya-ba phyag-rgya chen-po'i man-ngag*). bsTan-'gyur, Peking ed.: vol. *Mi*, fols. 95a–97a.

Sog-po Khal-kha chos-rje Ngag-dbang dpal-ldan. *Grub-mtha' chen-mo'i mchan-'grel dka'-gnad mdud-grol blo-gsal gces-nor zhes-bya-ba-las dngos-smra-ba'i skabs*. n. p., n. d.

Thub-bstan 'bar-ba. *Nges-don phyag-rgya chen-po'i sgom-rim gsal-bar byed-pa'i legs-bshad zla-ba'i 'od-zer*. n. p., n. d.

Thu'u-kvan bLo-bzang chos-kyi nyi-ma dpal bzang-po. *Grub-mtha' thams-cad-kyi khungs dang 'dod-tshul ston-pa legs-bshad shel-gyi me-long.* n. p., n. d.

Vimalamitra. *rDo-rje rtse-mo 'dus-pa'i rgyud* (in *rNying-ma rgyud-'bum*, vol. 5, 441–69).

Yon-tan rgya-mtsho. *(Yon-tan rin-po-che'i mdzod-kyi 'grel-pa) Nyi-zla'i sgron-me.* Reproduced photographically by Sonam T. Kazi. Gangtok, 1969.

g.Yung-mgon rdo-rje. *rDo-rje tshig-gi zab-don cha-tsam 'grel-pa ngo-mtshar rdo-rje gsum-gyi gzhal-med-khang* (in Smanrtsis Shesrig Spendzod, vol. 8, 425–49).

SANSKRIT

Āgamaśāstra. Edited, translated, and annotated by Vidhusekhara Bhattacharyya as *The Āgamaśāstra of Gauḍapāda.* Calcutta: University of Calcutta, 1943.

Hevajratantra. Edited by D. Snellgrove as *The Hevajra Tantra.* London: Oxford University Press, 1959.

Īśā-upaniṣad (in *Kalyāṇ*, 161–71. Gorakhpur, 1949)

Kāśyapaparivartasūtra. Edited by Baron A. von Steäl-Holstein. Shanghai, 1925.

C. TIBETAN WORKS BY UNKNOWN AUTHORS

(Rin-po-che 'byung-bar byed-pa) sGra-thal-'gyur-ba chen-po'i rgyud (in *rNying-ma'i rgyud bcu-bdun*, vol. 1, 1–205).

Thig-le kun-gsal chen-po'i rgyud (in *rNying-ma rgyud-'bum*, vol. 5, 124–288).

Rig-pa rang-shar chen-po'i rgyud (in *rNying-ma'i rgyud bcu-bdun*, vol. 1, 389–855).

Seng-ge rtsal-rdzogs chen-po'i rgyud (in *rNying-ma'i rgyud bcu-bdun*, vol. 2, 245–415).

rDo-rje sems-dpa' snying-gi me-long (in *rNying-ma'i rgyud bcu-bdun*, vol. 1, 315–88).

Mu-tig phreng-ba (in *rNying-ma'i rgyud bcu-bdun*, vol. 2, 417–537).

(Chos thams-cad rdzogs-pa-chen-po byang-chub-kyi sems) Kun-byed rgyal-po (in *rNying-ma rgyud 'bum*, vol. 1, 1–220).

Man-ngag thams-cad-kyi sdom (in *rNying-ma'i rgyud 'bum*, vol. 2, 208–26).

Rin-po-che 'khor-lo'i rgyud (in *rNying-ma'i rgyud 'bum*, vol. 4, 24–35).

rDzogs-pa-chen-po Kun-tu bzang-po ye-shes gsal-bar ston-pa'i rgyud (in *rNying-ma rgyud 'bum*, vol. 4, 548–63).

rDzogs-pa-chen-po thig-le gsang-ba de-kho-na-nyid nges-pa'i rgyud (in *rNying-ma rgyud-'bum*, vol. 5, 515–25).

Main Index

Index of Sanskrit and Apabhraṃśa Terms

Index of Tibetan Terms